MONEY AND THE ECONOMY:
CENTRAL BANKERS' VIEWS

Money and the Economy: Central Bankers' Views

Edited by

Pierluigi Ciocca

Central Manager for Central Bank Operations
Banca d'Italia

St. Martin's Press   New York

© Societá editrice Il Mulino, Bologna, 1983
English translation © The Macmillan Press Ltd., 1987

First published in the United States of America in 1987

Printed in Hong Kong

ISBN 0–312–54429–4

Library of Congress Cataloging-in-Publication Data
Money and the economy.
Includes bibliographies and index.
1. Banks and banking, Central—Addresses, essays,
Lectures.   2. Money—Addresses, essays, lectures.
3. Economic policy—Addresses, essays, lectures.
I. Ciocca, Pierluigi, 1941–
HG1811. M66   1986   332.1'1   86–1778
ISBN 0–312–54429–4

a Nicoletta,
in cammino

Contents

List of Tables and Figures

TABLES

FIGURE

Preface

Those who interface with reality from within the institutions responsible for economic policy often feel that academics tend to abstract and commentators to oversimplify. None the less, it is widely recognised that economic analysis in the domain of central banking may be on a course which, though not actually wrong, is probably less fruitful than in the not-so-distant past. It has become more difficult in both the teaching and the popularisation of economics to give an accurate picture of the potential benefits of a credit policy and of the obstacles encountered in its implementation.

The idea for this anthology developed, and was tested, in a series of lecture-meetings with students of economics in various universities and with bank officials who had recently completed academic studies. It grew out of the hypothesis that reading material other than the average monographic essay and the even more typical macroeconomics textbook can help to form a balanced critical view, especially in those who are preparing to face the complexities of monetary economics. In any case, it seemed well worth making some of the writings of central bankers more readily available by bringing together essays, often neglected and difficult to find, which are in themselves of considerable interest.

The promptness with which the authors agreed to have their essays reprinted and where appropriate and possible enriched by the addition of an unpublished retrospective comment, allowed the idea to be put into practice. The editor is particularly grateful to Professor Paolo Baffi for his generous encouragement and advice in the planning of the book. Fausto Vicarelli and Filippo Cesarano commented on a first draft of the introductory essay, and John Smith successfully sought to conserve the significance of the Italian essays in his translation. Responsibility for any remaining imperfections and for the general design of the collection lies, of course, with the editor.

PIERLUIGI CIOCCA

Introduction

Between 'a Science' and 'an Art': Central Banks and the Political Economy of Money

Pierluigi Ciocca

From the very beginning of industrial capitalism the evolution of the concept of monetary policy has clearly, though not always closely, paralleled that of both economic theory and central banking practice. The advances still considered fundamental for the regulation of money were coupled with equally important steps forward in monetary and credit analysis.

The major developments in this century probably took place between the 1920s and the 1950s. Ever since Sir Ralph Hawtrey in 1932 defined central banking as an art based on systematic reasoning,[1] there has been a steady reduction in the time it takes for improvements in the theory and practice of monetary policy to find their way into textbooks, and to be popularised in the literature and the press.

Of necessity, these processes are neither linear nor simple, and they vary in each historical period as regards their causal links and rate of development. None the less in recent years there appears to have been a pronounced weakening of the virtuous elements in the circle that links operational experience, analysis, and popularisation.

Specifically, the works used by students today show a clear tendency toward presenting the set of monetary policy instruments and objectives in ways that are only apparently rigorous and thorough – in reality, they are mechanistic and simplistic. Academic production is increasingly specialistic or has become caught up, because of the spread of 'monetarism', in a sterile return to issues that were discussed, probably on a higher theoretical level, fifty years ago. Extreme *laissez-faire* positions are put forward, albeit in updated forms, even though their shortcomings were clearly revealed by the critical analysis to which they were subjected in the 1930s.

3

If not a remedy, at least food for thought, can be provided by the reflections of central bankers on their own experience. Hence the idea for an anthology of both recent and not-so-recent writings by governors of central banks in several countries. The essays were chosen on the basis of four simple criteria. They were to be subsequent to full acceptance, in principle and in practice, of the concept of monetary management. They were to touch on a wide range of issues in different economic and institutional contexts. Their authors were to be distinguished not only as bankers but also as scholars and free from any taint of vague institutionalism or apologetic empiricism. In both approach and content they were to make it clear, in Menichella's words, how unproductive it is to look for 'the precepts of good credit management in well-ordered handbooks' in the absence of a critical attitude that only political economy and attention to experience and history can provide.

The introduction to an anthology does not allow thorough consideration of all, or even the most important, stages in the development of the relationship between the theory and practice of central banking on the one hand, and economic theory on the other. In monetary economics and policy the history of thought and the history of facts are particularly closely interwoven and therefore difficult to unravel, especially if more than just one country, albeit one as important as England, is considered. None the less, on balance the literature up to the 1960s confirms the following statements:

(a) monetary and credit policy has progressively come to be identified with the activity of central banks;

(b) the recourse made, in pursuit of the general interest in monetary matters, to an institutional body outside the executive necessarily entailed recognition of its autonomy *vis-à-vis* the government; on the other hand, arbitrary decision-making conflicts with the need for unity which is inherent in the very concept of economic policy;

(c) the banking nature of this body has always meant that its discretion and hence the effectiveness of the action it is required to take depend in part on its being consonant – albeit in a central position – with both financial intermediaries and the markets for loans, securities and foreign exchange;

(d) differences of opinion, to the point of feuds between schools, have been a regular feature of the history of monetary thought and of the activity of central banks; discussion has focused on the aspects of the economy that are most directly relevant to monetary policy and hence to the relationship between means and ends in central bank operations, never doubting, however, the *possibility* of establishing this relationship;

(e) a pragmatic approach to the implementation of monetary and credit policy, within certain limits, has always been considered appropriate. This was not only because of the banking nature of central banks but also because of the scientific tone taken by the discussion when the participants realised that the models underlying the analysis were liable to be refuted and that they could be used for economic policy purposes only with substantial modifications on the empirical and institutional level.

Confirmation, if not proof, of these propositions can be found in the path which central banking has followed and in the major monetary controversies that have accompanied its development.

The original role of the first central banks,[2] and in several cases the actual reason for their establishment, was to finance the government in connection with note-issuing privileges.

The inflation and expropriation associated with direct government production of money made this device necessary in order to overcome the difficulties which the public's distrust of government money created for the financing of public expenditure. Awareness of the need to avoid further inflationary excesses led to attempts, through various and varying institutional forms, to reconcile the financing of the borrowing requirement with healthy financial conditions in the economy. The solution was found in the principle that central banks should restrict themselves to advancing governments no more than they could expect to receive in the short term from taxes and sales of securities.

The relationship between governments and central banks thus rapidly took the form of a dialectical complementarity that excluded both the total subordination and the complete independence of central banks.[3] The shift to a note-issuing monopoly was the natural – though not unopposed – outcome of this approach. It accelerated both the change from a still largely barter-based society to a monetary economy and the replacement of coinage by paper money in everyday transactions. It also made it easier to link the task of ensuring a controlled supply of funds to the public sector with other central bank services to governments, acting as their financial agents and advisors.

As time passed this special relationship encouraged the development of close ties between central banks and the banking system. The solidity and flexibility inherent in being banker to the government made the central bank, *de facto* or *de jure*, the ultimate depositary of the liquidity reserves of other intermediaries and the performers of the 'bankers' bank' function.

Responsibilities in the public sector and a pivotal position in the banking system reinforced each other and helped to make central banks the lender of last resort, entrusted with general responsibility for the stability of credit structures and with the specific task of preventing liquidity crises in individual banks from causing widespread insolvency and thus from having serious repercussions on the whole economy.

In different ways and at different times these national developments were coupled in the nineteenth century with the commitment to satisfy and, if necessary, reconcile two general requirements: on the one hand, to maintain the convertibility of notes into gold or other precious metals at fixed rates and, on the other, to ensure a sufficiently elastic supply of credit and money to meet the seasonal and cyclical needs of domestic economic activity.

The last stage of the development of the modern institutional and operational structure of central banking was the progression from an awareness of the economic effects of central bank operations – on prices, economic activity, the financial system and the external accounts – to a full appreciation of the potential inherent in a deliberate use of these operations to achieve 'objectives' of general interest. The older central banks passed through this crucial phase in the period between the end of the last century and the 1930s:

> The central banks established since 1945 have therefore been based on the view that the main business of a central bank is to control the monetary system in a way conducive to the broad economic policies of government (high levels of employment, economic growth, stable prices, foreign exchange stability, etc.) by exercising the following powers: (1) action as lender of last resort at an announced rate of interest (Bank Rate); (2) open-market

operations; (3) fixing reserve requirements for commercial banks; (4) supervision of commercial banking; (5) banker to the government (generally involving important debt management functions); (6) adviser to the government on foreign exchange policy; (7) custodian of the country's international reserves; (8) administrator of foreign exchange restrictions; and (9) dealer in foreign currencies and gold. The relative importance attached to these powers varies greatly from country to country, reflecting the histories, institutions, and prevailing economic doctrines in the different countries.[4]

Attacks on the conduct of central banks have been frequent and sometimes ferocious in the debates on money that constitute one of the strands of the history of economic thought. Very rarely, however, has this led to the total relinquishment of the contribution that central banks' institutional independence and their ensuing discretion can make to the conduct of a policy for credit, or at least to the safeguarding of monetary systems (such as the gold standard) which are based on rules which, though rigid, cannot cover every contingency.

This interpretation appears to apply even to the first of these controversies, the thorough and fierce debate which involved English academics, businessmen and politicians – whose opposing views corresponded in part with those attributed to the Currency and Banking Schools – from the Restriction Act in 1797 to the Bank Charter Act of 1844.[5] I do not entirely agree with the view, widely held among historians, 'that at bottom neither school recognized the necessity for discretionary management of the currency';[6] even less acceptable, though widespread, is the opinion that 'neither side recognized the essential functions of a central bank, a fact which gives the entire controversy a somewhat dated appearance'.[7]

Both these arguments have been seriously undermined, though perhaps not rejected, especially in the masterly work of Henry Thornton, the banker who was the leading co-author and, together with Ricardo, the mind behind the *Bullion Report* published in 1810. He cannot be classified as a full member of the Currency School, however. The acuteness of some of his intuitions and the subtlety of his arguments stand him apart from the rest, including Ricardo. Thornton fully understood that an economy intrinsically exposed to inflation and unemployment required constraints of a monetary nature as well as degrees of freedom for credit, both to be applied with pragmatic firmness.[8]

This difficult responsibility could only be entrusted to the central bank, whose basic tasks Thornton defined – in the page which Schumpeter was to call the *Magna Charta* of central banking[9] – in a way that excluded its subjection to hard and fast rules:

> To limit the total amount of paper issued, and to resort for this purpose, whenever the temptation to borrow is strong, to some effectual principle of restriction; in no case, however, materially to diminish the sum in circulation, but to let it vibrate only within certain limits; to afford a slow and cautious extension of it, as the general trade of the kingdom enlarges itself; to allow of some special, though temporary, encrease in the event of any extraordinary alarm or difficulty, as the best means of preventing a great demand at home for guineas; and to lean to the side of diminution, in the case of gold going abroad, and of the general exchanges continuing long unfavourable; this seems to be the true policy of the directors of an institution circumstanced like that of the Bank of England.[10]

The responsibilities Thornton defined clearly cover the long and the short term in normal as well as in special circumstances. Any comment appears unnecessary,[11] except perhaps to underline the delicate balance involved in the 'limiting' or 'leaning to the side of diminution', without 'materially diminishing' and in the 'affording a slow and cautious extension' of money in the long run or a 'special encrease' under exceptional conditions.

None of the other participants in the debate came near the level reached by Thornton in his analysis. None the less, Ricardo, who was the most formidable opponent of the Bank of England and who also judged the short-term instability of the economy to be a secondary problem compared with that of the 'laws' governing its longer-term development, conceded that it was necessary to proceed along the path of deflation via a gradual absorption of excess currency which it was the task of the Bank of England to implement.[12] Moreover, when, shortly before his death, Ricardo reformulated his argument against the renewal of the Bank of England's note-issuing privileges, he claimed that its directors had failed to resist government pressure for monetary financing of the deficit, but he also confirmed that it was indispensable to remove note-issue from the executive and entrust it to a public, but independent, body (five 'Commissioners' appointed by the government but removable only by parliament) – conceptually no different from a properly-run central bank.[13] The Banking School, for its part, emphasised the impossibility of arriving at an unchanging definition of the stock of money. This did not so much prevent the object of monetary control from being specified as exclude the possibility of this control being entrusted to previously established rules:

> Working to rule is the antithesis of central banking. A central bank is necessary only when the community decides that a discretionary element is desirable. The central banker is the man who exercises his discretion, not the machine that works according to rule . . . We have central banks for the very reason that there are no such rules.[14]

Undeniably, the supporters of the Banking School were more categorical than their opponents in refusing the hypothesis of monetary control as a means to an end. Similarly, Ricardo strove to minimise the acquisition of government liabilities by his 'Commissioners' (formally excluding direct lending, but not the purchase of government securities in the open market). The subsequent period of reflection, however, was to see a more thorough analysis of the two pillars of central banking that had already begun to emerge – although they were not accepted, except by Thornton – during this first phase of the debate. It would later become clear that even limited flexibility in financing public expenditure presupposes an (inherently questionable) assessment of the threshold beyond which the equilibrium of the economy is jeopardised by financing public expenditure with money rather than securities or taxes. Once it was admitted that there was a need to regulate the liquidity position of the economy, which varies with preferences and financial innovations, full recognition of the advantages of its being assessed by an institution that was both 'public' and continuously present in the loans, securities and exchange markets followed.

The outcome of another major controversy – whether there should be one or more banks of issue – also depended on this admission. The debate continued for several decades until the 1880s, and was especially lively in continental Europe and the USA.[15] In contrast with the *querelle* over the concepts of money and liquidity, which has never died down since it broke out between the Banking and Currency Schools, this debate has never again caught on, notwithstandding attempts to revive it, including that made by Hayek.[16] Even Vera Lutz concluded her 1936 study by admitting that while the idea of a single central bank was not logically watertight it was so deeply rooted and widely accepted that 'to suggest its abandonment is to invite ridicule'.[17]

The reasoning that prevailed – over the arguments, and above all over the special interests opposed to it – was that a single, sound and 'public' but autonomous bank of issue would have made the monetisation of the economy a faster, fairer and more efficient process by spreading the use of banknotes, saving even the least informed agents from having to assess – on what basis, anyway? – the creditworthiness of a plurality of issuers. Above all, it was expected to ensure the stability of the banking system by acting as a last-resort lender, a function that necessarily involves decisions of both a 'political' and 'market' nature. The rescue of banks trapped between illiquidity and insolvency makes it necessary to assess and reconcile the general interest in the stability of the credit system and the special interests of competitors, managers, shareholders and creditors of individual banks in difficulty. With a sufficient understanding of the working of a credit economy, this 'active' approach would have made it possible to push the control of the monetary situation, exercisable with a single central bank to the point of conducting a systematic anti-cyclical policy.

It took time for the interventionist view of monetary policy to gain ground, both because central banks were themselves exceedingly cautious in embracing it openly and because economists only gave it the stamp of full legitimacy after a laborious critical revision of the quantity theory of money.

As late as 1867 – a year after the crisis of confidence triggered by the failure of the banking house, Overend & Co., a crisis that the Bank of England efficiently overcame by increasing its lending by 80 per cent in one year – Thomson Hankey, former Governor and member of the Court of Directors of the Bank of England, firmly stated that the Bank's role in the system was no more that that of a *primus inter pares*. Size apart, 'the more the conduct of the affairs of the Bank is made to assimilate to the conduct of every other well-managed bank in the United Kingdom, the better for the Bank, and the better for the community at large'.[18] This reluctance was clearly justified by the unpopularity of any form of control whatsoever, at a time when the rise of industrial capitalism was supported, if not by the practice, at least by the apologetics of *laissez-faire*. The large size of central banks, together with the close links between gold movements, exchange rates, and the level of economic activity under the gold standard, also allowed them considerable scope for stabilising interventions; the mantle was provided by the theory that these should be profit-oriented operations in the same way as those of any other bank, with the sole specific task of mechanically linking the currency in circulation and loan conditions to the flows of gold into and out of the country. 'If we add that fine steering looks like no steering, we cannot exclude the possibility that both the insight and the practice of the [central bank's] directors were above – and especially ahead of – what they have been credited with'.[19]

It is none the less true that Bagehot's *Lombard Street* marked a turning-point in the dual sense of being designed 'to knock into the heads of the magnates of the City, for the guidance of future policy, two or three fundamental truths',[20] and to render explicit, even to economists, that which had until then remained implicit.[21] Banker and journalist, Bagehot understood as clearly as Thornton, and set out with greater force, that an advanced credit system increases both the potential for growth and the risk of instability in the economy. The fragility of a system based on the minimisation of the reserves against liabilities, including sight debts, and on their being concentrated with the bank of issue is accentuated in industrialised economies by the probability of a financial panic being heightened by the fluctuations to which such economies are systematically exposed.[22]

The real prospect of a widespread financial crisis, with negative repercussions on both economic activity and the balance of payments, requires the central bank not to go against its commitment to lend freely, at high rates, on the basis of careful discretionary assessments of the macroeconomic aspects of the crisis and of its effects on the allocation of resources. 'Though the rule is clear, the greatest delicacy, the finest and best skilled judgment, are needed to deal at once with such great and contrary evils'.[23] An immediate increase in interest rates is needed to counter the foreign drain but may 'frighten the market' at home, and undermine confidence in firms and banks. On the other hand, countering a domestic drain through 'an alleviative treatment with large and ready loans'[24] may cause such easy credit conditions that it becomes advantageous to export capital. As for the effects on resource allocation of stabilisation policies, Thornton lucidly defined the nature of the problem: 'The relief [provided by the central bank] should neither be so prompt and liberal as to exempt those who misconduct their business from all the natural consequences of their fault, nor so scanty and slow as deeply to involve the general interests'.[25] In this connection I do not believe that Bagehot's contribution lies so much in having formulated the concept of a penalty rate,[26] as in having grasped that the announcement of the existence of a lender of last resort is in itself a decisive stabilising factor;[27] that 'one failure makes many, and the best way to prevent the derivative failures is to arrest the primary failure which causes them';[28] and that, to avoid rescuing bankers who are not only illiquid but also insolvent, the granting of credit must none the less be backed, independently of the technical form, by guarantees that the central bank judges to be acceptable.[29]

It is probably true that the *Lombard Street* 'analysis of depressions and the account of the process by which prices rise are rather confused and rather superficial'.[30] The very solution adopted by the Bank of England to the problem of scarce gold reserves in the twenty years subsequent to the book's publication tended more towards a resolute use of the discount rate than to a structural increase in the Bank's gold as advocated by Bagehot. The former was used in the domestic and international markets much more than foreseen in *Lombard Street*, and acquired the status of a signal that it has retained to this day. *Lombard Street* none the less established a solid analytical connection between the regularity of the business cycle, the fragility of the credit structure and the need for discretionary interventions to promote stability. Notwithstanding the prevalently quantity-theory-of-money approach 'after Bagehot the Bank's special position is taken for granted. It is not "just like any other bank"; it is the holder of the single reserve, the ultimate source of support for the country's financial structure in times of difficulty'.[31]

It is commonly held that the quantity theory dominated the scene, and not only the theoretical scene, throughout the nineteenth century and into the early twentieth century.[32] In the most coherent of the original versions, that of Ricardo, the proportional relationship between changes in M and changes in P was derived by assuming that the gold stock was exogenous, that the velocity of circulation was fairly steady and that money had no influence on output or relative prices.[33] Formulated in this way, quantity theory excluded any possibility of monetary management: the only indication it provided for economic policy – at least in the short term – was that circulation should be kept unchanged to counter any risk of inflation.[34] And yet this rigidity did not prevent the parallel development of an active concept of monetary policy and the growth of central banking. The necessary flexibility was provided not only by the pragmatism and caution that are always required when applying abstract models to reality but also by the analyses conducted in opposition to the quantitative theory, or those which took place outside and even inside the quantity school.

There was no lack of adversaries. Apart from Tooke, Senior, Anderson and Marx, who defined quantity theory as an 'insipid hypothesis',[35] 'it was attacked, vehemently and repeatedly, by a series of minor writers',[36] who 'were the majority' in countries like France and Germany.[37] This criticism did not lead to the formulation of an alternative analytical approach to replace that of the quantity theory of money. It none the less helped to remove theoretical prejudices and to collect empirical material, thus fostering other lines of economic enquiry that were largely independent of the question of the value of money. In addition to the fundamental contributions just mentioned, such as those of Thornton and Bagehot, the development of central banking owed much to the progress made in the independent and systematic study of cyclical fluctuations. It is probably not by chance that economists such as Tooke and Marx should have made important contributions in this field. Though very different, they both started from a partly empirical criticism of the quantity model. Equally important is the emergence of the general hypothesis of the non-monetary and endogenous nature of the mechanism-generating cycles. The economic and social problem of how to counter the instability of the productive system, a yardstick for central banks, thus became more and more clearly defined.

But even within the quantity school itself the number of leading economists holding the most extreme positions was very small indeed.[38]

Hume himself fully conceded that the effects of a monetary expansion were felt in employment, wages, labour productivity and output before working themselves out in price increases that were ultimately proportional to the amount of new money which is not hoarded.[39]

J. S. Mill's monetary theory was also eclectic, and this is partly why his *Principles* reigned unchallenged as the economist's bible until those of Marshall became widespread in the 1890s.[40] In his exposition, Mill moderated quantity theory by contemplating the possibility that, as the quantity of money increased, relative prices would vary, hoarding occur and banks change their ratio of liquid reserves to deposits.[41]

Although there was the precedent of Senior,[42] it was Marshall who introduced the cash balance criterion, which was subsequently formalised in the 'Cambridge equation'. He considered it complementary in terms of velocity of circulation; the former better suited to short-term analysis and the latter preferable for understanding the long waves of prices. But 'in expressing the Cambridge equation in words, it is natural to say . . . that "the public choose" or "elect" to keep $p(k+rk')$ in cash and balances, and this manner of speaking constitutes a psychological bridge to later, especially Keynesian, opinions'.[43] Furthermore, Marshall clearly considered $MV = PQ$ as an identity that was useful for a first selection of the variables relevant for an etiology of price movements that was none the less to be based on hypotheses whose realism required testing in each and every case.[44] Marshall also attributed considerable importance to credit in his analysis of the economic cycle; he recommended an elastic monetary system, and believed that monetary policy, entrusted to the discount instrument, was effective in promoting stability.

Wicksell moved along the lines of traditional quantity theory when he analysed an economy in which, despite the presence of a rudimentary capital market, money consists only of metal and notes, and changes in bank deposits reflect those in the velocity of circulation since banks have to keep a reserve equal to total deposits. In such an economy, the lack of bank reserves sets an upper limit on the fluctuations in prices and nominal income. However, in a 'pure credit' economy the premise of an exogenous stock of money – which is fundamental to the quantitative theory – breaks down: 'banking policy' fixes 'the' nominal interest rate exogenously, the quantity of money is determined endogenously by demand, the differential between the nominal and the real interest rate has cumulative effects on prices, unless steps are deliberately taken – in the face of difficulties that must not be underestimated – to eliminate the differential and prevent its reappearing as a result of the inevitable fluctuations or trend changes in the real rate of interest.[45]

Fisher, who put the quantity theory of money into mathematical form and with whose name it is most closely associated, also used the idea with major qualifications and was fully aware of the different degrees of robustness of each assumption. He recognised that the quantity equation holds only in equilibrium and not in transition phases; that economic activity, or the volume of transactions, can produce a feedback effect on both V and M; that the constancy of V is not an immutable institutional or technological given, but the outcome of complex forces; and that the equation only captures the proximate causes of price changes. In other words, it is quite true that 'Fisher stopped short of anything like a rigid quantity theory'.[46]

This rapid *excursus* into the history of economic doctrines confirms that until the turn of this century the work of economists did not create insurmountable obstacles to the development of central banking, even if it only occasionally provided explicit support:

> Economists enlarged indeed their conception of the functions of central banks, especially the controlling and regulating function of the 'lender of last resort'. But most of them were surprisingly slow in recognizing to the full the implications of Monetary Management, which as we have seen was developing under their eyes . . . Because of it control continued to mean – not wholly but primarily – control by discount policy.[47]

Central banks did not discard their early prudence and understatement in describing their philosophy and role in managing the credit system, both domestically and internationally, with the aim of curbing outbreaks of instability. 'Discount policy' normally sought to achieve the dual aim of stabilising exchange rates and domestic prices: 'Even mere stabilization of prices implies – as its main purely economic motive – concern with stabilization of a country's economic situation. But stabilization of employment was often mentioned explicitly'.[48]

Towards the end of the nineteenth century analytical and operational–institutional progress gathered pace. Evidence of 'the grafting of this theoretical work on to the notions of the central bankers themselves'[49] held in the immediate post-war period can be found in the *Cunliffe Report* of 1918:

> This report, aimed at the elimination of inflation and restoration of the international gold standard, pinpointed the central bank's discount rate (Bank Rate) as the proper weapon. In advocating the use of Bank Rate, the *Cunliffe Report* concentrated not, as might

have been supposed from pre-war practice alone, on its influence on international capital movements, but on its influence in reducing the volume and use of credit internally, thus causing reductions in prices and employment. The functions of central banks were now much under review; central banking became for the first time fully self-conscious; and the theory of the internal effects of Bank Rate changes quickly gained influence in many countries of the world.[50]

The debate on quantity theory took a new turn in the 1920s and 1930s. Notwithstanding the differences and sometimes open disagreements, the writings of Hawtrey, Pigou, Robertson, Hayek, Myrdal and even Keynes's *A Tract on Monetary Reform* and *A Treatise on Money*, can be seen as providing general confirmation of the fact that 'the quantity theory was in decline *before* the Keynesian Revolution. It was found to be theoretically inadequate and too mechanical or simplistic as a framework for understanding the role of money in the economy'.[51]

The serious problems faced in the 1920s – in restoring price and employment stability in Europe and establishing a lasting international monetary system – and those encountered in the 1930s – in coping with the Great Depression – accelerated the crisis of the quantity paradigm. At the same time they reinforced the analytical commitment, tightened the connections, by then out in the open, between interpretative models and monetary policy, and caused central banks to intensify their efforts and to collaborate internationally, which was a relatively new development. The ultimate expression of this labour was the *General Theory*. This work, variously mediated, is still the theoretical *point de repère* of modern central banking.

Before Keynes's *General Theory*, no one had ever taken analysis of the economy to the point of asserting that its inherent instability could actually produce states of unemployment equilibrium – that is, a waste of resources that was neither temporary, nor cyclical, nor necessarily susceptible to improvement by market forces alone.

The *General Theory* made it clear that only conscious economic policy action was, in principle, capable of guaranteeing the correction and prevention of such conditions. The theoretical trust traditionally placed in a fall in real wages as the price mechanism able to absorb an excess supply of labour, appeared to Keynes to be totally unfounded. In a monetary economy wage negotiations do not involve real wages but nominal wages; if these decline, prices – which are determined at the margin on the basis of variable costs – decline proportionally. In a system of industrial relations where bargaining is not centralised, each category resists cuts in its nominal wages to prevent them from falling with respect to those of other categories. In fact, employment does not depend on the real wage, but on effective demand – the result of consumer expenditure (a stable function of income) and investment expenditure (an unstable function of entrepreneurs' long-term expectations) – and aggregate supply, defined as the reaction of variable production costs to rising employment, given the intensity of competition, the endowment of physical capital and the technology. The exogenously determined level of nominal wages fixes the level of prices and of the real wage, which enables production and employment to respect the profit maximisation constraint.[52]

The vital link of the quantity theory was thus broken. Q could no longer be considered invariable at its full-employment value. Furthermore, the monetary theory of interest advanced by Keynes entailed the possibility of a link between monetary conditions and economic activity:

> The main determinant of the level of interest rates is the state of expectations. When bond-holders have a clear view of what is the normal yield which they expect to be restored soon after any temporary change, the banking system cannot move interest rates from what they are expected to be. It is the existence of uncertainty or 'two views' that makes it possible for the banks to manipulate the money market.[53]

The *General Theory* also provides the basis for resolving the question of the neutrality of money in Hayek's sense of a theoretical condition to be respected in order to prevent Walrasian general equilibrium from being upset by a cyclical instability which can only be generated in the model by the 'external' element of bank credit. Shifting brusquely from highly rarefied analysis to very practical issues, Hayek had narrowed the choice to the two following concrete possibilities: either to keep the money stock totally unchanged, entrusting the distribution of the fruits of technical progress to the fall in prices; or accepting cyclical fluctuations as the inevitable cost of the contribution that the banking system can make to long-term growth. Hayek's views were rejected by Piero Sraffa, who demonstrated both the difficulty of defining conditions for the existence and stability of a general equilibrium that were even minimally realistic and the total irrelevance of money as such in Walrasian models, and hence the improbability of the cycle having a purely monetary origin. The Hayek–Sraffa debate – to which Keynes himself actively contributed taking Sraffa's side – was conducted, at a very high level of abstraction, in the *Economic Journal* during 1932.[54] It is widely believed – though hardly ever openly asserted – that the debate did not influence the principles of economic policy. I do not share this view. Hayek was highly critical of the quantity theory, but widespread adoption of the new approach which he propounded would have entailed a clear, and perhaps conclusive, invitation to central banks not to act.

Rather, the outcome of the debate, together with the *General Theory*, helped to complete the framework of central bank tasks outlined by Thornton. Besides avoiding excessive surges in demand, allowing an elastic but not inflationary financing of long-term real income growth, averting incipient panics among creditors and countering imbalances in the external accounts, monetary policy was called on to do the utmost to rectify situations of unemployment equilibrium:

> The quantity of money is controlled by the banking system. When effective demand is beginning to rise, it induces an increase in average over-all velocity of circulation as money balances are moved from the inactive to the active circulation. If the banking system fails to allow the quantity of money to increase, the demand for active balances will tend to raise the level of interest rates, which causes V to rise to the required extent . . . In a period of unemployment, an increase in the quantity of money can do some good. It tends to lower interest rates and to permit the 'fringe of unsatisfied borrowers' to get finance. *Relatively to given expectations of profit*, a fall in interest rates will stimulate investment somewhat, and, by putting up the Stock Exchange value of placements, it may encourage expenditure for consumption. These influences will increase effective demand and so increase employment.[55]

Thus, not only was the scope for action defined; so were the limits to the effectiveness of an economic policy entrusted exclusively to monetary policy. The efficient working of the economy might require, in cases of conflicting objectives, supporting action through fiscal policy, intervention in foreign transactions and, the political climate and centralisation of wage-bargaining permitting, incomes policy.

The *General Theory* is undoubtedly one of the most difficult economics books ever written. Ever since it appeared it has been subjected to continuous interpretation which cannot be said to be concluded to this day. This interpretation has moved basically along two paths: pursued, on the one hand, by those of Keynes's colleagues and followers who were most directly aware of the radically innovatory general sense of his analytical message, as well as of its incompleteness, and, on the other hand, by those who believed that what was new in Keynes could be usefully grafted, in a new synthesis, onto the theoretical trunk that the great Cambridge economist had sought to supplant.

What is of special interest here is that both approaches stressed the importance of the role of money and of monetary policy. After the post-war revival of monetary policy, following the abandonment of the practice of pegging interest rates at a low level, both approaches made substantial contributions to the definition and predominance of active and scientifically-based central banking. With this as well as the 'Keynesian' label in common, they advanced in parallel despite the difference in their points of departure, until the authentic interpreters of Keynes considered their task of translating his thinking into a framework of reference for monetary policy to have been to all intents and purposes completed. This 'completion' can be seen as having coincided with the contributions of Kaldor, and especially Kahn, to the Radcliffe Committee in England at the end of the 1950s.[56]

Two aspects in particular of Keynes's thinking were taken over by the *Radcliffe Report*:[57]

(a) 'monetary measures cannot alone be relied upon to keep in nice balance an economy subject to major strains from both without and within. Monetary measures can help, but that is all';

(b) 'though we do not regard the supply of money as an unimportant quantity . . . it is the whole liquidity position that is relevant to spending decisions, and this can be influenced through interest rates'.

Kahn's memorandum sustained point (a) with an approach firmly rooted in the consistency between the objectives and instruments of a diversified economic policy, of which monetary policy is one of the strands. The case Kahn considered is the important one of conflicting objectives in an economy operating at a fluctuating and rather depressed level together with inflation and a trade deficit. The latter requires an 'adjustment of the terms of trade', in the extreme case accompanied by a 'bland selective control' of imports and support for investment in export- and import-substitution industries. The curb on the rate of increase in prices, apart from the case of pure demand inflation, is to be found 'in the sphere of wage negotiation'.[58] Economic activity has to be stabilised with a mix of monetary and fiscal policies that will protect investment and hence the potential for higher output and productivity. On the assumption that fiscal policy influences mainly consumption and monetary policy primarily fixed investment, every effort must be made to use the former to achieve restriction and the latter to establish expansion. In this delicate balance it is vital to remember that businessmen's animal spirits, which are decisive for investment, 'cannot be turned on and off at will'.

Point (b) is an almost literal reaffirmation of Keynes's view, forcefully argued by Kahn, that, apart from the case of credit-rationing, 'it is the lower level of interest rates, not the larger quantity of money, which exercises an expansionist influence . . . it is immaterial what changes in the quantity of money have to occur as part of the process of securing a particular desired behaviour of rates of interest'.[59] 'The quantity of money held in "inactive" form is closely related to the level and structure of rates of interest, but the relationship is not at all a stable one, so much depending on expectations about the future'.[60]

The other interpretative path can be traced back to Hicks's reading of the *General Theory* on the basis of the simplified framework that has come to be known as the *IS–LM* model.[61] It is now clear, even to the least pure of Keynes's followers that this model reflects his thinking only insofar as it incorporates the three basic functions of behaviour he proposed – consumption, the marginal efficiency of capital and liquidity. For the rest, they are employed to give a summary picture of a Walrasian exchange economy that is reduced, in the simplest versions, to the exchange of money, securities and one single product.

The differences between the 'true' Keynes and this 'formalised' version are enormous. It is sufficient to mention three, apart from the obvious consideration that the author of the *General Theory* was also a good enough mathematician to be fully aware of the impossibility of reducing the finer points with which he was concerned to the slopes of two curves. In the first place, 'what is the meaning of making the rate of investment a function of the rate of interest? Keynes's contention was that a *fall* in the rate of interest relatively to *given* expectations of profit would, in favourable circumstances, *increase* the rate of investment . . . he could never have said that a permanently lower level of the rate of interest would cause a permanently higher rate of investment'.[62] Further, 'One of the best known lessons of monetary history (which Keynes often repeated) is that a *fall* in activity leads to a collapse of confidence and a *rise* in interest rates, whereas, at a time of high activity, high expectations of profit affect the confidence of lenders as well as borrowers'.[63] And lastly:

> in dealing with the speculative-motive it is, however, important to distinguish between the changes in the rate of interest which are due to changes in the supply of money available to satisfy the speculative-motive, without there having been any change in the liquidity function, and those which are primarily due to changes in expectations affecting the liquidity function itself. Open-market operations may, indeed, influence the rate of interest through both channels; since they may not only change the volume of money, but may also give rise to changed expectations concerning the future policy of the Central Bank or of the Government.[64]

These, and other radical differences have led the most philologically faithful Keynesians to reject the *IS–LM* model *en bloc*; on the other hand, they have convinced the most rigorous critics of the whole neoclassical analytical construct to consider the Keynesian revolution as incomplete because of the contamination to be found in the *General Theory* between highly innovatory elements and the underlying reference to a theory of value, distribution and capital that is cast, though not irremediably, in an essentially neoclassical mould.[65]

These debates are still open to this day. Never the less, in the fields of enquiry of greatest relevance for monetary policy there have been analytical developments concerning the core of the *IS–LM* model in all its various versions that are undoubtedly important,[66] independently of whether they can be traced back to, or are compatible with, Keynes's teaching.

A reasonably complete survey is beyond the scope of this intro-duction.[67] The most important of these developments can none the less be listed under the following headings:

- the analysis of the determinants of the individual components of expenditure, disaggregated beyond the basic division into private consumption and investment;
- the analysis of the determinants of the demand for money, securities and other assets according to models of portfolio de-cisions in which budget and flow-of-funds constraints are re-spected;
- the dynamic analysis of the savings–investment relationship, seen as the central mechanism of cyclical and growth phenomena;
- the analysis of the money-supply function, based on the links between monetary base, its distribution between the public and banks, and the criteria underlying the microeconomic behaviour of the latter;
- the extension of the basic model to the foreign exchange of goods and international capital movements;
- the explicit consideration of the transmission mechanism of mon-etary policy impulses in the logical order of: instruments–inter-mediate objectives–final objectives;
- the compilation of statistical tables of flows of funds and of the composition of financial assets that are consistent with national income and wealth accounts;
- the econometric testing of single hypotheses of behaviour and the construction of 'large' econometric models with special care being paid to the quantification of the parameters, the structure of lags and the relationships between macroeconomic aggregates.

These analytical advances were especially relevant between the 1940s and the 1960s. Central banks gave ready acceptance to the theoretical and methodological implications, and made a decisive contribution of their own as far as the empirical–institutional aspects were concerned; they also gave practical application to these ad-vances in specific circumstances through 'political' assessments of their potential scope and importance for central banking oper-ations.[68] Handbooks of monetary macroeconomics, in their, turn adopted these advances to a great extent, though not completely, and appeared at a rate that permitted reasonably rapid updating together with an adequate degree of debunking. Above all, the best textbooks of the period, notwithstanding the differences in the emphasis they placed on the various basic analytical approaches and in the complexity of the problems studied and instruments employed, maintained an acceptable balance between critical appraisal and favourable exposition of the preferred conceptual system.[69]

In the 1960s this seam already showed signs of exhaustion and involution, signs that were to become all the more evident in the 1970s. Within the truly Keynesian school original contributions to the study of strictly monetary problems began to peter out, while the unwillingness of its members to publish textbooks and systematically popularise their views was confirmed.[70] A significant comment is to be found in Kahn's bitter reaction to the resurgence of hypotheses of private investment being crowded out by public deficits in situations of considerable unutilised human and capital resources:

> Is it really true that the notorious 'Treasury view' of 1929 has been resuscitated? How did it happen? Is it accepted by those who believe in it that the economy is in a strait-jacket? . . . How is it that Keynes's great lesson has been forgotten – that additional investment automatically results in the additional saving required to finance it? Did Keynes teach in vain? I conclude by admitting – shamefacedly – that Keynesians are heavily to blame for failure to destroy this odious weed.[71]

The model stylised by Hicks has been increasingly interpreted, and taught, as the canonical theory of interest and income in the short run. In successive expositions, the necessary critical caution has gradually been abandoned including that implicit even in simplified historical presentations (with the 'Keynesian model' set against the 'classical model'). Hicks himself has had to admit his dissatisfaction with this tendency, which has been especially evident in applied economic analysis.[72]

Rather than listing a series of bad textbooks and mediocre theoretical and empirical studies, it is probably more profitable to see how these works have generally treated the liquidity-preference function, the linchpin of Keynes's monetary analysis of interest. The theory of Markowitz and Tobin was intended to explain portfolio diversification between money and variable price assets.[73] The explanation was based on preferences for the expected yield and the risk, in a range of choice defined by a given distribution of the probabilities of the possible yields, with risks being insurable, in principle, by 'normal' *investors*, who are characterised by 'risk aversion'. This risk is clearly different from the state of uncertainty that Keynes considered relevant for *speculators*, who decide whether to invest all their funds in money or in securities with the aim of making capital gains on the basis of their conviction that they can beat the market in foreseeing non-random events. Since the two models refer to entirely different economic agents, they can usefully be considered complementary, albeit with the necessary analytical caution. Instead, Keynesian speculators have been allowed to drop gradually out of the picture with no good empirical or institutional reason. The 'speculative motive' has been reduced to the stereotyped assumption of an inverse relationship between the demand for money and the interest rate. The basic question of the inherent instability of the demand for money has been relegated to the background, notwithstanding Hicks's, perhaps tardy, reminder:

> We must evidently refrain from supposing that the expectations, as they were before April, of what is to happen after April were precise expectations, single-valued expectations; for in a model with single-valued expectations there can be no question of liquidity. And we must also refrain from the conventional representation of uncertain expectations in terms of mean and variance, since that makes them different in kind from the experiences that are to replace them.[74]

Despite the neo-Ricardian criticism of the theoretical basis of the marginalist explanation of value and distribution,[75] a comforting 'neoclassical synthesis' has been achieved,[76] according to which the special cases of 'Keynesian' underemployment can be overcome with demand policies, while market mechanisms of the Walrasian type should ensure a reasonably efficient allocation of resources. The inverse relationship found by Phillips between the rate of change in money wages and the unemployment rate led to a revival of the view that these mechanisms work even in the labour 'market'.[77] According to the interpretation of Samuelson and Solow,[78] this relationship enables another inverse link to be established between inflation and unemployment: a few points of inflation were seen as an acceptable price for socially and economically satisfactory levels of employment.

The twenty years of sustained and steady growth after the Korean war gave rise to genuine optimism with regard to the scope for suitable combinations of fiscal and monetary policy to prolong conditions of domestic and external equilibrium in economies with a natural bent for growth.[79] Bland incomes policies were thought sufficient to correct the trade-off between inflation and unemployment and to make the Phillips curve well-behaved. Forgetful of the perhaps excessive coolness with which Keynes had greeted Tinbergen's early efforts,[80] huge resources were invested in research into econometric modelling, blissfully confident that, with the analytical framework defined, the primary need was to quantify the links between the instrumental variables and those representing an equal number of intermediate and final objectives of economic policy. Economic analysis was thus transformed into a sort of stochastic macroaccounting, subcontracted on a *pro rata* basis to accountant-economists, who were urged to specialise in various sections of models made up of hundreds of equations, the underlying rationale of which was difficult and costly to modify once established. There was serious speculation as to whether the economic cycle had become a thing of the past.[81]

This approach spread to monetary policy and to research into money and the economy, though central banks – as the essays in this anthology evidence – refrained from excessive optimism. The 'mean-variance' formula was applied to the behaviour of every kind of agent, including financial intermediaries. The *raison d'être* of the latter came almost to coincide with their being part of a 'transmission mechanism' of the impulses of monetary policy. The question of liquidity preference was reduced to the empirical estimation of demand for money functions of exactly the same kind as those used for every other type of financial instrument. 'Control engineering' appeared applicable and fine-tuning feasible, even in monetary matters. Monetary policy was presented to students as a quantitative technique for the mechanical shifting of an *LM* curve in an econometrically known world, apart from random factors which could make it necessary to choose (once and for all? case by case?) between intermediate objectives to be specified in terms of quantities of money or interest rates depending on whether the instability of the *IS* curve was more or less pronounced than that of the *LM* curve itself.[82]

The world economic crisis of the 1970s rapidly dispelled this frankly simplistic air of confidence and, as often happens in such cases, triggered an opposite reaction in the form of a growing adoption of the 'monetarist' positions that Milton Friedman had already been developing for thirty-odd years and, more recently, of the theories of the so-called 'new classical macroeconomics', primarily linked with the name of Robert Lucas.[83]

Friedman consciously adopts a decidedly empirical epistemological approach based on the conviction that the soundness of a theory is not to be judged by the 'descriptive' realism of its assumptions nor – at least to any significant extent – by its completeness or logical consistency, but rather by comparing it with other theories in the light of the correspondence between their implications – above all, predictions for economic policy purposes – and actual experience.[84]

Set within an analytical framework inspired by what he considers to be the basic hypothesis of quantity theory – 'that what ultimately matters to holders of money is the real quantity rather than the nominal quantity they hold and that there is a fairly definite real quantity of money that people wish to hold under any given circumstances'[85] – Friedman's underlying conviction is that changes in national income are primarily caused by changes in the money stock. In his view statistical and historical analyses, particularly of the US case, allow for three deductions:

(1) that the demand for money is a stable function, in the econometric sense, of a small number of variables (and notably income) that can be determined by the model of portfolio decisions;
(2) that changes in the money supply are in the long run exogenous and 'that even during business cycles the money stock plays a largely independent role' *vis-à-vis* real income and prices;[86]
(3) that changes in the money stock have been important in the past, that they are the result of identifiable 'actions' by the monetary authorities and appear closely related to changes in income and prices, which they systematically precede during the cycle, albeit with long and variable lags.

The instability of the economy is thus seen as deriving primarily from bad management of the money supply, even though other factors also play a part:

The variation in timing means that there is considerable leeway in the precise relation between changes in the stock of money and in prices over short periods of time – there are other factors at work that lead to these variations and mean that even if the stock of money were to change in a highly regular and consistent fashion economic activity and prices would none the less fluctuate.[87]

The negative effects of these factors cannot be neutralised by a stabilising monetary policy:

> When the money changes are large, they tend to dominate these other factors . . . But when the money changes are moderate, the other factors come into their own. If we knew enough about them and about the detailed effects of monetary changes, we might be able to counter these other effects by monetary measures. But this is utopian given our present level of knowledge.[88]

According to Friedman, our ignorance, which is primarily empirical and almost impossible to overcome, concerns primarily the channels, manner and timing of money's influence on expenditure and the distribution of changes in nominal income between quantity and prices in a way that is consistent with the need to avoid divergences of the real wage, the interest rate, and hence employment, from their 'natural' values.

These 'natural' values are inherently changeable and unknowable. However, according to Friedman, confidence in the ability of economic agents and markets to behave 'as if' general equilibrium theory were consistent and demonstrated in every part justifies confidence in the internal stability of the system. Equilibrium values, of both prices and output, will tend to prevail and, even though they cannot be perfected with counter-cyclical economic policy devices, they will prove to be socially acceptable in the long run.

Monetary policy therefore cannot 'peg these real magnitudes at predetermined levels' and must stop trying to do so.[89] It has, instead, a triple task: '[to] prevent money itself from being a major source of economic disturbance' as had all too often been the case in the past;[90] '[to] contribute to offsetting major disturbances in the economic system arising from other sources' – the large-scale non-monetary disorders such as 'an independent secular exhilaration', 'an explosive federal budget' or 'the end of a substantial war';[91] to ensure that the quantity of money grows at a steady pace that 'would on the average produce moderate inflation or moderate deflation',[92] by providing 'a monetary climate favorable to the effective operation of those basic forces of enterprise, ingenuity, invention, hard work, and thrift that are the true springs of economic growth. That is the most that we can ask from monetary policy at our present stage of knowledge'.[93]

Having cut the need for discretion in monetary matters down to size, Friedman also draws on considerations of a political and institutional nature to conclude that monetary policy should be implemented by fixing monetary growth by law and removing it from the discretionary management of an independent central bank. In Friedman's view it is impossible for a central bank to be entirely independent of the executive and in any case such independence would be unacceptable in a liberal–democratic society, even in the form of 'a coordinated constitutionally established, separate organization'.[94] If it did exist, responsibility would be diluted, the distribution of monetary power would come to depend on the strength of character of those who exercise it; in other words it would depend on chance, and the intermingling of 'credit' and 'money' would result in the banking lobby having too much influence.

The support which Lucas's studies give to these conclusions is based on awareness that 'Friedman's case was built largely on the *presumption* of ignorance of the nature of business cycles'[95] and consists primarily of an attempt to define the boundaries and meaning of this 'ignorance' by rigorously establishing, on the basis of a still largely incomplete, theoretical programme, the knowledge needed to put counter-cyclical policy onto a scientific footing.

Lucas claims that *IS–LM* based econometric models, with excess demand or supply and involuntary unemployment, are irremediably inadequate for economic policy purposes. They do not allow policies to be compared since their structure does not change with the various options. Indeed, they do not envisage agents' reaction functions based on expectations that respect the double condition of cleared markets and optimising individual behaviour. In contrast, this condition is supposed to be respected in the Walrasian general equilibrium, 'the' equilibrium theory in Lucas's view. He sustains that economic policy must be put on an analytical basis by extending the equilibrium method to the study of the business cycle, not so much in the sense of its changing historical features as in that of the set of systematic 'co-movements' to be found in statistical series.

A theory of cyclical equilibrium tends to exclude the working of endogenous factors of instability. Like Friedman, Lucas sees the quantity of money as the only exogenous factor consistent with the fact that, thus defined, business cycles appear morphologically similar, and with the theoretical assumption that fluctuations in output and employment are produced by agents' reactions to price movements:

For explaining *secular* movements in prices generally, secular movements in the quantity of money do extremely well. This fact is as well established as any we know in aggregative economics, and is not sensitive to how one measures either prices or the quantity of money. There is no serious doubt as to the direction of effect in this relationship; no one argues that the anticipation of sixteenth-century inflation sent Columbus to the New World to locate the gold to finance it. This evidence has no direct connection to business cycles, since it refers to averages over much longer periods, but the indirect connections are too strong to be ignored: we have accounted for the pattern of co-movements among real variables over the cycle as responses to general price movements; we know that, in the long run, general price movements arise primarily from changes in the quantity of money. Moreover, cyclical movements in money are large enough to be quantitatively interesting. All these arguments point to a monetary shock as the force triggering the real business cycle.[96]

Lucas is fully aware of the incomplete nature of his research, but none the less he believes that the results already obtained are sufficient to decree the suspension of all counter-cyclical monetary policy until an equilibrium model of economic fluctuations that can be considered 'operational' is at hand. 'Monetarism' in all its aspects has been widely criticised through the years both in terms of content and methodology.

At the epistemological level the most serious economists have been anything but willing to entrust the choice between different theories to the conformity of their predictions to the 'facts'. There is still a tendency to continue to give priority to logical consistency, generality, simplicity, plausibility and relevance – rather than 'descriptive' realism – as criteria for assessing explanatory models. I believe that this tendency can also be found among students of the neoclassical school, who are the most exposed to neopositivistic and pragmatic influences.[97] Moreover, it is virtually essential for critics of neoclassical economics who attempt to construct a classical and/or a Keynesian theory of economics on a rational basis.[98] Tests alone cannot resolve theoretical controversies for many reasons: the conditions that allow predictions to be compared with the facts are not inevitable; there are several methods of empirical testing available and the choice is not neutral; a *ceteris paribus* constraint is always necessary in economics (a science that deals with the *economic* aspect of complex social phenomena) and it is always difficult to ensure that it is respected; and, finally, measurement of the variables normally involves considerable problems.[99]

Even in the 'naive falsificationism' practised by the majority of
monetarists, the 'concise' implications of monetarism receive little
support from statistical and econometric tests. The turbulent 1970s
have further undermined the hypothesis of a stable demand for
money. There has been increasing recognition of the difficulty of
determining whether this function is more stable than the consumption function, even with multi-equation models. As regards the links
between M and Y, causality tests – in the stochastic sense, with
reference to variables containing information that helps to predict
changes in other variables more accurately – have produced conflicting results in the USA and the UK and, moreover, the results depend
to no small extent on the concept of causality actually adopted.
Furthermore, econometric models able to test whether public expenditure tends to crowd out private expenditure are lacking. Finally,
the hypotheses of a natural rate of unemployment and rational
expectations have still to be empirically tested.[100]

Monetarism is also open to serious criticism in terms of both
economic history and the history of monetary thought. Business
cycles are not all alike; indeed they show differences that are probably more interesting, and certainly no less important, than the
similarities. The causes and manifestations of instability in an agricultural economy are not the same as those in an industrial economy;
the same is true of open and closed economies, of widely- and
narrowly-based productive systems, and of economic and institutional
systems that differ with regard to the organisation of markets,
public finances and credit. To limit 'theoretical' analysis of the
business cycle to repetitive co-movements, as Lucas suggests, would
amount to an unacceptably simplistic neglect of the above features.
The wealth of knowledge that the economic history of each cycle
provides cannot simply be set aside without critical assessment. The
etiology this literature develops cannot be summarised here, not even
at the bibliographical level. In any case, monetary factors are not
excluded; but they are not the only forces at work, nor are they
usually the decisive ones. Just about every monetary explanation of
individual business cycles is matched by other non-monetary explanations. The choice is complicated and has to be made case by case.[101]
This assertion is confirmed by events over the past one hundred years
in the USA itself, events that Friedman and Anna Schwartz – to their
merit – studied themselves from a historical as well as from a
statistical point of view.[102] Equally unjustified, in terms of the history

of thought, is Friedman's attempt to link his propositions to pre-Keynes quantity theory of money by invoking the 'oral tradition' of the Chicago school. In particular, neither that school, nor the economists under whom Friedman studied in Chicago – Simons, Knight, Viner and Mints – had denied the appropriateness of counter-cyclical policies, as today's monetarists have come to do so forcefully.[103]

The question of the so-called exogeneity of money has important historical and institutional features, as well as merely statistical ones. The identification of monetary policy with control of the quantity of money, by means of which monetarists tend to justify the hypothesis – fundamental to their theory – of exogeneity, is again an over-simplification of a complex reality. The mere existence of central banks increases the interest rate elasticity of the supply of bank money. Independently of official declarations of the central banks, their traditional mode of operating is to implement monetary policy by varying the restrictiveness of the conditions for their financing and thereby influencing market interest rates, expenditure, the demand for bank money, and hence its quantity.[104] The correlation between money and income can substantiate hypotheses of causality only if supplemented by a thorough historical and institutional analysis of the stance of monetary policy, as reflected in the changes in the conditions under which the central bank grants credit.

Just as business cycles are not all alike, inflation has been coupled with both high and low levels of profits, production and employment. In this respect 'what is wrong with monetarism is that it tries to put all the kinds of inflation into the same box'.[105] The monetarist attempt is based on the hypothesis that cases of cost inflation are always simply the tail-end of demand inflation, on the dual assumption that the labour market is a competitive market and that, owing to the rigidities of contracts, increases in wages lag behind excess demand. But 'it is just not true that money wages are determined by supply and demand'.[106] Furthermore, there is a downward 'Real Wage Resistance' that can lead to imported inflation, such as that from which the OECD area suffered in the 1970s. It would be absurd to counter this with the monetarist prescription of keeping the growth rate of the quantity of money unchanged.

The abstraction of considering the labour market 'as if' it worked in exactly the same way as the market for commercial paper – taken to its logical extreme by Lucas – lays monetarists open to the more general and basic objection that they are referring to the Walrasian paradigm while forgetting the limits of its applicability and the theoretical criticisms made against it, especially regarding the logical consistency of its treatment of capital accumulation.[107]

Compared with their modern followers, the great neoclassical economists against whom the Keynesian attack was directed in the 1930s were much more aware of the limitations of their model, even though they believed in it whole-heartedly. This is perhaps one reason why that debate was more fruitful than the present one. Impervious to the hail of criticism that has fallen on them, monetarists continue to make proselytes, especially in the English-speaking countries, among statisticians and applied economists, who have a greater propensity to 'use' the latest techniques of quantitative analysis than to test the suitability for the problem in hand of uncritically-accepted theoretical models that are often acquired indirectly and in simplified form. This fact has been fuelled, moreover, not only by the wave of neoliberalist scepticism set off by the failure of economic policies to cope with the stagflation of the 1970s, but also by monetarists having chosen the most watered-down and eclectic versions of Keynes's thought as their target of criticism. It is none the less worth adding that numerous economists still uphold these versions, firmly convinced that analytical controversies are to do with the values of the parameters of some simplified functions of behaviour and that they should be won, in every sense, with the quantity rather than the quality of views popularised in the mass media rather than discussed in scientific forums.

The bitterness of this judgement suggests that the debate on macroeconomic theory and monetary policy has reached a dangerous stalemate. A totally negative assessment of analytical developments in recent years would, of course, be unjustified. Together with other qualifications that such a judgement would require and which space does not permit,[108] it should be noted that in the wake of the basic contributions of Gurley and Shaw, Goldsmith and the *Radcliffe Report* itself, considerable progress has been made in the research into the structural features of the credit system, made up of bank and non-bank intermediaries and capital markets in the narrow sense.[109] The results have greatly increased our knowledge of the channels that transmit monetary policy impulses. Above all, they have provided an indispensable basis for controls and interventions designed to increase the stability and efficiency of the credit system over and above what market forces can achieve on their own.

The risk of involution, typical of a stalemate situation, extends in this case to the role that a longstanding tradition, strengthened over the years by experience and analysis, has attributed to central banks.[110]

Monetarism explicitly tends to diminish this role, based on the recognition of a discretion that is not arbitrary because it is rooted in the principle of a division of tasks within the framework of institutional mechanisms designed to recompose conflicts and restore the unity of economic policy. Apart from the justified grounds for analytical dissent, this is another reason why central banks are far away – indeed poles apart – from the monetarist position, despite convergence on specific points, particularly those of a technical and operational nature. The writings brought together here confirm this assessment. In some cases the criticism of monetarism is explicit, as in the essay by Zijlstra (Chapter 8 of this volume). More generally, it is implicit in the belief that the economy is basically unstable, in the trust placed in economic policy, in the conviction that domestic and external equilibrium require several strands of policy – budget policy, incomes policy and exchange-rate policy – to intertwine with monetary policy.

More generally, the whole controversy between monetarists and so-called Keynesians risks distorting our view of the functions of central banking and the delicate equilibrium among the prerequisites for their effective performance.

All the essays chosen argue or assume that our knowledge of how a monetary economy works means that the government of money cannot be reduced to measures directly stemming from the simulation of a multi-equation model. None the less, not only is our knowledge perfectible but it is not really so limited as to force us to rely on the repeated application of 'rules of the game' laid down once and for all and *a priori* to give up using the unending flow of new information.[111]

It is worth freeing the relationship between the central bank and the government from the alternative of subjection to the executive or flamboyant independence, which, through rationing of credit to the government, implies indirect powers of taxation and control of public expenditure. The first solution would reinvest the 'prince' with unlimited power to debase the currency;[112] the second would lead to the socially and institutionally absurd situation of taxation without representation,[113] or to the opposite but equally undesirable result of making the central bank the natural focus of political conflict.

The solution based on the correct, albeit imperfect, model of a pluralist democracy – on which there is agreement especially in the essays of Cobbold, Rasminsky and Ciampi, and towards which all the major countries are now oriented, though substantial institutional differences still remain – is, of course, that of providing the central bank with sufficient independence to permit a form of critical co-operation with the executive allowing for procedures and institutions – normally the parliament – to settle conflicts between monetary policy and fiscal policy.[114]

The essays by Einaudi, Menichella, Kamitz, O'Brien, Carli and Wallich call for reflection on the decisive importance for the nature of central banks of their being an integral part of the credit system. The delicacy of the balance that has to be maintained in stimulating, supporting and controlling a body of which the central bank is itself a part is matched by the social utility that can stem from success in achieving and sustaining that balance: more efficient and stable credit structures; more effective monetary policy, through awareness of its being mediated by a heterogeneous body of banking businesses; and finally a series of links between the central and the commercial banks, a necessary condition for the special relationship between the central bank and the executive to be justified and of the appropriate dialectical nature.

The international aspect of central banking is considered in the final part of the book, from two points of view. In a world of interdependent economies capital movements can either promote common progress or aggravate existing welfare differentials. In the essays by Hoffmeyer and Baffi, international financial markets and exchange markets are again seen as indicating the 'market plus intervention' combination as the only realistic and effective answer to the more general problem of giving a form to the monetary system that might reconcile growth and stability. In the essays by Patel and Horowitz, the overcoming of economic backwardness and the fostering of development raise the problem for monetary policy – without its assuming responsibility directly for the allocation of resources, which would tend to distort the function of the central bank – of the specific need to establish itself on an international footing, oriented towards co-operation between countries, which is the only way to relax the external constraint.

As regards methods, the pragmatism of central bankers is not only the result of their being aware of the need to combine wisdom, in the ordinary sense of the term, with analytical ability within the bounds of a discipline – economics – that is lacerated by unresolved controversies; it also owes much to the further recognition – particularly evident in Burn's and Emminger's respective interpretations, coloured by sociological and foreign policy overtones, of inflation in the USA and the strength of the DM – that economics, even when it aspires to the rank of 'political economy', is directed at only one of the many facets of a reality that has always been, and is indeed increasingly, complex.

Perhaps the sense of this complexity, with reference first and foremost to the central bank as an institution, is the most useful lesson that can be learnt from the essays in this anthology: 'Monetary policy lives on details, like all that is practicable and real . . . Of things which are indeterminate, the rule also needs to be indeterminate'.[115]

Notes

1. The passage in question is well worth quoting in full: 'If the subject of central banking is classed as an art and not as a science, it is not for that reason any the less scientific. The art of central banking is practical in that it teaches how to use a power of influencing events. It is concerned, not merely with the relation of cause to effect, but with the relation of means to end. But there is no less scope for systematic reasoning in the study of means than in the study of causes. The pursuit of wisdom is as scientific as the pursuit of truth. Economic theory, in every branch, deals with practical affairs. Its subject is human welfare, and it is never entirely dissociated from the practical question of how human welfare is to be promoted. But it is a special characteristic of the art of central banking that it deals specifically with the task of an authority directly entrusted with the promotion of human welfare. Human welfare, human motives, human behaviour supply material so baffling and elusive that many people are sceptical of the possibility of building a scientific edifice on so shifting a foundation. But however complex the material, and however imperfect the data, there is always an advantage to be gained from systematic thought. We may have to be satisfied with probabilities, but we can at any rate see to it that our probabilities make the most of the data we have', R. G. Hawtrey, *The Art of Central Banking* (London: Longman, Green, 1932) pp. vi–vii.
2. The central bank was founded in Sweden in 1668, in England in 1694, in France in 1800, in Holland in 1814, in Austria in 1817, and in Belgium in 1850. The Reichsbank (since 1957 the Bundesbank) was set up in 1875, the Bank of Japan in 1882, the Bank of Italy in 1893 and the US Federal Reserve System in 1913. Among the many works in this field, see the summary comparative study by M. Fanno, *Le banche e il mercato monetario* (Rome: Athenaeum, 1912); see also V. C. Smith,

The Rationale of Central Banking (London: King, 1936); M. H. de Kock, *Central Banking* (London: Crosby Lockwood Staples, 1974); R. S. Sayers, 'Banking, Central', *International Encyclopedia of Social Sciences* (New York: Collier & Macmillan, 1968) vol. II.

3. 'The case for giving to the central bank some special constitutional position rests on the fact that it is the creator of cash, and thereby offers standing temptation to improvident governments. The advantages which such governments enjoy, when they resort to easy finance at the central bank, are immediate and obvious; the disadvantages are not so readily perceived, but in the long run they are cumulative and can be disruptive to economic society. In recognition of this, most countries (including our own) have not been willing to reduce their central banks to the position of an ordinary department of government. The need to integrate the policy of the central bank with the broad economic policy of the government is generally accepted, but the central bank retains a special status which is something rather more than freedom to conduct its daily technical operations unhindered. It is rather, in the words of an outstanding Governor of the Bank of England, that the central bank has "the unique right to offer advice and to press such advice even to the point of nagging; but always of course subject to the supreme authority of the Government", R. S. Sayers, *Modern Banking* (Oxford: Clarendon Press, 1967) p. 67.

4. R. S. Sayers, 'Banking, Central', p. 6.

5. For an introduction to this debate, see E. V. Morgan, *The Theory and Practice of Central Banking, 1797–1913* (Cambridge: Cambridge University Press, 1943). A thorough account is to be found in C. Rotelli, *L'origine della controversia monetaria (1797–1844)* (Bologna: Il Mulino, 1982); but the best critical appraisal remains that of J. A. Schumpeter, *History of Economic Analysis* (New York: Oxford University Press, 1954).

6. M. Blaug, *Economic Theory in Retrospect* (London: Heinemann, 1970) p. 202.

7. Ibid.

8. For an interpretation in this sense of Thornton's major work, see J. R. Hicks, 'Thornton's "Paper Credit" (1802)', in *Critical Essays in Monetary Theory* (Oxford: Clarendon Press, 1967) especially pp. 181–8.

9. J. A. Schumpeter, *History of Economic Analysis*, p. 729.

10. H. Thornton, *An Enquiry into the Nature and Effects of the Paper Credit of Great Britain* (London: Hatchard, 1802) p. 295.

11. A summary comment can none the less be found in T. M. Humphrey, 'The Classical Concept of the Lender of Last Resort', *Economic Review of the Federal Reserve Bank of Richmond*, no. 61, 1975, especially pp. 3–4.

12. D. Ricardo, 'The High Price of Bullion: A Proof of the Depreciation of Banknotes', in P. Sraffa (ed.), *Works and Correspondence of David Ricardo* (Cambridge: Cambridge University Press, 1951) vol. III, pp. 94–5.

13. D. Ricardo, 'Plan for the Establishment of a National Bank', in *Works and Correspondence of David Ricardo*, vol. IV.

14. R. S. Sayers, 'The Theoretical Basis of Central Banking', in *Central Banking after Bagehot* (Oxford: Clarendon Press, 1957) pp. 1 and 7.
15. See the survey by V. C. Smith, *The Rationale of Central Banking*, which, though full of sympathy for the pluralist view, is thorough and penetrating. This book does not deal with Italy, even though the debate there was no less exhaustive and actually lasted longer than in other countries because of the survival of several banks of issue and the strength of regional forces. A useful bibliographical guide to the period after the unification of Italy is to be found in E. Vitale, *La riforma degli istituti di emissione e gli 'scandali bancari' in Italia 1882–1896* (Rome: Chamber of Deputies, Historical Archive, 1972). Among the writings of the politicians involved, the most interesting and lucid is that by C. Cavour, *Discorso sul progetto di legge per l'affidamento del servizio di Tesoreria generale dello Stato alla Banca Nazionale (14 novembre 1853)*, in Nuova Collana di Economisti Stranieri e Italiani, A. Garino Canina (ed.), *Economisti italiani del Risorgimento* (Turin: UTET, 1933) vol. II, pp. 214–29.
16. F. A. v. Hayek, *The Constitution of Liberty* (Chicago: University of Chicago Press, 1960) pp. 520–1; *Choice in Currency* (London: The Institute of Economic Affairs, 1976); and *Denationalisation of Money* (London: The Institute of Economic Affairs, 1976).
17. V. C. Smith, *The Rationale of Central Banking*, p. 172.
18. Quoted in W. Bagehot, *Lombard Street: A Description of the Money Market* (London: King, 1873) pp. 170–1. The data on the Bank of England's loans on private securities are given on p. 62.
19. J. A. Schumpeter, *History of Economic Analysis*, p. 697.
20. J. M. Keynes, 'The Works of Bagehot', *The Economic Journal*, 1915, p. 371.
21. J. A. Schumpeter, *History of Economic Analysis*, p. 1111.
22. W. Bagehot, *Lombard Street*, p. 123 and ch. 6.
23. Ibid, p. 57.
24. Ibid, p. 56.
25. H. Thornton, *Paper Credit of Great Britain*, pp. 185–6.
26. In his *Lombard Street* Bagehot actually talks of 'raising' and 'very high' interest rates (cf., for example, the passage on p. 56 quoted above) exclusively as the means of countering a foreign drain. The view upon which this reasoning is based is that if the risk of capital outflows were eliminated, a domestic drain would require unchanged or lower interest rates. However, see T. M. Humphrey, 'The Classical Concept of the Lender of Last Resort', for the opposite view.
27. W. Bagehot, *Lombard Street*, p. 71.
28. Ibid, p. 51.
29. Ibid, pp. 51–2.
30. J. M. Keynes, 'The Works of Bagehot', p. 372.
31. R. S. Sayers, 'The Development of Central Banking after Bagehot', in *Central Banking after Bagehot*, p. 9.
32. J. M. Keynes, *The General Theory of Employment, Interest and Money* (London: Macmillan, 1936) pp. 32–4. The only qualification to this view is that the critical approach which Keynes identified with the principle

of effective demand survived, after Malthus, in the 'clandestine' analyses of Marx, Gesell and Douglas. See also N. Kaldor's *The Scourge of Monetarism* (Oxford: Oxford University Press, 1982) p. 19.

33. J. A. Schumpeter, *History of Economic Analysis*, p. 703.
34. N. Kaldor, *The Scourge of Monetarism*, p. 42.
35. J. A. Schumpeter, *History of Economic Analysis*, pp. 702–3. On money in Marx, see C. Boffito, *Teoria della moneta* (Turin: Einaudi, 1973).
36. M. Blaug, *Economic Theory in Retrospect*, p. 615.
37. J. A. Schumpeter, *History of Economic Analysis*, p. 1103.
38. 'I maintain that Ricardo, before him Wheatley, after him James Mill and McCulloch, held the quantity theory in this sense and that no other major writers did', J. A. Schumpeter, *History of Economic Analysis*, p. 703. 'Ricardo turned a deaf ear to Thornton's suggestion and kept on repeating again and again – almost unintelligently – that "fictitious" capital cannot stimulate industry' (ibid, p. 724). 'Ricardo, there, is not much help to us. Though he did have a theory of the "world" value of money, explaining it in terms of the real cost of production of the money metal, it was a very long-run theory, an almost incredibly long-run theory, so long-run as to be uninformative', J. R. Hicks, 'Monetary Experience and the Theory of Money', in *Economic Perspectives: Further Essays on Money and Growth* (Oxford: Clarendon Press, 1977) pp. 48–9.
39. D. Hume, 'Of Money', in *Political Discourses* (Edinburgh: Fleming, 1752).
40. M. Blaug, *Economic Theory in Retrospect*, p. 180.
41. J. S. Mill, *Principles of Political Economy* (London: Longman, 1885) especially book III, ch. 8.
42. E. Eshag, *From Marshall to Keynes: An Essay on the Monetary Theory of the Cambridge School* (Oxford: Blackwell, 1963) p. 14.
43. J. A. Schumpeter, *History of Economic Analysis*, p. 1109.
44. 'I hold that prices vary directly with the volume of currency, if other things are equal; but other things are constantly changing. This so-called "quantity theory of the value of money" is true in just the same way as it is true that the day's temperature varies with the length of the day, other things being equal; but other things are seldom equal', A. Marshall, 'Evidence before the Indian Currency Committee (1899)', in *Official Papers by Alfred Marshall* (London: Macmillan, 1926) p. 267.
45. For a well-argued interpretation in this key of Wicksell's monetary theory, see J. R. Hicks, *Monetary Experience*.
46. M. Blaug, *Economic Theory in Retrospect*, p. 616. See also, in the same vein, J. A. Schumpeter, *History of Economic Analysis*, pp. 1101–2.
47. J. A. Schumpeter, *History of Economic Analysis*, p. 1112.
48. Ibid, p. 1077.
49. R. S. Sayers, *Banking, Central*, p. 4.
50. Ibid, pp. 4–5. For supporting evidence with regard to Italian central bankers' awareness of the effects monetary restriction could produce on income and employment as well as prices and exchange rates, see P. Ciocca, 'Note sulla politica monetaria italiana, 1900–1913', in G. To-

niolo (ed.), *Lo sviluppo economico italiano, 1861–1940* (Bari: Laterza, 1973) pp. 241–82.

51. M. Desai, *Testing Monetarism* (London: Pinter, 1981) p. 35. Schumpeter had arrived at a similar conclusion: ' . . . the chief progress of monetary theory in more recent times has been the result of a tendency to tear up the straitjackets and to introduce explicitly and directly all that the best presentations of the quantity theory relegated into the limbo of indirect influences', *History of Economic Analysis*, p. 1106.

52. J. M. Keynes, *The General Theory*, especially chs 3, 5, 20 and 21. For a critical guide to *The General Theory*, see V. Chick, *Macroeconomics after Keynes: A Reconsideration of the 'General Theory'* (Oxford: Allan, 1983). A simpler handbook with a similar approach is that published twenty years earlier by P. Davidson and E. Smolensky, *Aggregate Supply and Demand Analysis* (New York: Harper & Row, 1964).

53. J. Robinson, 'Quantity Theories Old and New: A Comment', *Journal of Money, Credit and Banking*, 1970, pp. 505–6.

54. For a recent appraisal of that far-off but decisive discussion, see M. Desai, 'The Task of Monetary Theory: The Hayek–Sraffa Debate in a Modern Perspective', in M. Baranzini (ed.), *Advances in Economic Theory* (Oxford: Blackwell, 1982).

55. J. Robinson, 'Quantity Theories Old and New', p. 505.

56. Committee on the Working of the Monetary System, *Principal Memoranda of Evidence* (London: HMSO, 1959). Kahn's contribution is to be found in R. Kahn, *Selected Essays on Employment and Growth* (Cambridge: Cambridge University Press, 1972).

57. Committee on the Working of the Monetary System, *Report* (London: HMSO, 1959) paragraphs 514 and 389 respectively.

58. 'I believe that negotiation of some kind of national wage structure, conceived in terms of relative wages, at least for the most important sections of labour, is an essential prerequisite to securing . . . a tolerable behaviour of the absolute wage level . . . Essentially it would be a matter for negotiation *between* trade unions, and to some extent *within* trade unions. It . . . would call for strong direction inside the trade-union movement', R. Kahn, *Selected Essays*, pp. 143–4 (my italics).

59. R. Kahn, *Selected Essays*, p. 146.

60. Ibid, p. 147.

61. J. R. Hicks, 'Mister Keynes and the "Classics"', *Econometrica*, no. 5, 1937.

62. J. Robinson, 'Quantity Theories Old and New', pp. 507–8.

63. Ibid, p. 508.

64. J. M. Keynes, *The General Theory*, pp. 197–8.

65. Cf., in particular, P. Garegnani, *Valore e domanda effettiva* (Turin: Einaudi, 1979).

66. F. Modigliani, 'Liquidity Preference and the Theory of Interest and Money', *Econometrica*, no. 12, 1944, pp. 45–88; L. R. Klein, *The Keynesian Revolution* (New York: Macmillan, 1947); A. H. Hansen, *Monetary Theory and Fiscal Policy* (New York: McGraw Hill, 1949).

Greater awareness of the neoclassical elements in this type of model is naturally to be found in D. Patinkin, *Money, Interest and Prices* (New York: Harper & Row, 1958).

67. Any selection of critical surveys of the main results of the research in this field is bound to be arbitrary, even if its purpose is purely bibliographical. It is none the less impossible to omit those sponsored between 1957 and the early 1960s by the Royal Economic Society in the UK and the American Economic Association in the USA. For a summary discussion of the leading large-scale econometric models constructed in the USA, see M. D. Intriligator, *Econometric Models, Techniques and Applications* (Amsterdam: North Holland, 1978) ch. 12. The most important example in Italy is the model constructed by the Bank of Italy; see the first description by Guido Carli in *Vincoli nella politica economica italiana*, a lecture given on 7 February 1970 at the Economics Faculty of the University of Parma in Brescia.

68. With reference to Italian experience, see P. Baffi, 'L'analisi monetaria in Italia', in *Studi sulla moneta* (Milan: Giuffré, 1965) and 'Metodi e programmi di azione monetaria in Italia: uno sguardo a due decenni', in *Nuovi studi sulla moneta*, (Milan: Giuffré, 1973); see also F. Cotula and P. de' Stefani, *La politica monetaria in Italia: Istituti e strumenti* (Bologna: Il Mulino, 1979).

69. Among such works, it is worth mentioning: G. Ackley, *Macroeconomic Theory* (New York: Macmillan, 1961); M. J. Bailey, *National Income and the Price Level: A Study in Macrotheory* (New York: McGraw Hill, 1962); J. S. Duesenberry, *Money and Credit: Impact and Control* (Englewood Cliffs: Prentice Hall, 1964); R. G. D. Allen, *Macro-Economic Theory: A Mathematical Treatment* (London: Macmillan, 1967); M. K. Evans, *Macroeconomic Activity: Theory, Forecasting, and Control* (New York: Harper & Row, 1969). Textbooks were also produced in Italy giving a full and critical description of the *IS–LM* model; outstanding among these, apart from anything else for the clarity of the writing, is that by F. Caffè, *Lezioni di politica economica*, published by Boringhieri, Turin 1978.

70. Strictly Keynesian textbooks on money and monetary policy have not been totally lacking, but they have appeared sporadically. An example is the lively and elegant work by A. B. Cramp, *Monetary Management: Principles and Practice* (London: Allen & Unwin, 1971). Of the famous Keynesians, it was again Joan Robinson who showed the greatest commitment to teaching – cf. J. Robinson and J. Eatwell, *An Introduction to Modern Economics* (London: McGraw Hill, 1973). Furthermore, not much research was done in this direction either. Among the exceptions of greatest interest, and also decidedly opposed to the main stream of US literature, the writings of H. Minsky occupy an important place; see, in particular, H. Minsky, *John Maynard Keynes* (New York: Columbia University Press, 1975).

71. R. Kahn, *The Development of Theories of Employment*, Lezioni Mattioli (Milan: Banca Commerciale Italiana, 1978) mimeo, lesson 5, p. 25.

72. '. . . the only way in which *IS–LM* analysis usefully survives – as anything more than a classroom gadget, to be superseded, later on, by

something better – is in application to a particular kind of causal analysis, where the use of equilibrium methods, even a drastic use of equilibrium methods, is not inappropriate. I have deliberately interpreted the equilibrium concept, to be used in such analysis, in a very stringent manner (some would say a pedantic manner) not because I want to tell the applied economist, who uses such methods, that he is in fact committing himself to anything which must appear to him to be so ridiculous, but because I want to ask him to try to assure himself that the divergences between reality and the theoretical model, which he is using to explain it, are no more than divergences which he is entitled to overlook. I am quite prepared to believe that there are cases where he is entitled to overlook them. But the issue is one which needs to be faced in each case.' J. R. Hicks, '*IS–LM* an Explanation', *Journal of Post-Keynesian Economics*, vol. III, 1980–1, pp. 152–3.

73. H. Markowitz, 'Portfolio Selection', *Journal of Finance*, 1952, pp. 77–91; J. Tobin, 'Liquidity Preference as Behaviour Toward Risk', *Review of Economic Studies*, 1958, pp. 65–86.
74. J. R. Hicks, *Causality in Economics* (Oxford: Blackwell, 1979) p. 85.
75. For a concise introduction to this criticism, see M. H. Dobb, *Theories of Value and Distribution since Adam Smith: Ideology and Economic Theory* (Cambridge: Cambridge University Press, 1973) ch. 9.
76. *De rigueur*, the reference is to the textbook bought by over 10 million readers, P. A. Samuelson's *Economics* (New York: McGraw Hill, 1980).
77. A. W. H. Phillips, 'The Relationship between Unemployment and the Rate of Change of Money Wage Rates in the United Kingdom, 1861–1957', *Economica*, 1958, pp. 283–300.
78. P. A. Samuelson and R. M. Solow, 'Analytical Aspects of Anti-Inflation Policy', *The American Economic Review*, 1960, pp. 177–94.
79. A classic example of this optimism is W. W. Heller, *New Dimensions of Political Economy* (Cambridge, Massachusetts: Harvard University Press, 1966).
80. J. M. Keynes, 'Professor Tinbergen's Method', *The Economic Journal*, 1939, pp. 558–68.
81. M. Bronfenbrenner (ed.), *Is the Business Cycle Obsolete?* (New York: Wiley, 1969).
82. W. Poole, 'Optimal Choice of Monetary Policy Instruments in a Simple Stochastic Macro Model', *Quarterly Journal of Economics*, 1970, pp. 197–226.
83. Friedman's writing and its derivatives now form a copious literature. For a preliminary guide, see T. Mayer, *The Structure of Monetarism* (New York: Norton, 1978); T. Congdon, *Monetarism: An Essay in Definition* (London: Centre for Policy Studies, 1978); D. D. Purvis, 'Monetarism: A Review', *The Canadian Journal of Economics*, no. 1, 1980. The major works by Lucas have been brought together in R. E. Lucas, Jr, *Studies in Business-Cycle Theory* (Cambridge, Massachusetts: MIT Press, 1981).
84. M. Friedman, 'The Methodology of Positive Economics', in *Essays in Positive Economics* (Chicago: University of Chicago Press, 1953). On

Friedman's place in non-rational epistemology, see W. J. Frazer, Jr, and L. A. Boland, 'An Essay on the Foundations of Friedman's Methodology', *The American Economic Review*, 1983, pp. 129–44.

85. M. Friedman, 'A Theoretical Framework for Monetary Analysis', *National Bureau of Economic Research Occasional Paper*, no. 112 (New York: 1971) p. 2.

86. M. Friedman, *The Optimum Quantity of Money and Other Essays* (Chicago: Aldine, 1969) p. 179.

87. Ibid, p. 181.

88. Ibid, p. 181.

89. M. Friedman, 'The Role of Monetary Policy' in *The Optimum Quantity of Money and Other Essays*, p. 105.

90. Ibid, p. 106.

91. Ibid, p. 107.

92. Ibid, p. 109.

93. Ibid, p. 110.

94. M. Friedman, 'Should There Be an Independent Monetary Authority?', in L. B. Yeager (ed.), *In Search of a Monetary Constitution* (Cambridge Massachusetts: Harvard University Press, 1962) p. 227.

95. R. E. Lucas, Jr, *Studies in Business-Cycle Theory*, p. 257, my italics.

96. Ibid, pp. 232–3. For a useful guide to the problems raised by the new classical economics, see A. Vercelli, '"Anti-Lucas", ovvero "La Nuova Economia Classica" e la rivoluzione Keynesiana', in *Keynes*, edited by the Cassa di Risparmio di Torino, Piemonte Vivo Ricerche, Turin 1983. Vercelli's essay brings out the merely instrumental nature of the so-called 'rational expectations' hypothesis within Lucas's programme.

97. 'Friedman's arguments can be taken as an injunction to look for good correlations and make no attempt to judge whether or not they are spurious. If this is what he means I must part company with him . . . It seems to me that one of the most convenient instruments for judging the appropriateness of our necessarily imperfectly realistic models is the examination of the plausibility of their assumptions. While ridiculous premises may sometimes yield correct conclusions, we can have no confidence that they will do so', W. J. Baumol, *Business Behavior, Value and Growth* (New York: Macmillan, 1959) p. 6.

98. '. . . specifications and identifications must be determined *a priori* by reflecting on what is essential to capitalist industrial institutions', M. Hollis and E. Nell, *Rational Economic Man: A Philosophical Critique of Neo-Classical Economics* (Cambridge: Cambridge University Press, 1975) pp. 20 and 265.

99. M. Hollis and E. Nell, *Rational Economic Man*, ch. 1, and M. Desai, *Testing Monetarism*, ch. 3.

100. M. Desai, *Testing Monetarism*, p. 189. This book also contains an excellent survey of the empirical literature on other monetarist propositions.

101. For an introduction to this issue, see the entry 'Crisi economiche' and similar in the encyclopaedia *Il mondo contemporaneo: Economia e Storia* (Florence: La Nuova Italia, 1978).

102. The most controversial example is, of course, the Great Depression.

For two non-monetary interpretations, see P. Temin, *Did Monetary Forces Cause the Great Depression?* (New York: Norton, 1976) and C. P. Kindleberger, *The World in Depression, 1929–1939* (London: Allen Lane, 1973).

103. D. Patinkin, 'The Chicago Tradition, the Quantity Theory, and Friedman', in *Essays on and in the Chicago Tradition* (Durham: Duke University Press, 1981). F. Cesarano is more open to the possibility of links with the older economists in the case of Friedman, but not in that of the new classical macroeconomics, see his 'The Rational Expectations Hypothesis in Retrospect', *The American Economic Review*, 1983, pp. 198–203.

104. An extreme version of this analytical approach is that which envisages a managed money supply function with infinite interest rate elasticity; see N. Kaldor, *The Scourge of Monetarism*, especially pp. 19–29, and also N. Kaldor and J. Trevithick, 'A Keynesian Perspective on Money', *Lloyds Bank Review*, no. 139, 1981, pp. 1–19. The resort to the announcement of quantitative monetary and credit targets by the central banks of several countries does not break the tradition. Dr Emminger's postscript in this book is confirmation of this affirmation, especially since the Bundesbank was the first central bank to make such announcements. In the final analysis they are an operational technique designed to enhance the effect of a restrictive and credible monetary policy in the short term by influencing expectations, with the aim of reducing the cost of bringing prolonged inflation down. For a discussion of the limits of this technique when it is not part and parcel of an economic policy mix that also curbs demand and costs, see A. Lamfalussy, *Observation de règles ou politique discrétionnaire: Essai sur la politique monétaire dans un milieu inflationniste* (Bâle: Banque des Règlements Internationaux, 1981) and J. Tobin, *Monetary Policy in an Uncertain World* (Tokyo: 1983) mimeo.

105. J. R. Hicks, 'What is Wrong with Monetarism', *Lloyds Bank Review*, no. 118, 1975, p. 1. For a survey of the very different natures of inflation in modern times, see P. Ciocca, 'L'ipotesi del "ritardo" dei salari rispetto ai prezzi in periodi di inflazione: alcune considerazioni generali', *Bancaria*, nos. 4 and 5, 1969.

106. J. R. Hicks, 'What is Wrong with Monetarism?', p. 4.

107. For a comprehensive example of the first type of criticism, see J. Tobin, *Asset Accumulation and Economic Activity* (Oxford: Blackwell, 1980). For the more systematic version of the theoretical criticism, see P. Garegnani, *Il capitale nelle teorie della distribuzione* (Milan: Giuffré, 1960). The difficulty of introducing money into the Walras–Arrow–Debreu model in a meaningful way has been made clear to both old and new monetarists on many occasions by Hahn, albeit to little effect. Cf. F. Hahn, 'Professor Friedman's View of Money', *Economica*, 1971, pp. 61–80; 'Monetarism and Economic Theory', *Economica*, 1980, pp. 1–17; 'Preposterous Claims of the Monetarists', *The Times*, 28 April 1981, p. 19; and *Money and Inflation* (Oxford: Blackwell, 1982).

108. In this connection Lucas's own caution, based on his methodological scrupulousness, needs to be remembered: 'From the point of view of

those involved in economic management, the position that policy should be dictated by a set of fixed rules seems at best a partial response to the question: What should be done now? . . . What advice, then, do advocates of rules have to offer with respect to the policy decisions before us *right now*? This question does have a practical, men-of-affairs ring to it, but to my ears, this ring is entirely false', R. E. Lucas, Jr, *Studies in Business-Cycle Theory*, pp. 257–8.

109. An overview of this vast subject together with a preliminary bibliographical guide is to be found in P. Ciocca, *Interesse e Profitto* (Bologna: Il Mulino, 1982). Among subsequent works that by G. Nardozzi, *Tre sistemi creditizi* (Bologna: Il Mulino, 1983) deserves mention for its comparative insights.

110. On the importance of tradition in the political and institutional 'legitimization' of central bank see the fine essay by K. E. Boulding, 'The Legitimacy of Central Banks', in *Reappraisal of the Federal Reserve Discount Mechanism* (Washington: Board of Governors of the Federal Reserve System, 1971).

111. In this connection one of the most sensible and effective criticisms of the hypothesis of predetermined monetary rules is by a member of the Chicago School. See J. Viner, 'The Necessary and the Desirable Range of Discretion to be Allowed to a Monetary Authority', in L. B. Yeager (ed.), *In Search of a Monetary Constitution*.

112. Cf., for example, H. G. Johnson, 'Should there be an Independent Monetary Authority?', in W. L. Smith and R. L. Teigen (eds), *Readings in Money, National Income and Stabilization Policy* (Homewood: Irwin, 1965).

113. For an echo of this view in Italy, though primarily with reference to the institutional order of Western Germany, see M. Monti, 'Più autonomia monetaria, meno poteri fiscali "occulti"', *Politica ed economia*, no. 1, 1983. The case is based on an interpretation of the 'constitutional' position of the Bundesbank that a large part of German legal scholarship itself rejects or qualifies, especially since the promulgation of the *Stabilitätsgesetz* in 1967. On the legal aspects of this question, see: R. Schmidt, 'La banca centrale della Repubblica federale tedesca: aspetti costituzionali', *Rivista Trimestrale di Diritto Pubblico*, 1982; F. Merusi, 'L'indipendenza della banca centrale nel dibattito della dottrina costituzionale tedesca', *Scritti in onore di Ugo Caprara* (Milan: Vallardi, 1975) vol. III; S. Ortino, 'La Bundesbank e la legge sulla stabilità economica', *Economia Pubblica*, April 1975.

114. '. . . independence, looked at practically, is a matter of degree, not of black and white', G. L. Bach, 'Federal Reserve Organization and Policy-making', in W. L. Smith and R. L. Teigen (eds), *Readings in Money*, p. 239.

115. 'Viner after Aristotle', in J. Viner, 'The Necessary and Desirable Range of Discretion', p. 274.

Part I
The Nature and Functions
of the Central Bank

1 Some Thoughts on Central Banking*

Lord Cobbold

In this chapter I propose to consider somewhat generally the place of the central bank in modern democracy and the part which it plays and can play both in domestic affairs in its own country and in international affairs in the world at large.

It is easy, in this field as in others, to make the mistake of taking things for granted and to assume that what happens now is the same as what happened fifty or a hundred years ago. Though it may be true that in their outer shell the older central banks have changed less than many other things, their structure, practice, and relationships have in fact been revolutionised in the past century. Evolution has been particularly marked in the last forty years.

In the domestic field the main structural problems which a central bank has to consider are:

(a) its relationship with government;
(b) its relationship with the banking and financial community;
(c) its relationship with the general public;
(d) the system of organisation and recruitment best suited to these various relationships and best designed to carry out the functions deriving from each.

The central bank is often described as the government's bank, and again as the bankers' bank: indeed these two headings comprise most of its functions. And both emphasise what I believe to be the first requirement – that a central bank should be primarily a bank, able to carry out banking operations efficiently, to give sensible and practical advice, and to gain the full confidence of its customers.

*This chapter originated as the 1962 Stamp Memorial Lecture, given by Lord Cobbold before the University of London on 13 November 1962, and was first published in London by the Athlone Press in 1962.

47

In its relationship with government the central bank has two main functions, advisory and operational. It is a common feature of modern central banks throughout the world that they have the main operational responsibility for official dealings, both in their own markets and in international markets: operational efficiency, both at the higher levels and in routine matters is therefore a *sine qua non*. The degree of final responsibility borne by the central bank for policy decisions still varies to some extent in different countries. Sometimes statutory authority for certain matters is placed directly on the central bank; sometimes the law provides, by such machinery as exists in this country for directions by government, that final responsibility for policy lies with government. In some cases again the central bank will operate in the money, stock and exchange markets as a principal; in other cases, for example in the handling of the British Exchange Equalisation Account, as the agent of its government.

But whatever may be the precise definition of statutory responsibilities, and the exact division between the functions of principal and of agent, it has seemed to me of recent years that the practice, and indeed the philosophy, of relationship between government and central bank has tended to become more uniform in the major centres. The conception, fairly widespread fifty years ago, that the central bank should get on with its own business and not pay too much regard to politics or governments, has steadily given way to the different conception that, though retaining much independence in its operations and in its thinking, the central bank should act in the closest harmony with government. It has become increasingly evident that with the growing preponderance of 'official' activity in business generally and in the markets, it could only lead to disaster if one part of the official machine pulled in one direction and the other part in another. And everywhere it has become increasingly recognised that monetary policy and general fiscal and economic policy are part of the same picture, in which the final responsibilities must lie with parliaments.

The details of this modern conception vary, as I have said, according both to statute and to local practice; the central bank has been described in one country as 'independent within the government', in another as 'independent subject to the final responsibility of government', and elsewhere by other phrases which reflect the different shades of relationship in different countries. But I think that few leading central bankers would nowadays dissent from the view that, at the end of the day, when all arguments have been put and thrashed out, in private and occasionally, if necessary, in public, the final responsibility for over-all policy must lie with government.

Central bank leaders would agree, I think, with equal insistence that they cannot properly carry out their responsibilities unless they enjoy a large measure of independence from government both in their technical operations and in their policy thinking. The importance of independence in operational matters is obvious enough. The need for an independent approach to policy may be more controversial, but I submit that it is no whit less important.

In a totalitarian state, in which government controlled virtually the whole commercial and financial apparatus, a central bank outside direct Treasury control would be wasteful and superfluous. But the free democracies of the world, in varying degree and with different emphasis according to the political philosophy of the government of the day, are in this century setting out to work a system which combines government control and influence with private enterprise and private capitalism. It is this combination of 'public' and 'private' which justifies the division of responsibility between Treasury and central bank: and it is in the working out of this combined system that a proper relationship between Treasury and central bank can give invaluable service both to the government and to the general public. Treasury and central bank are not, and should not be, the same sort of animal. Treasury ministers must always have their ear to the political ground: Treasury officials must be primarily concerned to serve, advise, and protect their ministers. The central bank, though it must be aware and conscious of developments in the political field, should not concern itself with them overmuch: it should concern itself with the general economic facts of life and above all it should be in and of the market, able to approach its problems in full knowledge and understanding of market actions and market thinking. The central bank can then form its judgements from a market and economic point of view, independently of politics: judgements which will often have a different slant from those formed by government, in which political considerations must obviously carry much weight. These two judgements can be put together and argued out at the top – often a useful and rewarding double check on policy.

I have often been asked whether I think the 'directions clause' in the UK Bank Act of 1946 is a good one, and what is the point of having it if it is never used. The clause provides that the Treasury may, if they think it in the public interest, and after discussion with the Governor, give directions to the Bank: this power covers any matter of policy, though the control of the domestic organisation of the Bank is specifically reserved to the Court in other sections of the Act.

My personal view is that for this country at any rate the clause is convenient, though I do not suggest that it would necessarily suit other countries in this precise form. It has the advantage of laying down where ultimate responsibility lies, thus helping to avoid difficulties and misunderstandings which have sometimes arisen elsewhere. Moreover, it seems to me to offer in certain circumstances a way out of an impasse. There could well arise disagreements which could not be overcome in discussion between central bank and government, but which were not so fundamental as to make the Governor feel obliged to resign, or, which would cause a much bigger crisis, to make the bulk of the Court feel obliged to resign with him. It has always seemed to me conceivable, though argument never reached that point in my time, that the central bank might be justified on occasions of this sort in saying to government 'Well, we do not agree and you know our views. But the final responsibility is yours and you know more about the wider picture than we do. We therefore suggest that you issue a direction and make it clear that the decision is yours and not ours'. Obviously this is not something which could happen often; if it did happen often, or if there was a loss of mutual confidence, more drastic remedies would be necessary.

Any use of powers of direction, whether in this particular form or in other forms, must obviously be handled with discretion. Indeed, the relationship between government and central bank on the sort of lines which I have indicated is at all times a delicate one and needs consideration and understanding from both sides. There is a perennial and almost universal lament by central bank governors that Finance ministers expect monetary policy to carry too much of the burden of fighting inflation without enough help from the fiscal side. There is an equally regular lament by Finance ministers that they are prevented from doing the things they would like to do by tiresome objections from central bank governors. But in my experience, and I believe that many of my colleagues in other countries would say the same, the partnership has on the whole worked out well and the relationship has been happy and productive.

I come next to the second heading, the relationship between central banks and the banking and financial systems. After the relationship with government, which is fundamental, this is the central bank's most important concern; one of its first duties is to interpret government thinking to the financial markets and market thinking to government. A central bank which is out of touch with its own financial community and does not enjoy their confidence can never be doing its job properly. Here I would say that confidence and praise are two quite different things. It is normal and natural for banks and financial institutions to be critical of the central bank's policy or lack of policy. That is healthy and often helpful. What is not healthy or helpful is that the financial community should have doubts either about the integrity or about the operational competence of the central bank, or that their leaders should not be on good and close personal terms with the central bank leaders. The ease with which contact between central bank and financial markets can be built up and maintained varies with many things, with tradition, practice, and, perhaps above all, geography. In a market like the UK, with long tradition and geographical concentration in London, it should be comparatively easy: but even then the central bank will be wise to take a close interest, and be seen to be taking a close interest, in much wider commercial and financial circles. It is most important that leaders of business opinion in main provincial centres should have frequent opportunity of seeing, hearing, and talking to top people in the central bank. In countries where traditions are less firmly rooted, where there are vast areas to be covered, or where there are several financial centres, the problem is much more difficult: it is further complicated where there is a federal constitution, with division of financial powers between central and regional governments. Everywhere it needs conscious and continuous effort, and on my list of hints to budding central bank governors I would put very high on the list 'Get to know your bankers and your financial leaders, and do not just sit in your office and expect them to come to you'.

Much more complicated is the question of relations between the central bank and the public, and the degree to which it is wise and useful for the central bank to explain, discuss, and forecast. It can be argued on one side that the more informed public opinion can be brought into the picture of the central bank's thinking, the more the public are likely to understand and co-operate in official objectives and the higher will be the level of public debate and criticism. On this line of argument it is maintained that, when there is a difference of opinion between central bank and government, both views should be fully presented in public so that the debate can be aired and the different views assessed. On the other side it can be held that the central bank is more likely to enjoy the uninhibited confidence of its customers (government, banks, and overseas authorities chief among them) if it maintains a certain discretion in its pronouncements and avoids too frequent dispute in public.

The ideal doubtless lies somewhere between the two extremes. The traditional secrecy which used to bind some of the older central banks, and even more the atmosphere of mystery and mumbo-jumbo which used to surround so-called 'high finance', are clearly out of date. Since the late 1930s, attempts have everywhere been made to make central banking better understood and to dispel the very silly air of mystery. In the 1950s especially, most central banks – rightly in my view – have adopted a generally more forthcoming approach. Policy in this field should not be static; it must evolve, often by trial and error; there will naturally and properly be variations in different countries reflecting the different formal responsibilities imposed on government and central bank respectively by statute or by usage. More often than not, decisions about when to speak out and when to keep silent will involve a judgement between desirable objectives which conflict.

No problem requires more constant attention from those responsible for a central bank than the methods of recruitment and organisation best designed to fulfil its various functions. Inevitably any major central bank has to perform a vast mass of routine work which must be done meticulously and accurately. At the same time it must be so staffed that at all levels the financial community will recognise in the central bank a technical competence at least equal to their own, and that first-class service can be provided to government in fields ranging from dealing in the gilt-edged and exchange markets to international negotiation. At policy level the governors must be able to count on advice, not only on markets at home and abroad, but also on the general economic picture. This involves a continuous integration of operational staff with people who have the time and the background for more basic thought: this in its turn must be achieved without turning technical operators into a study-group or leaving economic advisers to write memorandums to each other in an ivory tower. Whilst longer-term problems and longer-term policies can be batted around both inside and outside the central bank, there is a flow of market decisions which will not wait for long discussion but where a snap answer must be given often involving many millions of pounds.

I should like on this subject to digress a little from the general to the particular, because I feel that this question of personnel is fundamental, and obviously I know much more about the staffing

roblems of the Bank of England than those of other central banks. I
ave earlier used the word 'integration'. This has been the basis of
bjectives at Threadneedle Street. We have endeavoured progress-
vely, as the tasks falling to central banks progressively widen, to
ring together general financial and commercial knowledge, econ-
mic expertise, and technical banking skills, with a measure too of
xperience in handling outside negotiation at home and abroad. We
ave been immensely helped in this endeavour by the composition
nd role of the Court of Directors, which gives the 'professional' side
f the Bank continuous contact with very varied and world-wide
usiness experience. It has been the practice in recent years to fill the
op management from a mixture of men who have served the Bank
ll their lives, men who have had outside commercial or official
xperience, and men who have spent much of their lives in univer-
ities. In many cases it has proved possible to give men coming in
rom outside some years of apprenticeship in the Bank before taking
n top responsibilities. At the same time, as horizons have broad-
ned, men with academic qualifications have been increasingly re-
ruited to the regular staff, with two limiting factors always borne in
nind – that a large army needs other ranks than generals and staff
fficers, and that the bulk of a bank's staff must be trained profession-
lly to handle the bulk of a bank's business.

The criticism is often made, and superficially sounds very sensible,
hat there is not enough interchange between central bank and
Treasury personnel, and that promising men should be seconded for
few years from one to the other. I have never myself thought this a
ood idea. It would inevitably lead to a gradual assimilation of
pproach and thinking, and would ultimately destroy the advantages
which, I believe are great) of the central bank having a life and ethos
f its own.

I pass now to a few comments on the role of central banks in the
nternational field. Here I would repeat what I said at the beginning
f this lecture. People are apt to assume that things have always
appened in the way they do now. In fact the world-wide co-
peration between central banks which takes place today, and which
s almost taken for granted, is entirely the creation of the past forty
ears. Before the First World War, the older central banks had little
aste or competence for dealing with each other: many of the great
entral banks of today were non-existent or in embryo. Starting with
he contacts in the 1920s between the Bank of England and the
ederal Reserve System, going on with the formation of the Bank for
nternational Settlements in Basle and the creation of new central

banks throughout the Commonwealth and in many other countries, close collaboration on monetary matters has by now become a regular and accepted rule.

It is only when it seems to falter, as occurred for a brief moment at the time of the currency revaluations in Europe early in 1961, that one can see how much this collaboration is nowadays taken for granted. And indeed the very rapid and very effective 'gathering of the central banking clans' which followed that moment of uncertainty in 1961 gave more conclusive evidence than had been seen before of the practical value of the relations which have been built up.

The central banking profession has some great natural advantages in this matter of co-operation. It is always difficult to maintain continuous close relations with somebody else unless at least you have common interests and something practical about which to co-operate. On the whole central bankers throughout the world have much the same problems, and discussion with each other is invariably of practical as well as of purely academic interest. On top of that, many central banks are regularly operating together in markets, so that co-operation is more a matter of business necessity than of pleasurable *divertissement*. And continuity is usually easier than in inter-governmental negotiation, since both at the top and at the next executive levels tenure of office tends to be longer in central banks than in Treasuries.

Speaking personally for a moment, I think there is no side of my work at the Bank of England which I enjoyed more, or found more productive, than the very close and confidential relations which I formed with successive heads of the Commonwealth central banks, the Federal Reserve System, the European central banks at Basle, and others throughout the world.

Many of the comments which I have been making apply in the main to those central banks which have already grown to maturity and which work in the more developed financial markets. I pass now to say a word or so on the widespread development of central banking in recent years in the so-called 'emergent territories'.

This is a subject to which, during my later years at Threadneedle Street, we devoted much time and effort. The concept of creating a central bank at a very early stage in economic and financial develop- ment – a concept which has widely become a matter of national prestige – has its advantages and disadvantages. If managed wisely a central bank, even in these early stages, can play a helpful part in developing and regularising an internal financial market. It can also provide an additional and useful 'window on the world'. But, at the same time, where there is only a small and comparatively undeveloped banking system, it can be an expensive luxury. And, above all, too early reliance on a central bank can be extremely dangerous, if it is expected to provide cash to meet budget deficits or in other ways to provide some magic formula which will avoid facing the hard realities of economic life.

The older central banks have felt that they could make no better contribution to the development of these territories than by providing them with first-class people to get the new central banks off to a good start. Rewarding contributions in this direction have been made not only by the Bank of England but by many other banks both inside and outside the Commonwealth. In the result many of these new central banks have been able, with the guidance of senior officers on loan, to build up their own staff at all levels, to develop on sound lines, and to take their place in the international scene. Many of them, by now managed mainly or entirely by local officers, are already playing a most useful part. I take leave to emphasise the great responsibility which lies on the governments in these territories for the future of their central banks. They will need a long period of nursing and nurturing. Governments will be well advised to ensure both that their personnel is kept at first-class standards and that their facilities are never abused for any short-term advantage.

I have been talking primarily of international central bank business as such. But recent experience has shown that there are many ways in which central banks can help their own governments in the international field and can take an effective part in inter-government financial negotiation. I would attribute this partly to the close relations which the central banks maintain as a matter of course and not only of occasional necessity; partly to the speed at which central banks can often act as compared with governments; and partly because central banks can often mediate in situations where direct inter-government contact suffers from political inhibitions.

From the early experiments in the 1920s a whole apparatus of international co-operation has grown up – some at government level, some at central bank level, some, as in the Bretton Woods organisations, with active participation by both. The generalising of these contacts is certainly to be welcomed. But I would venture to hope that it will not be allowed to supplant what I believe to be the real raw material of effective co-operation in this field, the daily informal come-and-go between central banks and the intimate relations between their governors and senior officers.

Nothing is permanent in the world, and far be it from me to say that the division of tasks between government and central bank now generally accepted around the world will stay the same indefinitely. But I am convinced that in the next period the central banks have a material contribution to make. Having myself worked as Governor with seven Chancellors of the Exchequer and with governments of both major political parties, I believe that this rather curious position of the central bank, outside politics, half in and half out of government, inside markets both as operator and as watchdog, can be made to work to the great advantage of the public, both nationally and internationally.

POSTSCRIPT (APRIL 1983)

Although conditions in the international monetary field have changed since the early 1960s, there is, in retrospect, little I should wish to alter if I were writing this today. I should perhaps have laid even stronger emphasis on the importance of relations between central banks and governments and on close relations between central banks throughout the world. Especially in the exchange markets conditions have changed since the 1950s and the abandonment of Bretton Woods. We have seen the huge increase in the amount of volatile funds moving around the world and we have seen the uncomfortable, one could almost say hectic, movements of exchange rates and interest rates.

Clearly to return to Bretton Woods as such is not feasible. But I feel that there is an urgent need of some international structure, perhaps based on the International Monetary Fund, and worked up together by the governments and central banks responsible for the major currencies of the world; the BIS can also be helpful. To provide more stability in exchange rates, in particular on day-to-day movements, is surely a matter which should be given very high priority indeed in discussions on world-wide economic and financial policy.

Of course, stability in exchange rates must depend on the general economic and monetary policies pursued by governments. Central banks will be particularly concerned with monetary targets and interest rates. Here again I can only repeat what I stressed in 1962, that it is most important that there should be the closest relations between central banks and their governments and that they should have an intimate connection with the financial markets both domestic and international.

2 The Role of the Central Banker Today*

Louis Rasminsky

I propose to discuss some of the principal functions of the central banker as I see them, and some of the main problems with which he is confronted today and which he seems likely to face in the future. What I shall say is essentially based on my own experience in Canada in recent years. I ask you to bear this in mind because I would not wish to jeopardise my friendly relations with my central banking colleagues in other countries by pretending to talk for them. In saying this I have in mind my colleagues both in the highly industrialised countries and in the developing countries, some of whom I have had the pleasure of seeing regularly at meetings of the governors of the central banks of the American continent and at Commonwealth gatherings. The role of the central banker is necessarily greatly influenced by the system of government, by the stage of economic development, and by the organisation of financial markets; indeed, in underdeveloped countries, which are chronically short of capital, a great deal of the effort of the central banker may in fact be devoted to improving the structure of financial institutions so that the maximum amount of domestic savings may be mobilised for economically constructive purposes and the pressures for inflationary financing of development thereby reduced.

I will start with some very brief comments about the role of the central bank in the operation of financial markets. From there I shall move away from the world of finance towards the world of production and employment by outlining, again very briefly, my conception of how the monetary instrument operates and how it exercises its influence on the demand for, and the supply of, goods and services. This will lead me to a consideration of the relationship between monetary policy and other economic policies. In this section I shall

*This chapter originated as the 1966 Per Jacobsson Lecture, given in Rome on 9 November 1966, and published in the same year by the Per Jacobsson Foundation, IMF, Washington.

develop the central thesis. This is that, since monetary policy is just one element, albeit an important one, in over-all economic policy, the success of the central banker in using the instruments available to him depends primarily on the appropriateness of the whole set of economic policies: monetary policy cannot successfully compensate for the inadequacy of other policies. I shall then consider some of the practical problems that arise in achieving a proper co-ordination or mix of public economic policies. From this I shall move to some comments on the formal relationship between the central bank and the government. I shall then turn to some vexed problems of alleged conflicts between economic objectives and make some remarks about price stability and external equilibrium as objectives of economic policy.

THE CENTRAL BANK AND FINANCIAL MARKETS

In attempting a survey of the role of the central banker it is natural to begin with the position of central banks in the operation of financial markets. The powers accorded to a central bank, which enable it to influence the rate of expansion of the banking system, to act as lender of last resort to the banking system and the money market, and to act as banker and debt manager of the government, place it at the centre of the financial system. They make it a market-oriented institution. The central bank is naturally concerned that financial markets should function efficiently. They act as the channel through which the impact of monetary policy on the economy is transmitted and the channel through which the savings of the community are transferred to the ultimate users. In a world where a serious shortage of capital has become a chronic condition, concern about the efficiency of capital markets deserves high priority.

One way in which the central bank can make a contribution to the smooth functioning of financial markets is through the skilful handling of its own day-to-day operations. There is no set of rules to provide guidance here. A sensitivity to the working of the market is essential if the central bank is to take initiatives without producing perverse reactions and if it is to deal efficiently with disturbances that arise in financial markets for seasonal and other reasons. This sensitivity can be developed only through experience and must be supported by a steady flow of information from widespread contacts throughout the market.

The expertise which a central bank can develop in financial markets is of value not only in carrying out its own operations but also in assisting the government with its financial policies and debt operations. When the central bank's market expertise is reinforced by competent economic analysis it is able to participate fully and usefully in discussions of over-all economic policy.

The historic role of the central bank as the ultimate provider of liquidity in a financial crisis, is fortunately one of which we have heard rather little recently, but it is one that can never be completely absent from the mind of the central banker. Situations involving the danger of a spreading loss of confidence in financial institutions can still arise, though their origin may well be different than it was earlier in the history of central banking. In many countries institutions have grown up which are very much like banks in the sense that they obtain funds by issuing their own short-term obligations to the public and proceed to lend or invest these funds at longer term. These institutions usually lack a lender of last resort and they also differ from banks in the provisions governing their supervision, inspection, and liquidity. The central bank cannot, however, disregard any threat to confidence in the credit system, whether or not the source of trouble is an institution within the central bank reserve system. It cannot be unconcerned merely because it has no direct statutory powers or responsibility. An important part of the role of the central bank continues to be that of limiting the potential damage of shocks to financial markets and preventing extreme financial conditions from developing. Its concern with the liquidity position of particular classes of institution may, on occasion, have to be permitted to affect the course of monetary policy.

The question of the quality of credit, which is closely related to that which I have just been discussing, is one with which central bankers and other monetary authorities in all parts of the world have found it very difficult to come to grips. To a certain extent, the soundness of credit depends on the prevailing economic circumstances: credits that are perfectly sound under prosperous conditions turn out to be deficient if there is a chill economic breeze. But that is not by any means the whole story. A period of sustained economic expansion involving a substantial increase in the amount of credit outstanding brings with it the risk of a deterioration in credit standards – through the use of credit to finance basically unsound positions, or purely speculative positions, or positions involving an inadequate margin of equity or through the use of excessive amounts of short-term credit for purposes for which long-term borrowing is appropriate. Though he is aware of these risks, the central banker can hardly refrain from encouraging an expansion of credit to facilitate sound economic expansion solely because of the possibility that some of the credit may be misused. He must, however, always be mindful of the risk of encouraging credit conditions so easy that credit deterioration becomes a widespread danger. He must do what he can to remind credit-grantors of the need for prudence and to encourage investors, even and perhaps particularly in conditions of high prosperity, to apply searching and sophisticated judgements in their appraisal of credit risks.

MECHANISM THROUGH WHICH MONETARY INSTRUMENT WORKS

The objectives of the central bank in financial markets, and the smooth functioning of the financial system itself, are of course intermediate rather than final goals. In the last analysis, it is output, employment, and standards of living that matter. All central bankers must, therefore, proceed on the basis of some working assumptions about how the central bank exerts its influence on the level of economic activity. Views on this differ. Some central bankers concentrate their attention on the banking system which they regard as the main potential source of monetary instability. They tend to focus attention on changes in bank lending and bank deposits, or the supply of money. For my part, coming as I do from a country where, in addition to banks, there are many financial intermediaries and other borrowers which issue claims on themselves of varying degrees of liquidity, I have found it useful to regard the central bank as exerting its basic influence through its impact on credit conditions generally – that is, on the cost and availability of money throughout the economy.

The way I look at the matter, the central bank can exert a pervasive influence on the whole range of credit conditions by its operations in financial markets. It can directly influence the rate of growth of the banking system, of bank loans, bank holdings of liquid assets and private holdings of deposit claims on banks. If the central bank encourages an expansion of private money holdings, the growth of non-bank financial institutions is also facilitated. The expansion of banks and other financial intermediaries and the attempt by the public to employ its money claims in other types of liquid assets exert downward pressure on interest rates and increases the availability of credit throughout the system. Similarly, if the policy of the central bank is directed to restraint, this tends to raise interest rates and affect the availability of credit throughout the entire financial system.

Decisions to spend money on goods and services are influenced to some extent by the conditions in financial markets which confront those who wish to raise money and those who may be willing to acquire financial assets as an alternative to spending money on goods and services. These decisions, in turn, affect output, employment and prices. Decisions to borrow or invest outside one's own country are also influenced by changes in credit conditions.

This, in greatly simplified form, is the way it seems to me that the central bank exercises its influence on economic behaviour. It is only one of several possible ways of looking at the monetary process and the impact of central bank action. But no matter how one looks at it, one thing is very clear. The impact of central bank action on credit conditions, of credit conditions on spending, and of spending on employment, output, price levels, and the external balance, is very complex. We need more reliable knowledge of the magnitude and the time-path of the effect of central bank action. This can only come from intensive and sustained empirical research applied to statistics that are more up-to-date, more complete, and of higher quality than we now have.

A similar problem faces everyone with responsibilities in the field of economic policy. If policy actions are to influence the course of economic activity in the ways desired, the policy-makers must have up-to-date knowledge of what the economic situation is and they must know a great deal about all the main forces shaping economic developments. A decision to change some aspect of existing policies has to begin with an appraisal of the current position and a judgement as to what course future economic developments might otherwise take. In short, good policy requires good information and good forecasts.

The possibility of following rational economic policies depends crucially on a detailed and up-to-date knowledge of the facts, on the quality of the underlying economic analysis, and on the ability to look ahead into the future with some measure of confidence. I have to admit that it is in these respects that central bankers, like other economic policy-makers, often feel most inadequate. There is a great deal about economic behaviour which we simply do not know. We have every reason to strive to get fuller and more up-to-date information, to understand it better, and to improve our ability to forecast developments. Impressive resources are being invested in continuing economic research throughout the world – in central banks, in governmental and international organisations, at universities, and elsewhere – and we can look forward to a steady enlargement of knowledge and understanding of economic relationships. But there is still no general agreement on how, to what extent, and how quickly central bank action affects the behaviour of output, employment, price levels, and the external payments balance. So policy decisions unfortunately have to be taken in very much less than full knowledge of their consequences. The best that the central banker can do is to operate on the basis of a working view of the impact of monetary action which seems to him to fit the facts most closely. In framing his policy, he has to have a view of where the major risks facing the economy lie, and to be willing to alter his view in the light of new information received.

A number of economists, discouraged by the lack of precise knowledge to which I have been referring and profoundly mistrustful of the judgement of central bankers, have suggested that attempts to apply monetary policy in a discretionary manner should be abandoned. They have suggested instead that specific rules or criteria on which to base monetary operations should be adopted. These economists fear that if central bankers try to use monetary policy to moderate short-term fluctuations in demand, they are more likely than not to produce perverse results over a period of time. In their more extreme form the proposals of these economists would have central banks follow some very simple automatic rule, such as ensuring that the stock of money on some specific definition increases year in and year out, or indeed quarter in and quarter out, by a predetermined percentage. I do not consider these proposals realistic – I am afraid that it is impossible to encompass and resolve the full complexity of economic life in one or two very simplified relationships. The central bank has a responsibility to avoid the development of extreme financial conditions which would jeopardise the functioning of the financial system. In discharging this responsibility it may on occasion have to react to sharp shifts in investors' appetites for liquidity in a way which causes considerable short-term variation in the money supply. Though I do not regard the proposal for an automatic rule to govern the expansion of the money supply as a helpful one, there is something to be said for the view that central bankers should try to avoid over-reacting to minor and temporary shifts in the pressure of demand in relation to the economy's potential productive capacity, and that they should concentrate on using credit policy to help prevent more serious and prolonged bouts of underemployment or overheating of the economy.

No doubt in time the search for more reliable guides to policy will provide the central banker with a better knowledge of the facts and a better understanding of the precise impact of his actions on various sectors of the economy. Empirical research can be expected to do much to reveal the nature of these relationships. But I feel very certain that at the end of the day, after the computer has had its say, there will remain a continuing need for the central banker to exercise his judgement.

RELATIONSHIP OF MONETARY POLICY TO OTHER PUBLIC ECONOMIC POLICIES

In the course of the present generation, I think that central bankers have increasingly come to regard themselves as being concerned, not only with the management of the monetary instrument, but also with the way in which monetary policy is combined with other economic policies in the attempt to attain the broad economic objectives of the community. This shift in emphasis has arisen in part out of the continued accumulation of central banking experience. In part it results from developments in economic thinking and knowledge. It has been encouraged by the major reappraisals of the workings of the financial system that have been carried out in a number of countries. For the most part, however, it reflects the greatly increased responsibility that has been assumed by the governments of most countries, especially since the end of the last war, for the attainment of specific economic goals, and in particular for the maintenance of high levels of employment and rising standards of living of all sections of the population. This development has been accompanied by massive increases in public expenditure and in taxation which have proceeded to a point where in most Western countries 30 per cent or more of total national expenditure is made by governments or passes through the hands of governments in the forms of transfer payments to individuals.

With the growth of the public sector, government actions with regard to expenditure and taxation and the management of the public debt have come to have a very profound influence on the behaviour of the economy. Over the years, more and more attention has been paid to the way this influence can be exerted. I believe – and I hope I am not being too optimistic – that in recent years there has been a growing awareness that monetary policy is only one element in over-all economic policy, and that the chances of achieving desired economic goals depend very heavily on a proper combination of monetary policy and other elements in the totality of economic policy.

Since monetary policy is part of total public economic policy, its broad objectives must be the same as those of public policy generally. These objectives would be regarded in most countries as including high levels of employment and domestic and external monetary stability. Recently, great emphasis has also been placed on growth and rising standards of living. The new emphasis on growth has had a useful result in focusing attention on policies which can increase the output of the economy by operating on the 'supply' side, for example, policies which aim at increasing the mobility of resources and at improving the level of labour and management skills. As an inheritance from the 1930s, we have continued for too long to think of the maintenance of adequate monetary demand as the hallmark of good economic policy. Enough demand is a necessary but by no means a sufficient condition of satisfactory economic performance. It is an encouraging development of recent years that governments are now prepared to consider very carefully the need for 'supply' policies, including trade and tariff policies. These have a vital part to play in exercising a restraining influence on rising price levels and in improving rates of growth.

By their nature, however, 'supply' policies are long-range in character and cannot be altered quickly. While it is of the highest importance that they be given adequate weight in the total 'mix' of policies, and that they be co-ordinated with other aspects of public policy, it is in the area of monetary, fiscal, and debt management policies that the problems of co-ordination arise in their most immediate and continuous form. This subject-matter was dealt with very elegantly in last year's lectures and I do not intend to traverse the same ground again. I would like instead to refer to some of the practical problems that arise in attempting the co-ordination of monetary and fiscal policy.

It is only realistic for the central banker to recognise that there are a number of factors that inevitably work from time to time against the achievement of the best balance between monetary and fiscal policy. Fiscal policy is on occasion influenced by considerations other than the general economic considerations that apply to monetary policy. Changes in taxes and in government expenditure have very direct and specific impacts on groups within the economy and are therefore

subject to many pressures. While there is increasingly wide acceptance of the doctrine that fiscal policy should seek to stimulate the
economy (for example, through tax reductions) in periods of underemployment of resources and should help to restrain it (for example,
through tax increases) when the economy shows signs of overheating,
it appears that the first part of the prescription can be relied on with
greater certainty than the second. To the extent that there is inadequate use of fiscal policy when the economy is overheating, an extra
share of the burden of restraint falls on monetary policy and, more
importantly, the total job does not get done.

There is also a purely technical reason why this is a recurrent
danger. This is the fact that in most countries, government expenditure plans are normally presented only once a year and tax rates are
fixed by legislatures at that time. Between these annual dates, the
burden of meeting any inadequacy of fiscal policy resulting from an
original underestimate of the task to be performed, or from unexpected developments in the economic situation, tends to fall on
monetary policy.

The effective co-ordination of monetary policy with fiscal policy is
unusually difficult in federal states. A large share of government
expenditure may be made by regional governments who feel less
responsibility than national governments to use their fiscal power
with considerations of the over-all state of the economy in mind.
Where regional governments account for a large share of the total
government sector the central government can seek to obtain their
co-operation, but there is no doubt that the process of obtaining an
appropriate 'mix' of policies is more difficult in such circumstances.

I think that the general experience has been that in most situations
where the aim of public policy has been to 'cool out' the economy and
keep the aggregate of monetary demand from rising more rapidly
than the economy's real capacity to expand, an undue share of the
burden of restraint has tended to fall on monetary policy. This was
one of the main themes of the Report of the recent Royal Commission on Banking and Finance in Canada (published in Ottawa,
1964). This said 'Monetary policy is just not powerful enough to do
the job by itself over any reasonable range of credit conditions, even
if there were no international inhibitions about using it fully.' Most
central bankers would echo this view. Indeed, the present situation in
many of the large industrialised countries appears to provide a
striking example of this. The main share of the load of trying to
restrain the inflationary pressures which have emerged has again
fallen on monetary policy, and interest rates have risen to levels

which are very high by comparison with anything we have known in this generation. In many countries government financial requirements have increased the pressure on the capital markets. It seems clear that a different 'mix' of policies to restrain the inflationary pressures, with less emphasis on monetary policy and more emphasis on fiscal policy, would have been better in the circumstances.

There is much more involved here than the discomfort of the central banker in pushing the use of the monetary instrument too far. It has to be remembered that changes in credit conditions do not affect all parts of the community in the same way. Large corporate borrowers seem, on the whole, to be likely to feel the direct impact of credit restraint less and later than small borrowers: large corporations normally have substantial liquid resources on which they can draw and they have more ready access to the capital market if bank borrowing becomes difficult. There are differences in the ease of access of different categories of domestic borrowers in many countries to foreign capital markets or the Euro-dollar market, and there are differences in the response of different sectors of the economy to changed credit conditions. Housing expenditures are particularly likely to be affected by high interest rates. In addition to these inequalities, there is the real risk that excessive reliance on monetary policy may result in the development of financial conditions so extreme as to impair the functioning of the financial system and impede the flow of funds for productive purposes through capital and credit markets.

I would conclude and summarise this part of my remarks with two general observations: the first is that since the impact of monetary policy is more direct and powerful on certain sectors of the economy than on others it should not be pushed to extremes. It should be supported by and co-ordinated with other policy instruments in an over-all economic policy aimed at a rational combination of objectives. The second is that the appropriateness or inappropriateness of monetary policy cannot be judged in isolation but only in relation to the other public policies being brought to bear on the economic problems of the day.

RELATIONSHIP BETWEEN THE CENTRAL BANK AND THE GOVERNMENT

The formal status of the central bank varies a great deal from country to country. In any case this is a field in which the real inwardness of the situation is not likely to be revealed by the terms of the statute. Much depends on history and tradition and a fair amount even on the personalities involved. There is a variety of views as to the appropriate legal relationship between the central bank and the government. The extreme positions can be stated simply. At one end of the spectrum there is the view that the central bank should be little more than a technical arm of the Treasury, that no significant degree of independence for the central bank can be reconciled with the democratic process since the electorate must be able to hold the government responsible for every detail of public economic policy, including monetary policy. At the other end of the spectrum, there is the view that, human frailty being what it is, a wide separation between the power of the government to spend money and the power to create it is necessary if the latter power is not to be misused.

Between these two extreme positions there is room for varying degrees of independence for the central bank. My own opinion is that there are important advantages in arrangements under which the central bank has enough independence to insulate the management of its operations from the political side of government, and to ensure that the central bank can act as a formidable obstacle to the misuse of the monetary instrument. So far as basic policy is concerned, however, in most countries it would not be regarded as acceptable for the central bank to be able to thwart the government if the latter is prepared to take complete responsibility for bringing about a change of monetary policy in a way that causes the issues to be placed before the public in a clear and open manner. Arrangements which provide this degree of independence seem to me to have the advantage of putting both the central bank and the government in a position where there is no way in which either can avoid assuming responsibility for the monetary policy that is followed.

In Canada, where, as you know, we have had our problems in this area, the central bank has been operating for a number of years under the general arrangements which I have just outlined and I believe that on the whole they have worked well. In order that the relationship between the Bank of Canada and the government can be clarified in law, an amendment to the statute governing the Bank of Canada is now being considered by our parliament. The amendment makes it clear that there must be, as there is now, continuous consultation on monetary policy between the government and the bank. It provides a formal procedure whereby, in the event of a disagreement between the government and the bank which cannot be resolved, the government may, after further consultation has taken place, issue a directive to the bank as to the monetary policy that it is to follow. Any such directive must be in writing, it must be in specific terms, and it must be applicable for a specified period. It must be made public. This amendment makes it clear that the government must take the ultimate responsibility for monetary policy and it provides a mechanism for that purpose. But the central bank is in no way relieved of its responsibility for monetary policy and its execution. The public should always be entitled to assume that if the Governor were directed to carry out a monetary policy which, in good conscience, he could not regard as being in the national interest, he would, after taking steps to ensure that the issues involved were placed clearly before the public, resign.

As I have already indicated, however, I do not believe that the real position of the central bank in government is determined by the statutory arrangements under which it operates. In the final analysis the influence of the central bank on economic policy depends on the respect it can command for the objectivity and cogency of its views as judged in the light of experience and on the proven degree of competence it displays in performing its own specialised role. It depends too on the contribution that it is able to make to the public understanding of economic and financial issues in analysing, in understandable terms, the complex forces operating at all times on the economy and in elucidating the basic rationale underlying the policies it has followed.

PRICE STABILITY AS AN OBJECTIVE OF ECONOMIC POLICY

In the past two decades most countries have been having considerable difficulty in keeping prices under reasonable control. Not only have upward surges in price levels occurred when the economy was clearly overloaded but there has also been a persistent tendency for prices to move up even when capacity was not fully utilised. To some extent these developments have been encouraged by the great stress which modern economic thought has placed on the maintenance of demand as the key to successful economic performance, and by the increased role of government in providing, through social security programmes and in other ways, a firm underpinning of consumer demand. The maintenance of incomes has resulted in large flows of savings, but the persistence of inflationary pressures in many parts of the world, including some of the wealthiest, indicates a continuous danger that the flow of savings will tend to fall short of what is required. Rising population and incomes involve enormous demands for capital for agricultural and resource development, and even in the most highly industrialised countries the requirements for infrastructural development, for the provision of adequate educational facilities, and for harvesting the fruits of modern large-scale technology will continue to grow. To this must be added the huge capital requirements of the underdeveloped countries.

In most countries the goals of national economic policy are now taken to be high levels of employment, reasonably stable prices, a balanced external position and rising standards of living. Latterly, there has been a good deal of discussion on the question of whether these goals can in fact all be pursued with success at the same time, or whether some compromises – or trade-offs as they are called – may not be required. I am not proposing to try to add to the extensive and scholarly literature that has developed on this subject, but I do wish to make one or two observations in what I fear some will regard as a rather dogmatic vein.

The question most frequently raised is whether there is not some inherent conflict between the maintenance of reasonable price stability and high levels of economic activity, and whether we should not be prepared to sacrifice the goal of stability in the value of money in favour of economic expansion. For my part, I think it would be more relevant and useful to ask whether maximum sustainable growth is possible if there are serious price increases.

The views that central bankers in all parts of the world have expressed from time to time about the development of inflationary pressures have led some to describe us as being characteristically more alarmed about the threat of inflation than about the threat of high unemployment. I would deny this accusation. I do not think that it is in accordance with the facts to regard the central banker as having an inflation 'fixation', or as being determined to have price stability at no matter what cost in real output and unemployment. I suggest that the real difference between central bankers and those people who are not concerned about inflation lies in their assessment of what can be achieved over anything but a relatively short period of time by tolerating a certain amount of inflation, creeping or even more rapid. It may well be the case that if rising price levels are tolerated, real output will in certain circumstances be raised for short periods of time. But the public authorities have an obligation to take a longer view. Once it became clear to everyone that public policy, even without any explicit admission, was prepared to allow prices to rise at, say, 3 per cent a year indefinitely, then all members of society, including savers, would take whatever economic or political action was available to them to protect themselves against this erosion in the value of money. In this situation the stimulating effect of the 3 per cent per year rise in prices would fade away and there would be pressure for additional expansionary measures. These would cause prices to rise faster than the so-called 'acceptable' rate and the policies needed to keep the rise within the 3 per cent limit would appear to be 'deflationary' and would be associated with just as much difficulty as the policies that were formerly necessary in the attempt to avoid inflation altogether. Where would the process stop? Would not the end be greater and greater rates of price increase, involving more and more inequity – since in fact not all members of society are equally able to protect themselves against inflation – and culminating in a major economic dislocation?

I find it disturbing to see some economists taking the view that everyone can adjust to inflation, and others trying to measure the costs of inflation in some past period in order to compare them with the costs of potential output foregone in periods of unemployment. These approaches assume that an inflationary system can produce better results over the longer run. I do not think it can.

It seems to me that what is needed is not to decide how much inflation can be tolerated but to concentrate on trying to find ways of making the economy work at satisfactory levels without rising price levels. It is clear that we have a lot to learn about living with prosperity without permitting it to degenerate into inflation. But I am not prepared to give up hope. We are not necessarily helpless because on frequent occasions in the past the economy has thrown up unacceptable rates of price increase when running at low levels of unemployment. Policies aimed at increasing the mobility of our resources and improving labour and management skills can help to achieve stable prices by bringing about increases in productivity. Policies aimed more directly at relating the growth in incomes to increases in productivity and at limiting entrenched positions of market power may also be needed if we are to achieve a satisfactory combination of the goals of high employment and price stability. I know that this question is a very thorny and difficult one. There is the powerful argument that if monetary and fiscal policies prevent the emergence of excess demand there is no need for any special policy on prices and incomes, and if they do not do so such a policy will break down. There are, moreover, few brilliant successes to which one can point where income policies have worked when put to a rigorous test. But a basic assumption on which monetary policy (as well as fiscal and other policies directed towards affecting the level of aggregate demand) depends is that if total demand is not excessive, competition in the economy will ensure that reasonable price stability is maintained. If competitive forces cannot be relied upon to ensure that technical progress in production is reflected in the pricing policy of corporations and to keep income demands within reasonable bounds, that is, within the bounds of what the economy can really provide in the form of goods and services at reasonably stable prices, clearly some workable supplementary measures must be found. These supplementary arrangements cannot be a substitute for over-all policies which keep the increase in aggregate monetary demand within the real capacity of the economy to expand. But the experience of many countries suggests that monetary and fiscal policies need to be supported by some technique which mobilises the force of public opinion behind non-inflationary behaviour by those who are in a position to deploy strong market power.

EXTERNAL EQUILIBRIUM AS AN OBJECTIVE OF MONETARY POLICY

I turn now from the problems of domestic monetary stability to the problem of external stability. The two are obviously intimately related. If the authorities permit too great an erosion in the internal value of currency they are inviting a decline in its external value. The central bank is concerned with both.

In the heyday of the gold standard, central banks discharged their obligation to support the external value of their currency with surprisingly little in the way of gold and foreign exchange reserves. International flows of funds were very sensitive to movements in bank rate or to credit stringency produced by other means. Even if the mechanism of adjustment produced effects which were occasionally unfortunate on the domestic economy in terms of domestic levels of employment and output and prices, this was regarded as being in accordance with the rules of the game.

The situation today is completely different. The governments and peoples of all Western countries are firmly committed to various goals in addition to exchange stability, and in particular to high levels of employment and economic growth. The central bank, as I have indicated, is one of the instruments for the achievement of the general economic goals of the community. Though it must continue to regard itself as being very much concerned with safeguarding the external value of the currency this is no longer its exclusive aim. It has to seek, as best it can, to work for a combination of monetary and other policies which achieves external balance without sacrificing the other objectives of economic policy.

Since the end of the Second World War we have in fact devoted a great deal of effort to setting up institutional machinery which is basically designed to help countries adjust to imbalances in their international position without having to take action destructive of national and international prosperity. Indeed, we may, on occasion, be inclined to lose sight of the enormous progress which we have made along these lines in all the attention that is focused on the difficulties of particular currencies or on the need for further improvements in the international monetary system.

The International Monetary Fund stands at the heart of this system of collaboration. It has firmly established the principle that the level of exchange rates is properly a matter of international concern, it has established a code of good behaviour with regard to exchange practices, and it has mobilised large financial resources to help its members meet temporary balance of payments deficits and give them time to take corrective action when necessary. Under the Fund's General Arrangements to Borrow not only have large additional amounts of foreign exchange been made available which can be used to avert a threat to the international monetary system, but a forum has been provided in which, as in the Fund itself and in the OECD, the main industrial countries of the world can discuss in great frankness and detail problems of international liquidity and adjustment, and the impact of one country's policies on others. In addition to these new institutional developments, the traditional collaboration among central banks has been greatly expanded. Market-oriented as they are, and having a particular responsibility in regard to foreign exchange, the central banks of the main industrial countries have shown themselves capable of very rapid action in mobilising support for currencies under speculative pressure and in helping to maintain exchange stability during critical periods. Under the leadership of the Federal Reserve System and with the useful collaboration of the Bank for International Settlements, there has developed a network of mutual currency holding or swap arrangements among the leading central banks. In their nature these arrangements have to be of a short-term character. Central banks can hardly impose conditions on the recipient bank for the support they provide in these credits, since the corrective action required may fall within the purview of the foreign governments rather than central banks. These credits cannot therefore be treated as a medium- or long-term source of financing payments deficits. They can, however, provide the time needed to work out medium-term credits with the International Monetary Fund or elsewhere and for the authorities to initiate whatever corrective action may be needed.

The impressive development of the machinery of international collaboration does not, of course, eliminate the need that countries will be under from time to time to take domestic action to correct imbalances in their international payments. No country can, over an appreciable period of time, carry out domestic policies which result in it using up real resources – in consumption, or private investment or government programmes – in excess of its own capacity to produce, except to the extent that foreign lenders or investors are willing to go on providing those additional resources. The fact that occasions arise when the need to maintain external equilibrium places some limitation on the domestic policies that can be pursued has led to a frequent allegation that there is some inherent conflict between domestic expansion and external balance, with the implication either that a country which is concerned with expansion should leave its external accounts to look after themselves or that the amount of international liquidity available should be so great that external considerations provide no limitation on domestic expansion. The latter is, of course, an illusion. International liquidity is a claim on goods and services, and there is no reason to suppose that the countries which would be called upon to make good these claims would be prepared to cover other countries' deficits on a continuing basis. The necessary pendant to international liquidity is balance of payments adjustment.

External balance is indeed an essential condition for achieving the domestic goals of economic expansion and rising living standards, and in a world which has been as successful as ours has been throughout the post-war period in maintaining high levels of economic activity, it is a fundamental error to regard these objectives as being in conflict. It is true that if a country is willing to ignore the external effects of its domestic policies, it has greater freedom of action in the short-run. But the foundations of future success in attaining the domestic goals of expansion are inevitably undermined by policies which lead to external deficits which cannot be covered on a sustainable basis, just as they are undermined by ignoring considerations of domestic monetary stability.

The task of reconciling the objective of external balance with domestic economic objectives is by no means a simple one and requires a willingness to deploy all the instruments of economic policy and to avoid excessive reliance on monetary policy. The simple case of a payments deficit which is due to excessive pressure of domestic demand does not raise any problem of conflict of objectives – in this case the payments pressure serves as an early warning signal which alerts the authorities to the need for restrictive action both for domestic and external reasons. Other circumstances call for a more sophisticated combination of policies. A country experiencing payments pressure under conditions of only moderate demand pressure and less than satisfactory employment, and whose exchange rate is not out of line, may require a stimulating fiscal policy to encourage domestic expansion combined with a restrictive monetary policy to attract capital inflows. A country which is experiencing a payments surplus combined with excessive demand pressure may require a combination of a strong fiscal policy to restrain the demand pressures and low interest rates to encourage capital outflows. To meet the challenge of so-called conflicting objectives, there is clearly need for enterprise in expanding the policy instruments and skill and resourcefulness in using them in concert. And this skill is needed not only in the countries which are experiencing deficits in their international accounts but also by those which are experiencing surpluses and are not subject to the same financial pressures to move in the direction of equilibrium.

I am afraid that we have not shown as much skill or as much determination in this respect as the situation has required during the past few years. The great reliance which has been placed on monetary policy as the prime instrument for combating inflation by countries which have been gaining reserves, as well as by those who have been losing reserves, has impeded the restoration of international balance and has led to a level of interest rates and a degree of international monetary stringency which carries with it all the disadvantages and the risks to which I referred a few moments ago. Not the least of these is the threat of a sharp strain on domestic and international liquidity leading to a major curtailment in the international movement of long-term capital for productive purposes from which the world has derived such great benefits during the mid 1950s and the mid 1960s.

Central bankers have recently participated actively in the extensive discussions that have gone on concerning the next steps in the evolution of the international monetary system. These have focused on the means of making the creation of international reserves a matter of international responsibility. I believe that sooner or later we shall have to take a major step forward in providing the machinery for creating reserves by deliberate collective action, and that it is important to resolve our differences about the precise form of such machinery as soon as possible. What we are seeking is more orderliness in the system of providing reserves and more scope for the exercise of judgement as to the amount and timing of changes in reserves outstanding. It would not be helpful, in my opinion, to create new machinery quite separate from the International Monetary Fund for this purpose. On the contrary, it is essential to preserve the central position of the Fund in the international monetary system. At the same time, the arrangements must be such as to ensure that the decisions taken are supported by a substantial majority of countries whose international trade bulks large in the total and whose currencies are widely used throughout the system. The form of the new reserves is a question of less significance. What is essential is to retain flexibility, and to move, as circumstances permit, toward the evolution of forms of international money that are generally acceptable. The aggregate supply should be brought under collective international control, and this control should be exercised in such a way that liquidity is neither so scarce as to force countries to restrictive or harmfully deflationary action to balance their international accounts, nor so plentiful as to encourage deficit countries to avoid dealing with domestic inflationary pressures and thereby help to spread inflation around the world. The success of any new arrangements we may agree upon will depend in large measure on the efforts of central bankers and their colleagues in government not only to deal effectively with their own problems but also to understand the problems of their opposite numbers in other countries, and to seek for solutions which take the general interest fully into account.

The main theme that I have put forward is that the central banker today is a public servant as well as a banker. His role is to operate one of the instruments of public policy for the attainment of the economic objectives of the community. He does not have a separate set of objectives of his own, though he must seek to influence the articulation of the community's objectives and the combination of policies chosen to attain them. He must also seek to reconcile his own and his country's policies with those of other members of the world community. This view of the role of the central banker was shared by Per Jacobsson, who always urged central bankers to remember that monetary policy was only one aspect of over-all policy.

I have denied that the central banker has a fixation with respect to price stability, but I believe that many of us feel a special responsibility to act as the conscience of the community in this respect. No one else is likely to do so. Inflation in its early stages is popular, it creates a feeling of ebullience and well-being which does not tempt people to ask too many questions about the future. Keynes once said that the perfect standard of good manners for a gentleman attending a party is to maintain precisely the same level of sobriety or inebriety as the rest of the company. If this is so, then central bankers cannot aspire to be gentlemen. Their role is rather the unpopular one of acting as the chaperon who has to take away the stimulant just when the party is getting into high gear.

The central banker of today works in an imperfect world, with an instrument whose influence is only imperfectly understood, in seeking to attain objectives that can be defined only in broad general terms. It is not surprising that the profession is full of interest but not free of uncertainty and anxiety. I think that most of my colleagues would join me, echoing Pastor Rheinhold Niebuhr, in saying that what we need to play our role adequately is the serenity to accept what cannot be changed, the courage to change what should not be accepted, and the wisdom to distinguish the one from the other.

POSTSCRIPT (MAY 1983)

This chapter was originally the second lecture in the Per Jacobsson series, given in 1966 when the long period of economic expansion that Canada had enjoyed since the end of the war was beginning to be threatened by persistent inflation at levels which, though modest by today's standards, nevertheless seemed to hold serious threats for the future. The central thesis is that *monetary policy does not operate in isolation* and cannot be expected to compensate for the inadequacy of other public policies (especially fiscal policy) and that the essential job of the public authorities is to obtain a proper mix of policies which will help to achieve the objectives of non-inflationary economic expansion and a balanced international position. The chapter expresses scepticism regarding the desirability of the central bank forming its policy in terms of any fixed set of rules, such as a constant rate of increase in the money supply, however defined, and argues that while the money supply is an important variable, such an approach takes too simplistic a view of the economic process, and that in the final analysis there is no substitute for the exercise of judgement.

The experience of the ten years 1973–83 has strengthened my conviction that this view is correct. I have been increasingly impressed by the important part which fashion plays in the development of opinion in economic issues. The persistent inflation of the late 1960s and 1970s and the dissatisfaction which it engendered towards economic performance and policy led to a shift of opinion towards monetarism. This became the prevailing style, not only in academic circles, but also among central banks. But it turned out that, for a variety of reasons, adherence to a strict monetary rule was no more effective in controlling inflation than the judgemental credit conditions approach. What was wrong was not the technique of monetary policy but the substantive mix of all economic policies – monetary policy, fiscal policy, wage policies, supply-side policies, etc. If the mix had been appropriate to the economic circumstances, the credit-conditions approach would have worked reasonably well and so would a policy which laid stress on a regular growth in the money supply (if some adequate definition of this could be found).

In the same way, the pressures on exchange markets which developed in the late 1960s and in the early 1970s led to the breakdown of the Bretton Woods system. The system of adjustable fixed rates went out of style and flexible exchange rates became fashionable. But these proved no more conducive to international payments equilibrium than the system of fixed exchange rates had been. The trouble did not lie in the exchange system as such but in the failure of the total mix of policies followed to cope with the great forces of international disequilibrium. If these policies had been adequate, either exchange system – fixed rates or fluctuating rates – would have worked reasonably well.

Finally, I comment on the relations between the central bank and the government. In my lecture I develop the reasons Canada had for formalising the traditional theory of joint responsibility of the central bank and the government for monetary policy. In the ordinary course of events the bank should be responsible for monetary policy but the government should in the final analysis have the power, in case of a sustained conflict, to issue a formal directive to the bank. The bank would then have to carry this out, but the governor would not be relieved of this personal responsibility and if he felt that he was being directed to carry out a policy which was against the public interest, he would presumably make way for someone who did not share his view.

These suggestions were incorporated in legislation (Bank of Canada Act, 1967) subsequent to my lecture. No directive has ever been issued. Recently some opinion has developed that the power given to the governor is too great – that his resignation would always precipitate a crisis and therefore keep the government from exercising its right to issue a directive. Under this view, democracy requires, in effect, that the central bank become a branch of government with little or no independence.

I do not agree with this view: the risks are too great. The time horizon of the central bank is in the nature of things longer than that of the government; it is often alone in having an abiding concern with the value of money. The influence of the bank – and the consequence of the governor's resignation – are not automatic; they flow from the respect the community develops (or fails to develop) for the objectivity of the bank's views and the respect in which it, and the governor, are held in the light of experience. An important part of the role of the central bank is to provide one source of authority in the country which the community feels is striving to obtain as much monetary stability as possible, for without this there can be no sustained economic progress. It would, in my view, be a mistake to weaken this confidence in the central bank by destroying its independence.

3 The Functions of the Central Bank in Today's Economy*

Carlo A. Ciampi

The choice of this subject and its treatment here reflect the need to ascertain how far the institutional structure allows the central bank to perform the tasks required of it by a modern economy. This need stems not only from the seriousness of the problems facing the Italian economy but also from the tendency in all the industrial countries for the links between the economic and the institutional and between the juridical and the operational to increase and tighten. This tendency is confirmed by plentiful evidence, which is open to both analytical and value judgements, but which on this occasion needs only to be registered: first, the mere fact that institutional factors are still seen by many as constraints on the working of markets; second, the oft-repeated wish for more complementarity between the 'market' and 'planning'; and third, the greater efforts to take an interdisciplinary view of the problems.

The basic function of a central bank is to control the creation of money with the aim of maintaining the internal and external equilibrium of the economy. It performs this function through its administrative and market relations with the credit system, the Treasury and the foreign sector. Each of these three sets of relations constitutes a channel for the creation or destruction of monetary base. Through these channels and via a complex causal sequence, the central bank influences the formation of expectations, aggregate demand for domestically produced and imported goods and services, and external capital movements.

This chapter was originally presented as a lecture under the title *Funzioni della banca centrale nell'economia di oggi*, at the Scuola Normale Superiore di Pisa on 12 September 1982, and was later published by the Banca d'Italia in the series *Documenti*.

The final objectives of monetary policy have evolved in parallel with the emergence of new values in modern societies. None the less, central banks still perform the task – not so much traditional as innate – of maintaining the stability of the currency. Furthermore, even when this task is taken into account in the constitution or in other laws, it has to be performed in the light of its complementary relationship with another basic aim – full employment of resources in conformity with the external constraint. In many countries, including Italy, this basic function has been increased by entrusting the central bank with structural interventions and the supervision of the credit system. This has entailed the attribution of a series of powers and instruments designed to promote the efficiency and stability of financial intermediation. There are several reasons why the assignment of this additional task is institutionally appropriate.

Monetary policy and banking supervision must not be in conflict in view of the close connection between money and credit. Specifically in its choice and dosage of the various operational instruments monetary policy must take account of the ability of credit intermediaries to transmit the impulses that financial variables are meant to convey to real variables. Supervision, for its part, must consider the general monetary conditions when assessing the profitability and soundness of individual intermediaries. It must be stressed, moreover, that the monetary policy function itself implies control of credit intermediaries since they have access to central bank refinancing. Finally, the two functions are both bound by the constraint of 'allocative neutrality'. This does not mean that the central bank' monetary policy and supervisory measures have no effect on the utilisation of resources or the distribution of income and wealth. What has to be remembered is that such effects should not be pursued with reference to specific aims or, in the extreme case, individual financial intermediaries.

Monetary policy, even when it cannot avoid pursuing selective ends, is directed towards the major components of aggregate demand and supply together with the corresponding structure of credit flow and interest rates. Interventions and the control of the credit system are designed, in turn, to develop institutional and market configurations that will enhance the ability of the system together with other allocative mechanisms, to produce the best choice both of investment projects and of the firms to implement them.

Operational autonomy is basic to central banks. Its extent and form have varied from one period and from one country to another, but it has never decreased without the institutional role of the central bank and the usefulness of its action also tending to diminish.

Going back two or three centuries, it can be seen that one of the reasons for setting up the first central banks was the public's lack of confidence in government banknotes, the result of repeated episodes of heavy depreciation. Central bank mediation appeared a necessary condition for controlled, though not inflexible, financing of the government. Even at that early stage and with such a limited purpose, the independence of the central bank was indispensable for its control of money as well as for the management of the public debt, which remained the responsibility of the Treasury.

This independence is all the more necessary today with the completion of the transformation of the central bank from banker to the king, to agent of economic policy, equipped with flexible instruments of intervention.

Consideration also needs to be given to the aspects of central banking connected with participation in international bodies such as the International Monetary Fund, the World Bank and the EEC institutions entrusted with the co-ordination of monetary policy and, in particular, the running of the European Monetary System. Participation in the Bank for International Settlements provides access to a forum in which the representatives of the central banks of the major countries exchange views and discuss common approaches to monetary policy. The central bank's independence is thus confirmed at the international level.

The risk of independence deteriorating into arbitrariness is reduced by the code of behaviour that has been built up over the years on the basis of analysis and practice. What for a long time has been known as the 'art' of central banking has taken on more the aspect of a 'science'. Economists have made a decisive contribution to this shift from 'art' to 'science' in terms of both theory and empirical research into the causal and temporal links between the instruments and objectives of monetary policy and the interventions to modify financial structures. This accumulation of experience and theory provides parliament and public opinion with a yardstick for the *ex post* control of the technical measures used by the central bank to perform its institutional functions within the framework of the guidelines established by the political authorities.

The need for independence, as the necessary condition for central banks' effectiveness, is reflected in the Bank of Italy's institutional status, which is the outcome of complex legislative developments. The Bank of Italy was set up in the form of a joint-stock company in 1893, following the merger of three banks of issue. It operated in 'limited competition' with the two banks of issue in southern Italy until 1926, when it was granted the exclusive right to issue banknotes. The same year also saw it assigned responsibility for the first, embryonic system of banking supervision.

The 1936 Banking Law transformed the Bank of Italy into a public-law institution. The shares in circulation were reimbursed and the capital divided among suitable holders, most of which were public 'economic' bodies. The bank's governing organs continued, however, to represent the subscribers of the capital, though it was laid down that some appointments were to be approved by the very highest political authorities. By prohibiting the Bank of Italy from granting discounts to non-bank firms, the Banking Law formally recognised its position as the banker's bank. Simultaneously, the bank's new statutes made the issue of banknotes an exclusive institutional right and thus brought to an end the previous system of temporary government concessions.

The Banking Law made substantial innovations in the system of banking supervision with the introduction of a special body – the Inspectorate – that was formally incorporated in the civil service though it was closely linked with the Bank of Italy, to the extent that the Governor was head of both institutions. A 1947 decree formally assigned the functions of banking supervision to the Bank of Italy in replacement of the Inspectorate, which had been abolished in 1944.

The evolution of the legislative framework has profoundly changed the bank's functions and, more generally, its role as agent of monetary and credit policy, while it has made little impact on its constitution. Despite the disappearance of the profit-making function typical of joint-stock companies, the bank's corporate organisation model proved well-suited to its new tasks.

The bank uses private-law contracts to conduct its operations. Moreover its public function of regulating the money and financial markets does not affect the choice of instrument and is performed through market mechanisms rather than administrative orders. The cornerstone of this organisational framework is the bank's independence, in the sense both of responsibility for the correct application of guidelines rather than single actions, and of ability to adjust rapidly, without external constraints, to the changing needs of the economic situation.

The fact that the Bank of Italy is entrusted with banking supervision is not in conflict with the above model. On the contrary, it is precisely in this form of organisation that the technical aspects of supervision – which is designed to safeguard the efficiency of the banking system – find a suitable setting. This argument was already appreciated in 1926, when the first set of limited supervisory powers was entrusted to the Bank of Italy. At the time it was maintained that only a banking business could supervise the credit system. Such supervision, as I have pointed out, is in a sense a development of the control that the central bank automatically exercises over individual banks through its refinancing facilities, by continuously monitoring and protecting their liquidity and solvency without interfering in the merit of their decisions. The structure that was established in 1947 confirmed the logical and operational connection between the functions of banker's bank and supervision.

The Bank of Italy thus has two sets of instruments with which to regulate the money and financial markets via the credit intermediaries. They are legitimised in two separate laws: on the one hand, the typical central bank refinancing of banks, which, besides being foreseen in the statutes, is provided for in an old law incorporated in the Codified Law of 1910 and, on the other, the constraints on banks' assets that the Bank of Italy can impose in its capacity as the supervisory authority under the provisions of the 1936 Banking Law.

The 1910 legislation is based on the classic model of a central bank and its relations with the government and the market. It distinguishes between the two traditional forms of refinancing – discount and advance – and makes the Treasury minister responsible for fixing the official discount rate in accordance with the indications of the Governor of the Bank of Italy. The outcome is a system that – apart from the relative rigidity of the discount rate, which has to be varied with a ministerial decree – gives the Bank of Italy full independence in all operational decisions, especially those regarding quantities.

The refinancing situation today does not fully correspond to this model. Discounts now play only a minimal role and the traditional current account overdraft, which leaves banks free to draw on their credit, has been flanked for some time now by the fixed-term advance. This enables the Bank of Italy to keep a more accurate check on each bank's liquidity needs and the compatibility of the monetary conditions with the refinancing required.

A further technical refinement in connection with the Bank of Italy's interventions in the securities market to regulate the economy's liquidity was made in the early 1980s with the introduction of repurchase agreements based on government securities. Possessing highly flexible terms and yields, these agreements greatly facilitate the short-term control of liquidity, providing and absorbing it a necessary through interventions aimed at the market as a whole rather than at individual banks.

As regards the instruments of supervision, it should be noted that in many cases their scope was extended when they were assigned to the central bank. In particular, the power to impose constraints on banks' assets was originally conceived for precautionary reasons but can also be used for monetary and credit-policy objectives.

The most important example of this development is that of the regulations governing banks' compulsory reserves. Initially seen primarily as a guarantee of banks' liquidity and solvency, they came to be considered as an instrument of monetary policy so that the reserve requirement has increasingly become both the condition and the means of controlling total liquidity. Compulsory bank reserves are now a standard weapon in the armoury of every central bank.

More recent expedients – made necessary by the precarious state of the Italian economy but also adopted, sometimes permanently, in other countries – are the ceiling on the expansion of bank-lending and the requirement that banks should invest a part of their assets in securities.

Refinancing operations are based on the principle of autonomy, are implemented by means of contracts, and reflect a market approach; measures constraining banks' assets are based on the principle of authority, are implemented by means of administrative rules and reflect a regulatory approach. The former are the ordinary instruments of central bank intervention; use of the other instrument for the purposes described above is only justified to satisfy an urgent public need and until more suitable measures can be taken by the responsible authorities. The early abolition of the import-deposit scheme confirms it another field the intention to use administrative instruments only in so far as the urgency and scale of problems make this imperative.

here have been even more important developments in the relations etween the Bank of Italy and the Treasury. In the primordial state f central banks, financing the Treasury could almost be considered a uty, in a way the counterpart of the privilege of issuing notes ranted by the sovereign. When note-issuing ceases to be a privilege nd becomes an institutional attribute of the central bank, which thus cquires the role – sometimes recognised in the constitution – of uaranteeing monetary stability, financial relations with the Treasury ecome more complex and their dialectical aspects require compo- ition.

In the pre-war period this was achieved through consensus in Italy. n Article 2 of the Ministerial Decree of 31 December 1936, the Minister of Finance used the powers granted to him in Royal Decree Law 1647 of 5 September 1935 to indicate 'agreement' with the Governor as the key to new Bank-of-Italy advances to the Treasury vhenever extraordinary government requirements made such ad- ances necessary'.

The system underwent a radical change after the Second World War. The basic legislation governing financial relations between the Bank of Italy and the Treasury is now Legislative Decree 544 of May 1948. On the one hand, this establishes the overdraft limit on he Treasury's current account with the bank as a percentage of udget expenditure and, on the other, lays down that 'no additional xtraordinary advance may be made without special legislation spe- ifying the amount'.

These provisions can rightly be considered of constitutional im- ortance: not only because limiting the monetary financing of the ublic deficit tends to ensure price and exchange-rate stability and hus implements the constitutional principle of protecting savings contained, together with that regarding the government of credit, in Article 47 of the Constitution); not only because it completes and uarantees the constitutional requirement that the finance for every ublic expenditure should be specified in advance (Article 81 of the Constitution); but above all because it makes parliament the ultimate olitical mediator of any conflict between the defence of monetary quilibrium and the need to finance public expenditure.

The constitutional framework thus forbids the Bank of Italy from ccepting Treasury requests for financing that are anomalous in form or not transparent, since to do so would be to usurp parliament's rerogative. In reality the 1948 law does not so much forbid as assign responsibility: forbidding the Treasury from requesting and the Bank of Italy from granting extraordinary advances is instrumental in assigning ultimate responsibility in this matter to parliament.

The synthesis of the divergent aims of the Treasury and the central bank is made easier by the existence of a deep and competitive money market. This provides greater scope for the placement and management of the public debt. Furthermore it reflects the pressure of public borrowing on real and financial saving more rapidly and accurately.

The Bank of Italy has worked continuously over the years to promote the development of such a market. What has come to be known as the 'divorce' between the Bank of Italy and the Treasury i part of a process that, although rendered irregular by the need to compromise between conflicting short-term requirements, has been under way for many years.

The central bank's decision in 1975 to take up the Treasury bill unsold at auction was itself connected with other measures designed to make the money market more efficient and complete: non-bank operators were permitted to take part in auctions; these operator were allowed to present multiple bids amounting to a virtual demand schedule; the Bank of Italy, which had previously had to purchase unsold securities at their base price, was allowed to take part in auctions directly and to make its interest-rate views felt in its residual purchases. The thinness of the secondary market at the time forced the Bank of Italy to pursue its control of the monetary base via these securities, primarily by intervening in Treasury bill issues. Further more, when the decision was taken, budget deficits were neither as large nor as structural as in the early 1980s. The ratio of the public debt to GDP rose from 53 per cent in 1975 to 67 per cent in 1981 while the ratio of Treasury bills to the total public debt tripled. In these later conditions, automatic Bank-of-Italy purchases of unsold Treasury bills risked breaching the spirit of the legislation I mentioned.

A large public sector borrowing requirement that is growing fast and irregularly tends to reduce the scope for stabilising monetar policies. The underlying risk is that *de facto* negation of the central bank's independence will reduce it to a mere printing works and provoke a relapse into the primordial relations between the sovereign and his banker. This would amount to allowing inflation to get out of hand and balance-of-payments deficits to become chronic.

By contrast, the problem of putting public finances back on a sound footing must be allowed to appear in all its gravity, expendi ture must be curbed and its composition improved, taxes must be increased and made fairer, and the best distribution of costs sought between the present and future generations.

If it proves hard to progress along this road, which must aim at the elimination of the public deficit on current account, it becomes all the more important to safeguard the role of monetary policy by allowing the central bank to determine the general conditions of credit availability and cost that will best help to bring down inflation, keep expectations under control and defend the exchange rate.

Even though public debt management can affect the structure of interest rates and the composition of credit flows and financial assets, it must not be allowed to influence the basic features of monetary policy.

Coming now to the third channel of liquidity management, the foreign sector, one is struck by the complexity of the institutional organisation of the central bank's functions, a situation peculiar to Italy. Notwithstanding the intimate relationship between the functions of monetary control and exchange rate management, whereby the central bank pursues the objective of monetary stability in terms of both the domestic and the external purchasing power of the currency, in Italy all exchange matters are entrusted to a body that is formally distinct from the Bank of Italy: the Italian Foreign Exchange Office (Ufficio Italiano dei Cambi, UIC).

This situation has its origin in the fact that the UIC was created in 1945, to replace the National Foreign Exchange Institute, which had been set up in 1917 to run the foreign-exchange monopoly. This was introduced as a wartime measure, abolished in 1919, and then revived in 1934.

The law establishing the UIC refers explicitly to this monopoly when it lays down that 'as long as the exchange monopoly is in force, the UIC shall undertake all business in foreign currencies and in any other means of payment abroad'. The exchange monopoly thus gives substance to the detachment of the exchange function from the Bank of Italy and its assignment to a separate organisation. Furthermore, monopoly in the strict sense implies a centralised management of foreign currency and its allocation among operators in accordance with criteria of political and administrative rationing. Nothing could be more in conflict with the market orientation that must underly central banking.

The exchange monopoly has been a dead letter now for many

years, at least in the sense just described. The process of liberalisation got under way in the early post-war years and led to the decrees of 1955 and 1956. These are still the basis of the current exchange legislation and allowed banks considerable freedom to deal in foreign currency as well as the creation of a foreign exchange market. In turn, this liberalisation was one of the prerequisites of the convertibility of the lira – announced in 1958 – and of Italy's integration in the European and world economies, of which EMS membership is the most recent and important development.

As matters stand, however, Italy still has stricter exchange regulations than most other countries, and these entail the continuance of controls by the UIC as the government's technical organ. Besides, the assignment of the management of the reserves to a body separate from the Bank of Italy clearly illustrates the strength of the historical influences mentioned.

There is a sharp distinction between the functions of exchange control and management of the reserves as regards instruments and objectives. In its typically central-bank function the UIC employs market instruments. This is provided for directly in its establishing law, which states that the UIC's 'purpose is to make spot and forward sales and purchases of gold, foreign currencies, foreign banknotes, foreign securities, Italian securities issued abroad, and Italian securities denominated in foreign currencies'. In particular, the investment of foreign currency reserves is designed to reconcile the need for a high yield with safety and marketability.

As the government's executive body in exchange matters, the UIC employs the instruments typical of public administration. By ministerial delegation the UIC has broad powers of authorisation, whereby it makes what amounts to a prior control of the merits of a whole series of transactions between residents and non-residents. In addition, the UIC like its predecessor the National Institute of Foreign Exchange, has general responsibility for 'the supervision and control of the regular observance of the exchange regulations in force' and for this purpose is entrusted with far-reaching powers of inspection.

The actual scope of these powers of investigation, control and repression depends directly, of course, on the restrictiveness of the exchange regulations in force at any given moment. After a prolonged period of liberalisation, penalties were stiffened considerably during the crisis provoked by the first oil-shock, but – judging by the recent proposal the government has submitted to parliament – policy now appears to be moving closer into line with the majority of Western countries.

The assignment of exchange functions pertaining to the central bank to a different organisation is partly compensated by the close institutional links between the UIC and the Bank of Italy: the latter provides the UIC's endowment fund, and the Governor is by law its Chairman and hence able to guide its activity in accordance with the general objectives of monetary policy. For many of its operations the UIC makes use of the structures of the Bank of Italy and the accounts of the two institutions are published on a consolidated basis.

Harmonious performance of the exchange and monetary policy functions in the defence of the domestic and the external value of the lira is thus assured. It is produced by the close links between the level of the exchange rate, interventions in the exchange market and variations in the monetary base, especially via the foreign sector.

In economies with downward wage and price rigidity, combined management of the exchange rate and domestic demand is a necessary condition for balance-of-payments adjustment to proceed without the utilisation of productive capacity diverging too far from the normal level.

With a high rate of inflation the dosage of adjustment measures is even more difficult, both because there is a third objective – to bring down inflation – and because the increased importance of expectations makes the links between the variables more complicated and less stable.

The action taken in 1981 to control demand through monetary policy, on the one hand, and to maintain competitiveness through exchange-rate management, on the other, allowed an improvement in Italy's external position. In 1981 the current account of the balance of payments on a transactions basis closed with a deficit of around 9 thousand milliard* lire (8.4 in 1980) as a consequence of the worsening of the terms of trade caused by the rise in the dollar and energy prices. However, there was a marked improvement during the year – the seasonally-adjusted deficit fell from 4 thousand milliard lire in the first quarter to less than 1 thousand milliard in the last.

The productive system reacted to the credit restrictions and to the depreciation of the lira by cutting back imports and boosting exports,

---

* For denominations above one million, the book follows the British system of numeration.

thus confirming the resilience of a large part of the industrial sector. Though temporary factors, such as the destocking that accompanied the stagnation in output, contributed to this result, monetary and exchange-rate policy have succeeded in recreating conditions that will allow broader and more effective economic policy measures designed to consolidate Italy's competitive position by reducing inflation. Even though inflation has slowed since last summer, the annual rate of increase in consumer prices in Italy is still nearly twice the OECD average.

Today, even more than in the past, the Bank of Italy's monetary policy and supervisory functions are united by the economic and social imperative of fighting inflation. In view of the nature of Italian inflation, the central bank can contribute by controlling demand and raising the efficiency of the credit system.

The control of nominal demand is designed primarily to produce results in the short term by forestalling production bottlenecks, cooling inflation expectations, protecting the channels of fixed-investment financing in the capital markets, and defending the country's international creditworthiness and hence the scope for exchange-rate management. However, the effects of this control extend beyond the short term and have to foster the slowing of inflation in the medium term as well – a result that can only be achieved through voluntary wage restraint or an incomes policy, a rehabilitation of public finances, and clear choices coupled with determined implementation of energy, industrial and agricultural policies.

Banking supervision and intervention in the credit sector produce their disinflationary effects primarily in the long term. But this does not mean they should be underrated. Italian inflation is rooted in sectoral and territorial imbalances coupled with the persistence in many sectors of the economy of inefficiency that can only be eliminated through a different use of resources. In this respect, an even more substantial contribution than in the past is now required of the credit system in conjunction with structural policies and the other allocative mechanisms.

The Bank of Italy has prepared guidelines for the organisation and operation of financial structures that should increase their efficiency especially as regards the key aspect of banking – assessing the creditworthiness of loan applicants. The separation of subsidies from credit, the organisational structure and role of public sector banks, the range of operations of special credit institutions, the strengthening of the capital base of financial intermediaries, and top manage ment appointments in banks are some of the major problems for which solutions have been studied and often put into practice.

As always, the Bank of Italy has based its action in the present economic crisis on the principle of seeking to stimulate entrepreneurial banking within the existing institutional framework, with special attention being paid to the risks and yields of intermediation.

Inflation reflects the economic dualisms and centrifugal forces in society and, in turn, helps to generate them. The institutional order entrusts the central bank with the task of eradicating this ill without damaging the country's productive fabric. The central bank can produce lasting results if its action is part of an economic policy that intervenes directly on the real disequilibria in the economy. If inflation were curbed only by means of credit restrictions and not coupled with cost savings, investment could fail to revive and, even if it did recover, it would tend to be labour-saving and thus leave the employment problem unsolved.

In the early 1980s, there has been increasing awareness of this need. Thus one of the necessary conditions for a return to price stability is being satisfied. The constrast with behaviour that remains antithetical to the achievement of the objective is becoming sharper and sharper. In May 1981 I outlined a new monetary statute which necessarily includes some strictly non-monetary elements: a clearer specification of the central bank's autonomy in its financing of the Treasury, a balanced budget on current account, and some reduction in the indexation of incomes and wealth to prices.

After ten years of inflation, stability cannot be recovered without sacrifice. There is no easy way, no short cut. The will to fight inflation is not strengthened by extending indexation instead of reducing or eliminating it. Just as seeking higher real wages for workers with jobs will not help to increase employment, focusing exclusively on the short-term aspects of the budget will not help to eradicate the deficit.

Belief in the validity of these views encourages the firmness and, if I may say so, the tenacity with which the Bank of Italy seeks to implement the monetary policies adopted, albeit with the pragmatism needed to adapt its interventions to its interpretation of the changing conditions in the economy. Another expression of this belief is the commitment to give an account of its actions, starting with the Bank's Annual Report. An account that is backed by analysis and statistics and which eschews shock messages; for, while these may appear effective in the short run, they risk creating useless noise' that misleads economic agents, thus increasing instead of reducing monetary instability.

Part II
Experience with Monetary Management

4 The Contribution of the Banking System to Monetary Equilibrium and Economic Stability: Italian Experience*

Donato Menichella

THE LESSONS OF FOUR EXPERIENCES

In Italy the formation of the complex structure of a unified modern economy took place in a relatively short time. The crises which inevitably accompany such a process of amalgamation and growth were over within the space of a few generations and, in the case of the banking sector, were more acute than in those countries where capitalism and the tradition of unity were of less recent origin. Only in one other recently-formed nation perhaps – the USA – have these crises been anything like as violent as those which have occurred in Italy.

These crises, however, were not suffered in vain; each one of them taught us a lesson and marked a decisive step forward in the development and improvement of the institutional framework.

Thus the first crisis of which I am going to speak, and which developed towards the end of the last century, involved, as the principal figures, the banks of issue and the institutions engaged in providing medium- and long-term credit; and it showed how serious can be the consequences of abandoning the principles of prudence by which both these types of bodies must necessarily be guided, if they are to function properly, in balancing the sources from which they obtain their funds, on the one side, against the manner in which those

This chapter originated as a lecture delivered to the Zurich Economics Society on 15 February 1956. It was subsequently published in *Banca Nazionale del Lavoro Quarterly Review*, vol. IX, 1956.

funds are used, both as regards term and as regards risk, on the other.

Another crisis – which took place between the two world wars and which I shall briefly describe – provided proof of how necessary it is to intervene early and vigorously enough in order to nip in the bud incipient inflationary developments instead of allowing them to reach a more critical stage necessitating excessive repressive measures at a later date.

A later experience – the inflation in the period after the Second World War – taught us also that it is necessary, if the liquidity of the economic system is to be kept under control, that the bank of issue should be provided, in our country too, with certain means of action which had been tried out elsewhere. Thus the rational and practical character of the present system is due not merely to a detached clinical observation of the practices of other countries but also to actual operations carried out, in pain and suffering, on the body of Italy herself.

Finally, still another experience, of very recent years, has confirmed the value of a rule of conduct which it might be extremely dangerous to abandon. I refer to the necessity of maintaining cordial and permanent contacts between the central bank and the commercial banks. Such contacts make it possible to keep a close watch on situations which, by their very nature, are constantly changing, and to correct undesirable trends early on, thus avoiding the necessity of frequent recourse to dramatic remedies, of which the aim and scope is not always correctly understood.

All these experiences, viewed together, give an idea of how difficult and delicate are the tasks of the central banks and of the commercial banks – or, in a word, of monetary policy – in trying to achieve and to maintain monetary stability.

THE SCOPE AND LIMITS OF MONETARY POLICY

In all cases it is only a contribution to stability that can be given. This needs to be said quite clearly, especially because, alongside those enlightened people who do not expect of monetary policy (which has finally come into its own again) more than it can achieve, there are some who, less well-informed and more impatient, expect of it things of which it is not by itself capable. And since the victims of these misplaced demands are very often the central banks, to one of which I have the honour to belong, I should like, before going on to recoun the experiences which form the principal theme of this chapter, to take advantage of the present occasion in order to refer to another aspect of the subject of credit policy. I should like to draw your attention for a moment to the difficulties that are encountered by the central banks in regulating the volume of credit, and to explain how necessary it is that they should meet with understanding in their work. For if we who belong to the central banks do not ourselves seize every opportunity of ensuring that the difficulties with which we are every day confronted are seen in the proper light, it is most unlikely that anyone else will, since it is, alas, the fate of the central banks to be without friends, as are all those who often say 'No' and only rarely say 'Yes'.

It so happens that the recent return to the use of the traditional instruments of monetary policy, following the neglect of so many years, has appeared to some as a new discovery, as is always the case when one political form is replaced by another – often its extreme opposite – in response to the innate human desire to make a 'change'. The world which had grown accustomed to the system of fixed interest rates, usually kept low with the object of promoting full employment, realised, quite suddenly, that this system might induce inflation or make it harder to combat – at the monetary level – an inflation due to other causes.

As is well known, the clarion call announcing the revival of these instruments of monetary policy rang out in the USA in March 1951, when the agreement was concluded between the Treasury and the Federal Reserve System concerning 'the debt management and monetary policies to be pursued in furthering their common purpose, to assure the successful financing of the government's requirements and at the same time to minimise the monetisation of the public debt'. In Europe the revival reached a culminating point in November of the same year, when Great Britain once more had recourse to an alteration in its bank rate, which had remained practically unchanged at the level of 2 per cent for twenty years.

Because the traditional instruments had been forgotten for so many years, the return to them seemed to many people to represent a 'new doctrine' and – what is more – an infallible remedy, sufficient by itself, to ensure the stability and the orderly development of an economy. This caused some people to forget, to gloss over, or to make light of, the conditions which ought to exist, but often do not exist nowadays, if these instruments are to be used with full effect.

The result has been a deterioration in the psychological climate in which the monetary authorities and, in particular, the central banks have to operate. It is essential to the performance of their task that the public should realise that in an economic system of which the movements are governed by a great many different but closely interdependent factors, it is extremely rare that the use of a single lever alone can achieve all the results desired. The reason is that there are nearly always present certain ineradicable factors working in the opposite, or at least in an unharmonious direction.

In particular, the central bank's task of achieving monetary equilibrium by means of the so-called 'classical' corrective measures is made extremely difficult. And it frequently meets with almost insuperable obstacles of a psychological and technical nature if the policy of public spending simultaneously being pursued by the state, or by central and local government bodies, is such as to aggravate the conditions which the monetary measures are intended to correct.

Not infrequently, moreover, monetary disequilibrium is produced by major variations in the components of the balance of trade, attributable not to disparities between domestic and foreign prices – for such disparities are responsive to the influence of monetary policy – but to the sudden winning or losing of markets as a result of important changes in the particular conditions affecting certain exporting or importing countries. And as far as the general balance of payments is concerned, the corrective action of capital movements, which operated in the past, is now in abeyance almost everywhere, and the normal measures of monetary policy have not succeeded in bringing it back to life.

Monetary policy encounters particular difficulties, also, when it conflicts with wage policy. It sometimes happens that long periods of lull in the wage sector, or large and general wage increases, are due not to reasoned estimates of the level, or the rate of increase of productivity in a country, but to the behaviour of trade unions or entrepreneurs, actuated by various motives, not excluding political ones. In consequence the volume of demand may increase considerably when it ought to remain stable or to rise very little, and may thus cause an inflationary movement. Or, contrariwise, demand may fail to increase when productivity conditions would allow it to do so, with the result that a climate tending to induce a recession is created. It may be observed too, that a tendency towards inflation or recession that is caused by a disparity between labour productivity and labour earnings is certainly more difficult to combat by the use of monetary instruments alone than is, for example, an expansion or restriction of market liquidity caused by balance-of-payments factors. In the first case, indeed, the discrepancy affects the whole of the consumer sector of the economy, and a very large number of individual budgets, whereas, in the second, the only direct and immediate effect is on the liquid resources of commercial banks and business units. It can, therefore, in this latter case be discovered and corrected before it has caused any more widespread development, or any sharp contraction in fixed capital investment.

It is often argued, moreover, and in perhaps too dogmatic or categorical terms, that at a time of full employment it is sufficient for monetary policy to bring about a little unemployment in order to check an incipient inflationary movement.

The reason why I am bringing up this point is not, of course, that it specially concerns Italy, where there is still, unfortunately, a great deal of structural unemployment. It is quite generally true that the application of the instruments of economic policy ought to give useful results without inflicting on people, be it only on a few, undeserved suffering. The problem must moreover always be considered in the light of individual circumstances, and of phenomena which may vary, in nature and intensity, as between different times and places. In particular, it must be borne in mind that trade-union policy some-times tends to overlook the question of the level of employment. Thus insistent and unreasonable demands for increases in wages may be made even in situations where full employment does not exist. Not infrequently, indeed, the pleas advanced and the pressures applied by those in employment prevail, within the sphere of the trade-union organisations, over and against the claims of the unemployed. It may also happen that, given the high degree of specialisation among wage-earners in modern economies, an indiscriminate policy of rais-ing the cost of money, or, more generally, of credit restriction, will leave large sectors of production in a state of full employment without the wage level in these sectors being affected by the increased unemployment in others.

Another difficulty encountered by monetary policy comes from the fact that the investment decisions of industrialists are influenced first and foremost, and perhaps predominantly, by their firms' own possi-bilities of self-finance. Only to a subordinate extent, and very indi-rectly, do they depend on the changing terms on which the commercial banks grant short-term credit, the form of accommoda-tion which is usually most rapidly affected by movements in the discount rate, by the use of open-market policy and by changes in compulsory reserve requirements. Moreover, once a large-scale programme of investment in a new industrial plant has been started, it is difficult to stop it before completion, so that in such a case a change in monetary policy is very slow to take effect.

The methods of monetary policy and of central-bank action in general cannot therefore be rigidly systematised, nor can they always be fully effective. One need only think, here, of the difficulties, the misery, and the loss of wealth which may follow a policy of attempting to force an equilibrium in the market by endeavouring at all costs to maintain the exchange rate of the domestic currency in terms of foreign currencies, as was done in Italy in one of the 'experiments' I shall describe later on, and in a number of other countries.

For the reasons I have mentioned, and also because the instruments of monetary policy have only recently been restored to a place of honour, these instruments have during the last few years held a central position in discussions among economic theorists, among those concerned with practical economic policy, and between these two groups. These discussions have naturally dealt with the nature of the instruments, the conditions under which they can operate more or less effectively, and the results which they may be expected to achieve. There have thus been lively debates concerning the powers of the central banks *vis-à-vis* the action taken by the respective Treasuries, and concerning the relationships which should be established between these two bodies. The question has been discussed of whether they should both be autonomous to the point of ignoring each other's existence, or whether each should retain the ultimate right to make independent decisions though working together on a basis of permanent co-operation, and if so, what possible forms such co-operation might take.

Equally animated and interesting were the debates concerning the relations between central banks and commercial banks, the powers which should be given to the former and the duties which should be assumed by the latter, the question of whether these powers and duties should be defined by law or merely be subject to administrative regulation, or whether, finally, the co-ordination of their activities should be the result of action inspired by mutual goodwill and free from all constraint.

For some years now there has been a general realisation that the progress achieved in understanding the nature of economic phenomena, particularly in the monetary sphere, has helped and will certainly help in the future to mitigate the severity of crises compared with those of the past, so that it is probable that there will be no further depressions as intense and as prolonged as that of 1929. It seems certain, therefore, that within a few years our knowledge of how the instruments of monetary policy can be used to best effect will cause us, in the particular instances as they arise, to be more single-minded in our choice of action, to reach our decisions more quickly, and to put our instruments to better use.

In studying these problems we shall be able to profit not only from the progress which is being made and will go on being made in the field of scientific research, but also of the increased knowledge now available of various countries' experiences in monetary matters under different economic conditions.

In passing on to my brief illustration of the role of credit policy at various periods of Italy's economic history, I fully realise that in all countries the study of credit problems both in theory and in practice has made great advances in the last few years, so that past events, especially when they lie as far back as some of those which I am about to describe, can be of but little help to those who are called upon to operate in this sector of economic life today.

But even little streams make great rivers. I feel, therefore, that it is not a waste of time to try to highlight the similarities and dissimilarities, however small, between problems of the past and those of today. I hope, at least, that I shall succeed in showing, if only by the law of opposites, that events support my conviction that the corrective instruments of monetary policy, though not always completely effective, can often achieve very useful results, especially if they are applied in time and in sufficient strength, and especially also if the central bank's task is facilitated by the existence of good relations and a spirit of co-operation between it and the commercial banks. Whether central banks have complete and clearly-defined responsibility, as in some countries, or a more limited and less obvious role, as in others, the burden they have to shoulder in endeavouring to maintain monetary equilibrium and economic stability is a heavy one.

THE BOOM OF THE 1880s AND THE CRISIS OF THE 1890s

The first experience which I should like briefly to describe has, one might say, an archaeological flavour. It took place before most of us were born. I refer to it only in order to give an idea, by way of comparison, of the great progress which has been made in some seventy years in the system of granting credit and in the organisation of the central banks. It will not be possible, of course, to learn from what I shall say anything that might be valid today regarding the use of the instruments of credit control. My story will merely provide further proof of the unfortunate results which may ensue from a rash credit policy and from acute rivalry between banks.

In the years 1880–93, the period in which the events I am relating occurred, there were in Italy no fewer than six banks of issue, all in fierce competition with each other. The newly-achieved political unity of the country had not yet affected the organisation of the monetary system. Self-interest and misplaced considerations of prestige on the part of the various regions, which had formerly been independent states, were, in fact, destined for another third of a century to prevent Italy from establishing a single central bank.

On the slender basis of a generally poor agricultural economy and at a time when world-market prices were slumping, people in the new capital began feverishly to put up numerous large office buildings and dwellings to house a population which was growing so rapidly that it was to double itself in less than twenty years. To this excessive building activity was added the burden of railway construction and of military outlays for the Eritrean campaign.

A large proportion of the necessary capital was borrowed abroad. As a result of the tabling of a bill introducing convertibility of banknotes into gold, the premium of gold over banknotes dropped from 9–13 per cent in 1880 to 0–3 per cent in 1881. Though this appreciation of the lira naturally led to a worsening of the balance-of-payments situation on current account, it greatly encouraged the flow of foreign capital into Italy. Part of this took the dangerous form of short-term inter-bank credit (overdrafts, rediscounts of commercial bills, and securities repurchase operations). This influx of private capital has been put at some 500 million gold lire, equivalent to about 5 per cent of the annual national income at that time; in relation to the present national income, this percentage would represent one milliard dollars. To the influx of private capital was added a roughly equivalent amount of gold which the Italian government received, at the time of the restoration of convertibility in 1883, as a result of the placing on the London market through Hambro's and Baring's of a large 5 per cent loan issue. Further public loan issues were placed abroad during the following years, so that at the end of the crisis I am describing, that is, in about 1894, the external public debt amounted to some 1700m gold lire.

Of the large volume of monetary metal acquired by means of these foreign loans part was absorbed by the active circulation, and part went to increase the reserves of the banks of issue, thus enabling them to undertake a credit expansion to which they were encouraged by the spirit of mutual competition. Discount operations, which had amounted to 2.5 milliard lire in 1884, rose to 3.6 milliard in 1885 and to 4.4 milliard in 1886.

The additional operations were mainly of the nature of real-estate credits, building credits and stock-exchange credits granted to speculators, aside from operations, which – though less abnormal – were also influenced by the business boom, such as import credits. Between 1883 and 1887 import credits increased by about one-quarter, while exports decreased by more than 15 per cent.

The rush to buy land and building plots had become spasmodic; the prices of land bought with the aid of borrowed funds increased in many cases by as much as fifty times in the space of a year or two!

At the beginning of 1887 there was a change in the trend. On top of the depressed conditions in the agricultural sector, which was unable to pay off its bank debts, and the difficulties which had arisen in trade with France, there came the collapse in quotations on the Paris Stock Exchange, which also involved Italian government securities which had been placed on that market. The result was a general movement by foreign banks to withdraw their capital, so much so that the Italian banks, which were obliged to pay up, suddenly found themselves without funds to continue the financing they had undertaken to carry out, particularly in the building sector.

After a few attempts had been made to save the situation, several banks collapsed under the weight of the withdrawals of deposits.

Among them were two institutions which were giants of their day: the *Società generale di credito mobiliare italiana*, which had been modelled on the similar French institution (the *Crédit mobilier*), and the *Banca generale*. The most important concerns in the country, ranging from the railways to building contractors, and from the steel mills to farms, had relied on these banks for their financing.

The heated discussions which ensued made it impossible at the time to examine objectively what had really happened; and many leading bankers were even cleared of all blame, being regarded as the victims of the perfidy of others. Few people realised that the main cause of these events was the abandonment by the banks of issue, by the banks granting medium- and long-term credit, and by the ordinary commercial banks, of all the rules of prudence, and their unrestrained competition with each other to obtain deposits and financing contracts.

It took a long time, some fifteen years in fact, for the effects of the crisis to be worked off; and the banks of issue themselves suffered substantial losses. The losses were heavy even though the realisation of assets took place at a time when conditions had become very favourable for Italy, as for other countries. In that first decade of the twentieth century, in fact, world prices, which had been sinking in the previous thirty years, began to move upwards again, partly as a result of the working of the Transvaal gold mines.

THE INFLATION OF THE 1920s

Another unhealthy economic episode was the inflationary movement which lasted, with a few short interruptions, from the autumn of 1924 until August 1926 and which was again followed by an acute depression. This episode was largely due to the easy availability of bank credit, to the abuse of short-term financing for the purpose of covering the budget deficit, and to the absence of instruments of control such as compulsory reserve requirements, which were unknown at that time.

An idea of the extent of the inflationary movement which took place at this time is given by the fact that between December 1923 and August 1926 wholesale prices rose by about 30 per cent and the cost-of-living index in Turin and Milan by 32 per cent. There was also a rise in the index of money wages, but, as usually happens when a rapid inflationary process is under way, this increase fell short of that in the cost of living. Thus, for example, the wages paid in certain industries in Milan went up by only 26 per cent. All this happened six years after the end of the war, and following four years of relative price stability; in some sectors, indeed, there had even been a decline in prices.

From the external point of view, this period was characterised by a substantial depreciation of the lira. The dollar rate rose by about 20 per cent between October 1924 and July 1925. Subsequently the authorities intervened vigorously in order to check the rise, but as soon as intervention ceased the rate jumped up by 27 per cent in the short space of three months, from the end of April to the end of July 1926.

The inflationary movement was certainly not caused by any large budget deficit – in fact there were budget surpluses in the two fiscal years 1924–5 and 1925–6. Nor was it caused by the monetisation of balance-of-payments surpluses, for in 1925, the middle year of this period of difficulty, imports actually increased by 35 per cent and the trade deficit by 58 per cent.

On the other hand the period was one of high production and heavy investment activity: the productive capacity of many plants was utilised to the maximum, steel output was higher than in the most feverish period of the war, and the construction of hydroelectric power stations and of roads was proceeding at an extremely rapid rate, with the result, *inter alia*, that the demand for cement ran ahead of supplies despite the continual rise in prices.

The total nominal capital of the joint-stock companies increased by 55 per cent in the two years 1924 and 1925; and the index of share quotations rose by 70 per cent in the 14 months from December 1923 on. Unfortunately no complete statistics are available for bank credit; but the annual balance sheets of the principal banks reveal that the item *saldi debitori* (under which overdrafts are included) expanded by 32 per cent in 1924 alone.

What was the basis which had enabled the money and capital market to develop to such an extent as to allow a movement of general recovery and expansion in production to turn into a boom of such unhealthy dimensions that the total capital of all joint-stock companies increased in two years by 55 per cent and the volume of bank lending rose by 32 per cent in one single year?

The answer is that the banks of issue had greatly expanded their lending operations during the period in question, and that large amounts of Treasury bills and certificates were cashed in by the banks and by private investors. In the case of the Banca d'Italia alone the average annual total of discounts and advances outstanding rose from 4.7 milliard lire in 1920 to 8.5 milliard at the end of 1921, 9.3 milliard at the end of 1924 and 11.7 milliard at the end of 1925.

What happened was not, however, due to any course of action voluntarily adopted by the banks of issue. Their action had been dictated by the necessity of limiting the effects of a serious banking crisis which had broken out towards the end of 1921. One of the country's four big commercial banks had gone bankrupt as a result of a run by depositors, and this event had led in turn to substantial withdrawals from certain other banks. In order to make possible at least partial repayment to the depositors of the bank which had collapsed, pending the liquidation of its assets, and to sustain other banks which were in a precarious situation, the banks of issue had to intervene.

The resultant large injection of new cash led to a considerable flow of funds to those banks which had not been affected by the crisis, and this had the effect of widening their lending potential. This in turn gave an excessive impetus to productive activity and meant that the available physical resources were no longer sufficient to meet the demand, so that prices began to rise rapidly; and this movement was sustained – instead of curbed as it should have been – by the action taken in the field of credit. The process was aided by the monetisation of Treasury certificates which had been taken up by the banks and by private individuals during the years immediately after the First World War when they were issued to finance the large budget deficits.

Recourse was had to measures of intervention on the stock exchanges, a margin requirement of 25 per cent being introduced for security purchases. Changes were also made in the official discount rate, which was raised three times – altogether from 5.5 to 7 per cent – in the space of a little more than three months. After the Treasury Minister who had been responsible for these measures had been replaced, they were not pushed further, and perhaps this was one of the reasons for which they proved inadequate. It seems proper to conclude that the nature, the magnitude and the causes of the phenomenon which had occurred, would have called for a bold application of the methods which are most suitable for the sterilisation of excess market liquidity: that is, the creation and sale of substantial quantities of long-term government securities or the imposition of high compulsory reserve requirements, such as would have reabsorbed the large volume of cash which had been created as a means of facilitating the liquidation of the bank that had failed and of preventing others from failing. But these means of action were unknown at that time in Italy, as they were, indeed, in many other countries too. The boom came to an abrupt halt in August 1926 and turned into an acute recession as a result of a change in the psychological attitude of businessmen and traders. For these had been struck by the firm determination shown by the government towards the end of the same month to oppose any further decline in the purchasing power of the currency and, above all, by the measures adopted to block the issue of banknotes, and compulsorily to convert into long-term securities the very large volume of short- and medium-term Treasury certificates outstanding, of which the medium-term ones were about to fall due. This consolidation affected Treasury certificates to the value of more than 20 milliard lire, corresponding to about 1200 milliard present-day lire, or 2 milliard current dollars. All the market's liquid reserves having thus been mopped up, there was a severe restriction of credit, and this had the effect of sapping the nation's powers of resistance to the world crisis of 1929.

These were extraordinary events, events which perhaps could not have occurred elsewhere, since, as we have seen, they were essentially due to very large-scale financing by the banks not of short-term commercial loan operations but of operations which were of quite a different kind, and to the abuse of short-term financing by the Treasury.

It is true, of course, that banks of issue also intervene, though generally on a smaller scale, whenever the afflux of foreign capital to a country assumes abnormal proportions, or when an export boom occurs as a result of exceptional circumstances in countries where the bulk of the foreign exchange assets are held by the banks of issue themselves or by bodies financed by them. And a state of excessive liquidity may also come about as a result of a rapid amortisation of the public debt or the failure by subscribers to renew their holdings of government paper.

This brief description of events in Italy shows how limited is the effectiveness, in such cases, of changes in the discount rate. And it makes one realise that in these cases it is necessary to take direct action to reduce the volume of available resources by mopping up excess liquidity through a bold open-market policy or by the strict application of high minimum reserve requirements to the banks – or, perhaps better, by the use of both methods together, so that not only the banking system but business firms and private individuals as well may be affected.

THE STABILISATION OF 1947

I also have to say a few words about a further development which has been of great importance for Italy. At the time when it took place the credit system was undergoing the serious difficulties by which the whole Italian economy was beset less than two years after the end of the Second World War, and the corrective action then taken laid the basis for Italy's present monetary policy.

I refer to the action taken in the second half of 1947 to call a halt to the open inflation which had then been particularly virulent in Italy for about the last year. This event is well known and has been the subject, both at home and abroad, of such thorough and detailed studies that I need now only recall the salient points of the situation in which it arose. I shall then give a brief description of still more recent monetary events which have brought the further development of the principles of action underlying the measures taken in 1947.

There is no doubt that the 1946–7 inflation in Italy was due to a marked disequilibrium between, on the one hand, the excessively large volume of liquid resources which had been accumulated, during the war and immediately afterwards, both in the economic system in general and in the credit system in particular, and, on the other, the small amount of physical resources available for economic reconstruction. The disequilibrium was aggravated by the poor crops of 1947, by the paralysis of large sectors of the railways and of the system of maritime transport – one of the most serious effects of the war – and by the inadequacy of power supplies.

As a result of the running-down during the war of the normal stocks of raw materials and finished products by industry, trade and private consumers, the volume of discounts and advances had fallen to only 25 per cent of total bank deposits; a portion of the remaining 75 per cent was invested temporarily in Treasury bills and other government securities, but the greater part was held in the form of cash or sight funds with the central bank.

The provision of the financial backing for the reconstruction of the country could therefore be assisted, as in fact it was, by the large unused lending potential of the banking system. In the first few years after the war the banks were receiving a large and constant flow of banknotes, coming from the exceptionally large holdings of the public, for, particularly during the last few years of the war, Italian citizens who had left their homes to take refuge from the air-raids had accumulated, as an easily transportable personal reserve, large amounts of banknotes which, as soon as peace was restored, they once again deposited with the banks.

The nation's determination to undertake the rapid reconstruction of the country, backed by the strong spirit of initiative and enterprise which has never been lacking in Italians, thus derived considerable financial support from the high degree of liquidity of the banking system. At the same time, however, it came up against a serious difficulty in the form of shortages of raw materials and foodstuffs, together with a number of other obstacles created by the wartime destruction of the means of transport and by the deficiency of power supplies.

These disequilibria inevitably led to a rapid rise in prices, since everyone sought to obtain at all costs the means of production and goods available.

Such a process, provided that it is not stimulated by further inflationary injections of funds into the economy by the Treasury or the central bank, is bound to come to an end in due course through the re-establishment of equilibrium between the volume of money and the price level on the basis of the available supplies of goods. In 1947, however, only one of the two conditions described was fulfilled in Italy, for, though the central bank abstained from creating any additional purchasing power by way of its normal operations, the Treasury was running a very heavy deficit and had recourse to the bank of issue for accommodation. In the financial year from July 1946 to June 1947 the payments made by the state were almost double its receipts, without allowing for the large expenditures that were incurred during the year and not yet paid. It was not possible to increase tax revenue despite the goodwill shown by tax offices, which had been disorganised by the war and which inflation, either by altering the monetary yardstick or by bringing about rapid changes in private incomes, had gradually deprived of the very basis for their assessment of taxable incomes.

Finally, even if the stimulus to inflation deriving from the recourse which, despite the successful placing of certain public loan issues on the market, the Treasury still had to the central bank for financing its deficit, had not existed, it would have been inadvisable to wait passively for the restoration of equilibrium between the money supply and the price level. Two factors counselled more positive action: one was the impossibility of foreseeing under what conditions and at what price level such an equilibrium would be re-established and the other was the rapid decline in the foreign exchange reserves. The suffering inflicted on the general public by inflation would certainly have been increased by a further period of waiting and might have led to violent and uncontrollable social unrest. In addition to the action taken by the government in the form of issues of loans, the reorganisation of the fiscal system and the restriction of expenditure, it was also necessary to take resolute measures to sterilise a large part of the liquid resources held by the banking system. Such measures were taken in the summer of 1947, when the compulsory reserve system was revised and the new rules were strictly enforced.

Italy's experience has proved that, under certains conditions, even a very strong appeal from the central bank to the commercial banks is not sufficient. For since January 1947 the central bank had in fact strongly urged the commercial banks to limit their lending operations. These admonitions from the central bank were not very effective, for two reasons probably. One was the extent to which inflation had spread. The other was the fact that no bank likes to appear too clearly to be taking steps to restrict its lending unless it can show that other banks are following the same course, for fear that it may be considered to be in a weaker financial position than its competitors or that it may lose the goodwill of its customers. In the spring of 1947 the inflationary movement became particularly pronounced on the stock exchange, where there was a very rapid rise in quotations. This development was reflected, especially in the summer, in the brisk competition for imported raw materials and finished products, with the result that foreign exchange reserves fell to an extremely low level despite the full utilisation of the American aid received by Italy.

It was not until August of the same year that it became possible to set up an interministerial committee endowed with adequate powers of control over the credit system. Once the executive powers had been entrusted to the central bank, new rules concerning the holding of compulsory reserves by the banks were worked out and immediately put into application. Thus the inflation was brought to a speedy end.

The slowing-down of the rate of bank lending as a result of the blocking by the central bank of the banks' liquid resources and of the requirement that the banks should tie up, at the central bank or the Treasury, a large proportion of their new deposits, led owners of commodity stocks to offer them for sale. This caused, first, a halt in the price rise and, then, a fall in the prices which had risen most (that is, those of foodstuffs) and a decline from the peak prices which had been reached in some other sectors in the last few months. Moreover, many firms which had based their development plans mainly or entirely on expectations of the availability of additional credit facilities or of further price rises had to revise those plans.

The rate of production declined, as was natural, but the contraction was limited in amount and duration. Within six months production had begun to go up again – this time on a sound basis, that of a healthy currency.

At this time Italy avoided two errors which might have transformed the preceding strong inflationary movement into a no less serious and prolonged recession. When an inflationary movement is stopped or slowed down, there is a sudden fall in the velocity of circulation of money, as the public once more begins to hold on to banknotes. If the money supply thus becomes inadequate, the result is not merely a halt in the price rise but an actual fall in prices, which may turn out to be neither negligible nor of short duration. The movement then becomes continuous and is intensified by the reluctance of the public to buy anything which is not strictly indispensable; this in turn leads to a reduction in activity in many enterprises and to the spread of unemployment.

In 1926–7 these considerations did not influence the government then in office, which wanted above all to see the success of its effort to arrest inflation actually reflected in the stabilisation, or even in the reduction of the volume of banknotes in circulation, and took every possible step towards this end. The result was a downward price spiral which, even though it was accompanied by some reductions in wages, caused economic difficulties which in Italy added to the difficulties which were brought a few years later, to every country, by the world depression of 1929.

It was because they had profited by this experience that the Italian monetary authorities did not take fright at the rapid increase in the note circulation after the measures of August 1947. In 1948, while the wholesale-price and cost-of-living indices remained stable or even showed a slight tendency to decline, an increase of as much as 22 per cent occurred in the Banca d'Italia's note circulation; whereas in more recent years – from 1952 to 1955 – the average annual increase has been only 6.8 per cent, despite the substantial and continual growth in the national income.

The second mistake which was avoided in 1947 relates to the nature and the effects of credit restriction. It is often claimed these days that the banks do not apply credit restriction in an 'equitable' manner, since the measures taken by them are of a general nature and it may thus happen that their best customers are favoured at the expense of those who are less good or less influential.

There is a good deal of truth in this criticism, although the fact is often overlooked that today the best and most powerful enterprises are almost everywhere practically self-sufficient financially, and have relatively little recourse to bank credit. This was not the situation which prevailed in Italy in 1947, and there was a very real danger that the slowing-down in the rate of increase of bank credit, at which the measures taken in August were aimed and which they in fact achieved, would, in the case of many enterprises, actually lead to a reduction in the volume of credit at their disposal. In particular many sectors of the engineering industry were in a critical position at that time, since, after having worked to full capacity during the war, they were now passing through a difficult stage of adjustment of their production to civil requirements. It was thought that the needs of these enterprises might be disregarded under the new tighter credit conditions, and steps were consequently taken to create a government fund to provide finance for the engineering industries. This fund called the *Fondo Industrie Meccaniche*, carried out, in a very short space of time, lending operations totalling 35 milliard lire ($60m). Since the process of its liquidation began a few years ago it has recovered part of the funds lent, and is at present collecting that part of the remainder which is still recoverable. This was the price which had to be paid in order to overcome the objections – which were many – of those who saw in the monetary measures adopted the destruction of the illusion they had created for themselves that prices would go on rising indefinitely.

The events just described help to demonstrate that measures of monetary nature do not in themselves have any absolute validity, and are not universally applicable at all times and in all economies. The wisest policy, therefore, is to apply them with the degree of vigour and flexibility which seems to be called for by the technical, political and social conditions prevailing in the country concerned.

THE EXPERIENCE OF THE EARLY 1950s

As a result of the measures taken in the autumn of 1947, a close bond was established between the central bank and the commercial banks, especially the larger of these. Care has been taken since that time to preserve this link, and to strengthen it in various ways whenever developments in business conditions have tended to make it weaker.

The instruments used are of various kinds. The central bank can allow or refuse the commercial banks rediscounting facilities and advances on securities. The Italian Foreign Exchange Office, which, in turn, is financed by the central bank, may grant or refuse the commercial banks loans in foreign currencies. The banks can be requested to be more liberal, or more sparing, in their use of credit facilities granted to them by their foreign correspondents, especially American or British banks. The central bank can apply, with varying degrees of liberality, its powers to authorise the commercial banks to grant credits which exceed a certain percentage, fixed by law, of their share capital and reserves. Finally, a constant watch is kept on the level of the funds held by the banks in the form of free or tied deposits at short term (eight or fifteen days) with the central bank.

In this last respect it is perhaps not without interest to note that the experience of the last few years has taught the management of the central bank, and the managers of the commercial banks, a great deal about the magnitude of seasonal movements in the cash position of the banks, so that they are able to recognise quite easily phenomena which are at variance with what experience has led them to expect.

The use of the instruments which I have described, and the constant contact maintained between the central bank and the commercial banks, especially the larger of these, in order to induce them appropriately to control the volume of their liquid resources, independently of the application of the rules concerning their reserve requirements, has been supplemented since 1950 by the issuing, in the early months of each year, of nine-year government bonds, the so-called *Buoni del Tesoro Novennali*. These bonds, which are placed on the market by the credit institutions, serve to absorb the excess liquidity which usually appears in Italy towards the end of the year. And the placing of them tends to neutralise the inflationary effects which would otherwise be produced by the budget deficit. Other government issues have been launched in recent years, largely with the same object, whenever it has seemed opportune. These have been mainly twenty-year bonds issued for the purpose of providing the state railways with the funds needed for improving their equipment.

Since it is the central bank which, in Italy, handles all in-payments and out-payments on behalf of the government, the repercussions of movements in the Treasury accounts are directly felt by the central bank. Being in close contact with the market through the commercial banks, the central bank tries to offset the effects which may ultimately be produced on the market as a result of the operations of the Treasury combined with those of the commercial banks.

Lastly, the central bank, acting in its capacity as the executive organ of the Interministerial Credit Committee, gives this body its views on issues of shares and bonds which industrial, commercial and financial companies, and long- and medium-term credit institutions propose to launch. In this field, too, an examination of the liquidity position may justify, as an auxiliary policy measure, action aimed at preserving or restoring the financial balance of a market which, in Italy, has over the last few years always been extremely active so far as investment is concerned. Indeed the limiting factor here has come, and still comes, primarily, from the necessity of maintaining equilibrium in the balance of payments.

The instruments for limiting rediscounting and advances were used with particularly marked effect during the Korean crisis of 1950-1.

Under the Italian system regulating the relations between the central bank and the commercial banks there is no fixed ceiling up to which the commercial banks are entitled to draw on the central bank for funds. It was thus possible in the very first months following the outbreak of the war to take fully effective action to limit the rush which, in Italy as elsewhere, had started among consumers, producers and traders to pile up stocks.

The central bank, to which have to be submitted all applications for the granting of credit to any one firm in excess of a certain fixed percentage of the capital and reserves of the bank in question had, therefore, at that time two instruments at its disposal. It had the power to expand to a greater or lesser extent the volume of rediscounting facilities and of advances; and it had the power to grant or refuse permission to increase the amount of large individual credits. It used both these instruments. It allowed the commercial banks to be more liberal in the granting of credits that were to be used to finance imports of raw materials and finished products, but it was very strict as regards the accomodation it was ready to give the banks in the orm of rediscounts and advances, keeping this far short of the amount that was requested. The result was a tight credit situation which implied, of course, a marked slackening in the rate of increase of bank deposits – both on savings and on current accounts – which had until then been high. The final outcome, however, was that prices were prevented from soaring upwards. Domestic prices, in fact, rose only moderately, so that Italy may be counted among the countries which, after the events in Korea, succeeded better than most in checking the depreciation of their currencies.

Between July 1951 and September 1952 Italy went through a phase of high liquidity. This was due in the first instance to the very favourable trend – which lasted until March 1952 – in the export trade. This was in turn primarily attributable to the heavy sales abroad of textile goods, which were in particularly strong demand in those overseas countries which had rapidly increased their foreign exchange earnings as a result of the sharply increased prices of the raw materials which they produced. In the course of 1952 the liquidity of the market was further swollen by a rise in budgetary expenditure and larger outlays for workers' old-age pensions.

Such additional rediscounts and advances as had been granted – even if their amount was modest – in the preceding phase of credit shortage which I have just described were not renewed and steps were taken to persuade the principal commercial banks to exercise restraint in granting fresh·discounts and advances to customers. Never the less, despite the normal annual issuing of long-term Treasury bonds, the banks' liquidity remained very high, and it was feared that it might give rise to an excessive expansion. This danger was, however, forestalled mainly because at that time world-market prices were continually moving downwards.

A day-to-day watch was kept on the situation and the central bank would not have hesitated to intervene by raising compulsory reserve requirements if there had been evidence that its appeal to the commercial banks was not being heeded.

From 1953 up to the present time there have been no disturbances of note in the economy. The excess bank liquidity of the preceding period had been gradually absorbed as a result of the moderate expansion of credit which, on the basis of an improved balance-of-payments position, accompanied the increase in investment activity associated primarily with the programme of developing Southern Italy. The ratio between the liquidity reserves and deposits of credit

institutions was in consequence appreciably reduced by comparison
with the high level it had reached in the autumn of 1951, and it has
scarcely varied in the course of the following five years.

CONCLUDING REMARKS

The object of the account which I have just given of certain difficult
periods in the economic history of my country has been to give some
examples of disturbances of monetary equilibrium and economic
balance in which credit policy has played a decisive part in inducing
movements of important dimensions towards the expansion or contraction of economic activity.

A review of the monetary events in a country comes close to being
an outline of the course of its economic history. For the stability of
or the fluctuations in the purchasing power of its currency do, in the
last analysis, summarise the events – happy or unhappy, favourable
or adverse – of its economic development.

Thus, in the very turbulent years of the first period of monetary
difficulties to which I have referred, which occurred towards the end
of the last century, not long after the unification of Italy, the economic progress which was being made was not easy to discern; and in
any case the rate of progress was slowed down by the destruction of
capital and the acute recession caused by the mistaken credit policy.

These years were followed for Italy by a prosperous period of
economic development extending over the first fifteen years of the
present century, during which the conduct of the country's monetary
affairs was exemplary. A factor aiding the stability and economic
progress of this period was the well-balanced activity of a group of
newly-formed and well-organised commercial banks, which were
engaged in healthy but not excessive competition with each other and
which were continually expanding in a manner which was neither too
violent nor too spasmodic.

The central banks which had survived the economic storm which
ended in 1893 with the liquidation of one of their number and the
merging of three others to form the Banca d'Italia took determined
action during these years to mitigate abnormal movements of credit
they gradually transformed the frozen assets inherited from the past
into liquid resources, and converted a substantial proportion of these
into foreign-currency holdings deriving in large part from the rapid

growth in emigration. During this period the ebb and flow of these reserves of foreign currency safeguarded the monetary equilibrium of the country.

The difficulties which characterised the period between the two world wars were, on the other hand, particularly unfortunate. In addition to the factors productive of instability and crisis which had their origins elsewhere and which naturally spread to my country, other factors were at work which were peculiar to the Italian economy itself and which on several occasions brought about serious disturbances in the economic and financial system.

In some of these instances the credit system itself was responsible for serious deviations from the line of conduct which it ought to have followed in order to help to maintain, or restore, economic stability. In particular, a very harmful influence was exerted by the excessively rapid expansion of certain banks and the unrestrained competition between them.

The situation was sometimes aggravated by the obligation imposed on the central banks to create large amounts of money for purposes other than the maintenance of a healthy and steady development of production, and by the excessive use of short-term Treasury bills to cover budget deficits. In other cases, it was regrettable that the powers of the central bank – which was at last reduced to a single institution in 1926 – did not include the authority to take measures, such as the imposition of minimum reserve requirements on the banks, which are particularly suitable for correcting – if necessary gradually – the dangerously unbalanced liquidity situations which are sometimes produced by exceptional events.

On the other hand this authority was exercised to the full, and with great success, in order to put a stop to the inflation of 1946–7. Since that time the national income of Italy has been increasing substantially year by year. A far-reaching transformation is in progress, under the impulse given by the development of the southern part of the country and by the increasing share of our manufacturing industries in world trade, which is owed partly to the almost complete liberalisation of trade with the vast area represented by the European Payments Union. Both these factors have made possible a fuller utilisation of existing industrial plant and considerable increases in productivity.

Not since before the First World War has Italy known such a prolonged period of marked and continuous economic development as that which she has been experiencing in the period 1949–56. This development has been accompanied, moreover, by a high degree of monetary stability and by the accumulation of ample foreign exchange reserves which have made it possible to correct temporary disequilibria in the balance of payments.

In the field of public finance, this period has been characterised by the renewed effectiveness of fiscal instruments, which had been almost destroyed or rendered inoperative by the war and by inflation. This new efficacy of the instrument of taxation has made it possible gradually to cover an increasing part of the government's expenditure by tax revenue, so that the budget deficit has been progressively reduced and is still falling. The consequence has been a considerable slackening of the tendency towards excess liquidity which usually results from budget deficits and afterwards has to be mopped up by monetary policy.

Among the many causes which have helped to bring about these favourable and encouraging events, on which Italy is basing its hopes of an ever-growing development of productive investment and of increasing well-being for its population, I must mention the by-no means unimportant role played by credit policy. Though far-reaching and penetrating, bank lending has not overstepped the limits beyond which it would have encouraged speculative movements characteristic of inflationary processes and would have created balance-of-payments deficits larger than could be covered by available foreign investment capital, including foreign loans.

The close ties which were established between the central bank and the commercial banks in the autumn of 1947 have contributed much to this very harmonious development of credit policy, which has stimulated and accompanied the increase in the national income over these years. This system of inter-bank co-operation has been fostered in a number of ways, so as to make possible the prompt correction of temporary disequilibria affecting the liquidity of the market.

This is really the gist of what may be learnt from Italy's experience in the period since the Second World War. While making use of the ever more-highly-developed means of action adopted elsewhere, Italy has also benefited and drawn strength from the lessons, sometimes painful, which she has learnt from her own past.

Adequate use has been made of the appropriate instruments of monetary policy whenever there have been very marked disequilibria to be corrected; when, on the other hand, the disequilibria have been minor and temporary in character, an important contribution to the redressing of the position has been made by the cordial relations existing between the central bank and the commercial banks, and by the constant contact maintained between their leading officials. These contacts have made it possible to reconcile each commercial bank's own requirements with the need for the banks, both as individual concerns and as a group, to bring their policy into line with that of the government in its efforts to promote the growth of production on a basis of monetary equilibrium.

In conclusion, my insistence on the need for reciprocal esteem and constant co-operation between the central bank and the commercial banks could seem – like the use of the instruments of monetary policy – to be merely a 'rediscovery' of the rules of good conduct which were always considered essential for success. And it will seem utterly pointless to those who expect to find the rules of sound credit management in handbook form.

The sound conduct of credit policy merely consists in the tackling of innumerable difficulties which can be overcome only by patient daily effort, sometimes in the face of considerable obstacles, which differ from country to country. The results are consequently nearly always fairly far removed from the original goals.

In drawing up the rules of sound credit management one must not overlook the question of how and when they are to be applied by those in charge of monetary policy. The principles of economic theory must, therefore, at all times be 'married' with the art of the banker.

Our scientific knowledge teaches us that dear money and restricted credit are necessary to stop inflation or check a boom, and that cheap and plentiful money must be called into play as part of the effort to combat a recession. But the art of the banker consists in judging when is the most suitable time for taking action and how far it should go; for the best results are obtained when measures are adopted before the need for action has become clearly apparent in the statistics.

5   'Noise'*

Luigi Einaudi

The explanation of Donato Menichella's *fuge rumores* helps to highlight a part of his code of conduct that is of much greater importance
for Italy than an academic nomination that did not terminate in the
normal affixing of seals. With the consent or co-operation of the
Minister of the Treasury, the Governor of the Bank of Italy can use
two powerful weapons – the discount rate and the banks' compulsory
reserve coefficient – to dominate the lira, the stock exchange and
industrial and commercial activity.

The discount rate is a traditional and almost immemorial weapon.
When economic agents go crazy, get carried away and buy securities
careless of price and yield, over-build plant, invest without discretion, run up inventories of fuel and raw materials, and produce for
stock, the central bank increases what is known as the price of
money. The discount rate rises from 3 to 4, to 5, to 9, to 10 per cent.
Perpetrate your follies, behave as though the Huns were at your
heels, as if wasting a minute in the rush to buy and to borrow meant
ruin, but you shall pay for your excesses dearly.

If the commercial banks and savings banks follow the example of
the central bank and money becomes generally expensive, there will
sometimes, but not always, be an inflow of footloose foreign capital
in search of profitable investment, from which the balance of payments benefits.

When, by contrast, economic agents are in low spirits, and, for
various and varying reasons, disinclined to embark on new projects
or carry on those in hand, a reduction in the official discount rate
might encourage the undecided if an abundance of bank deposits
resulted in a general reduction in the cost of money. If with a 6 per

Originally published under the title 'Rumore' in *Corriere della Sera*, 1 October 1960.
In an earlier article on Donato Menichella's retirement from the Bank of Italy,
Einaudi had referred to Menichella's having declined to become a full member of the
Accademia dei Lincei a few years before, attributing this to Menichella's desire to
avoid publicity – 'noise' – in connection with his name, or in other words, to avoid
being put in a 'new and different' position in Italian banking and industry, one of
intellectual superiority compared with the heads of banks and firms'.

cent discount rate – which becomes *en route* 8 or 10 per cent at the banks – there is no incentive to invest in new plant and production lines that are expected to yield no more than 8 or 10 per cent, there may be an incentive if the discount rate is lowered to 4 per cent and the cost of money to 7 or 8 per cent. The outcome is not certain; but if other factors combine to overcome the lack of confidence, the lowering of the discount rate is certainly advantageous.

Countries with deep markets for short-term securities, such as Treasury bills, resort to so-called 'open-market' operations. This means that banks, following the advice of the central bank, either sell short-term securities from their portfolios at times of euphoria, and thus absorb the deposits considered in excess while raising the cost of money to over-ambitious entrepreneurs, or, on the other hand, when the market is languishing for lack of business, they buy short-term securities and thus supply it with money.

The short-term securities market in Italy is not sufficiently deep to allow sales and purchases on a scale that would have a significant influence without substantially affecting prices. Consequently, in 1947 the authorities preferred – in the light of experience in America, followed only this year by the Bank of England – to require commercial banks to place a part of their deposits with the Bank of Italy. The proportion was initially fixed at 25 per cent, but it was meant to be raised whenever it was judged advisable to prevent commercial banks from granting excessive advances and discounts to over-optimistic customers, and lowered whenever it was felt necessary to increase commercial banks' resources so as to expand their lending to customers, while encouraging borrowers with decreases in the cost of money.

A dead letter. During Menichella's Governorship changes in the official discount rate were few and far between, and to all intents and purposes the proportion of bank deposits placed with the central bank remained unchanged at 25 per cent.

Curious to find out the reason for this behaviour, on the surface so different from what was expected, I again came to the conclusion that the now honorary Governor of the Bank of Italy does not like 'noise'. Silence is part of the tradition of the Bank. Staircases, rooms and corridors are silent and spotless. The ushers are few, properly dressed and polite. Voices are hushed, there is no irritating noise.

Menichella has applied this tradition to the management of the discount rate and the compulsory reserve requirement. An increase in the discount rate from 3.5 to 4 per cent and then to 5 and 6 per cent or more as necessary, makes a 'noise'. Newspapers blow up the news and arouse public opinion; financial columnists come close to forecasting doom. Stock exchange falls are predicted together with the impossibility of obtaining discounts or advances. Those with credit lines hurry to exhaust them to be safe against a credit restriction, even at the risk of depositing the funds elsewhere at a low rate of return. If, on the other hand, the discount rate is lowered from 6 to 5 to 4 to 3.5 per cent, anyone would think the golden age had come. The cautious are careful to move, but second-rate men have already become a nuisance. Bankers are hard pressed to get them out from under their feet. Political columnists rail because there is no investment. Why is there no investment? What is more, the investment must be on a 'massive' scale, otherwise it is of no account. If the private sector does not make up its mind, why does the state not intervene to take up and use the milliards that are 'lying idle'? Is not the Mezzogiorno crying out for investment? Let one or two hundred milliards be used to build a truly enormous plant. What does it matter if the number of workers employed is small compared with the many more who would be employed in less striking projects, undertaken by someone who might also be risking their own money? Speed is of the essence, the milliards are there and the important thing is that they should not be left to 'lie idle'. Somewhere in Italy the war led to the decision to mine a very poor-quality coal with a low yield, even lower than the advantage of its low price, and with a sulphur content that ruined the insides of boilers – coal that nobody would have bought unless forced to do so by some calamity, such as the war. The loss sustained was substantial, milliards of lire, and had to be paid for as usual out of the taxpayer's pocket. But since the reduction in the discount rate, or in the commercial banks' compulsory reserve requirement, which amounts to the same thing, indicates that there are milliards to spend, let us invest them in a plant that will use this terrible coal to produce electricity; and, since no one on the spot would buy it all, let us invest a few more milliards to transport it elsewhere, overseas if need be. What does it matter if the employment is minimal compared with the milliards invested? What is important is to invest on a 'massive' scale in order to use the milliards that are 'lying idle'.

If such things occur, or are threatened in Italy, even when the official discount rate and the compulsory reserve requirement are dormant, it can well be imagined what would happen if they were deliberately raised or lowered! Who stands to gain from the uproar, rumours, and newspaper articles? It was sufficient that after years of untiring effort – which began on the day we were in London together in 1947, painfully obliged to beg the US Treasury Secretary for a few million dollars to cope with a difficult situation – Menichella succeeded in building up a gold reserve able to protect Italy against the constant possibility of temporary balance-of-payments or public-finance needs, for there to be a flurry of proposals to invest or waste a share of these reserves on wild ventures in the four corners of the world.

This is why Donato Menichella does not like 'noise'. He preferred, I imagine, to receive bank managers – his friends or devotees – and the heads of large and small firms in his study, a quiet room, into which visitors are shown by dignified ushers, through vestibules and along corridors free of the dust and cobwebs that are, or were, to be seen in certain ministries and public offices. Orders are not given in the Governor's study; there is discussion, the situation is examined, intricate problems are disentangled and advice is given. As an alternative to raising the discount rate, commercial banks could quietly reduce some credit lines and increase the interest rates on the lending to be cut back? This advice, which in practice amounts to an order, is coupled with assistance – if at 25 per cent the compulsory reserve requirement is sometimes high, the central bank can increase the amount of its discount lending to the needy bank. Without 'noise', without bringing journalists flocking, situations are discussed one by one and, one by one, the most appropriate solution is sought.

Sometimes the difficulty of a situation may be attributable to the managing director or general manager of a minor bank, a savings bank or a rural bank. The Governor of the Bank of Italy is the first to be informed of offences, oversights, faults and sometimes even crimes. His inspectors have given him a complete list of all the improper operations undertaken by that bank – a detailed list giving names and a detailed description of every irregularity.

The dilemma is painful: according to a debatable interpretation of I-don't-know-which article of the penal code, coupled with that of an article of the Banking Law, the Governor is in duty bound to report transgressions to the public prosecutor. *Fiat justitia* above all, and let justice run its course. Unfortunately, this course would lead to disaster. Credit is that most delicate of plants rooted in silence, trust and other invisible and intangible factors. Bad news about losses, favouritism and excessive lines of credit has a habit of leaking out of the public prosecutor's office; nobody knows how, it just leaks out.

People talk, the local paper makes insinuations. Savers run to withdraw their deposits, at first a trickle and then a flood. The bank has to close. If a bank closes, the nearby ones come under suspicion and the run on deposits spreads. Should the Governor of the Bank of Italy, who knows all this in advance, denounce the transgressions in conformity with the principle that kingdoms are saved in the first place by rendering justice? Or is it not morally and socially preferable to run the risk of breaking the law, to avoid 'noise' and try to staunch the wound in time? Is it not possible for the suspect managing director or general manager to be called to account and, if unable to prove his innocence, above all condemned to pay and to make his wife and relations pay? If the transgression is manifest, is it not better that the transgressor should pay? And the punishment should fall not only on his head but also, even if they are not directly responsible, on the blockheads and softheads of his chairman and fellow-directors. If all that is not enough, the various associations of commercial and savings banks have an interest in supporting rescue operations. Since the crisis bank none the less has a tradition, depositors and borrowers that are worth something, the central bank may advise a merger with some other sound bank, which sacrifices something and in turn acquires goodwill, deposits and customers. By avoiding 'noise', the guilty are forced to give up what is left to them, credit is saved and depositors are not even aware of the risk they have run. Is it better to solve difficult situations in this way if possible or is it better to obey at any cost the commandment, 'let justice be done'?

Sometimes there is a close race between the attempt to rescue the bank in the public interest and the arrival of an anonymous accusation on the public prosecutor's desk; between protecting depositors and paying homage to pure justice. If, at the end, depositors are saved and, a minute later, the anonymous accusation arrives on the public prosecutor's desk, justice is done and, at the same time, the public interest is protected.

If Donato Menichella really embraced the principle of *fuge rumores*, let it also serve as a lesson to those who have the very delicate responsibility for public credit.

6 Thirty Years of the Deutschmark*

Otmar Emminger

THE 1948 CURRENCY REFORM

On 20 June 1948, the Reichsmark, which had been eroded by the war and the post-war disorder, was replaced by the newly created 'Deutschmark'. In March 1948 the Bank Deutscher Länder was established by a law of the allied military authorities, as the first joint public institution of the three western zones of occupation. This common West German central bank was an essential prerequisite for the technical implementation of the currency reform. The reform itself, however, largely followed the conceptions of American experts and was the responsibility of the allied military government alone. The Bank Deutscher Länder, together with the Land Central Banks, was entrusted with looking after the new currency, that is, the issue of new money and monetary policy. It was thus made the 'guardian of the currency', a task that was passed on in 1957 to its legal successor, the Deutsche Bundesbank, on its creation by a German law.

The currency reform of June 1948 was a turning-point not only in the economic but also in the social and political life of our community. It was the basis on which Professor Ludwig Erhard, then director of the Department of Economic Affairs of the 'Bizone', ventured in a bold step to abolish the price freeze and rationing and to take the plunge into the cold water of a free market economy. This, together with the new healthy currency, unleashed tremendous energies, just as Professor Erhard had predicted. This marked the beginning of the 'German economic miracle', which raised German workers from the subsistence-level existence of the early post-war years to the level of the world's best-paid workers, made the Federal Republic of Germany the second largest exporter in the world, and

*Originally published as an article under the same title, in *Monthly Report of the Deutsche Bundesbank*, June 1978.

Table 6.1   **Development of the cost of living in various countries, 1949–1977**

Country	Total increase	Average annual increase as %
Federal Republic of Germany	113	2.7
Switzerland	135	3.1
USA	154	3.4
Italy	350	5.5
France	422	6.1
UK	469	6.4

provided the financial basis for a social security system that is unsurpassed, at least among the major countries.

The thirty years from 1948 to 1978 were not without serious economic and social problems. The destruction that occurred in the war and the post-war period had to be remedied; more than 14 million refugees and displaced persons from other parts of Europe had to be accommodated and integrated in West Germany; in the early years until about 1955 the unemployment rate was far higher than in 1978; later on, recessions and international economic difficulties had to be faced. Never the less, those thirty years taken as a whole brought West Germany not only economic expansion and an unprecedented improvement in the standard of living but also a political and social stability which contrasts very favourably with the economic, social and political upheavals of the preceding thirty years, from 1918 to 1948. A comparison with this earlier period, which was characterised by economic, monetary and political crises, also makes it clear how much the better performance of the thirty years, 1948–78, owes to economic stability based on a healthy monetary system.

THE DEUTSCHMARK'S ROUTE TO A STRONG CURRENCY

The development of the Deutschmark during these thirty years has been marked by two basic tendencies:

- externally the position of the Deutschmark has become steadily stronger, so that today it ranks among the small number of 'strong' currencies the value of which *vis-à-vis* numerous other currencies, including the US dollar, has been increasing for years;

- at home it has become more and more difficult to safeguard the purchasing power of the Deutschmark, even though over the entire period price rises in Germany have been smaller than in any other industrial country.

Externally, the Deutschmark did not start from strength. On the contrary! In 1948 it began as a weak currency. At that time West Germany had no official reserves. Its balance of payments was in deficit and, but for the US Marshall Plan, not even the most vital products could have been imported. In September 1949 the Deutschmark had to join the wave of devaluations against the US dollar triggered off by the pound sterling (although its devaluation rate, at 20.6 per cent, was below that of the pound and several other currencies, at 30.5 per cent). In the autumn of 1950 Germany was faced with a serious balance-of-payments crisis which obliged it to adopt a very restrictive monetary policy; temporarily to suspend the partial liberalisation of imports, and to take up a special credit from the European Payments Union (EPU). Germany, which in later years was to become the 'extreme creditor country' of the EPU, was initially the first 'extreme debtor country' of this European monetary institution, which was set up in 1950.

1951–2 saw the beginning of the period of balance-of-payments surpluses which – albeit with a number of interruptions in the second half of the 1950s and the first half of the 1960s – characterised Germany's external position. In part this has been due to Germany's better stability record, that is, to the relatively greater price stability in Germany, especially by comparison with prices in most other European partner countries. But German foreign trade also benefited from the structure of German exports, which enabled our exporters to derive special advantages from the sustained world-wide boom in capital investment.

The increasing strength of its external position caused Germany in the 1950s to pursue a good-creditor policy, in particular to dismantle import restrictions rapidly, to lower customs duties, to promote capital exports and to ease exchange controls. This development culminated in the transition to *convertibility* at the end of 1958 simultaneously with the other OEEC countries. Germany went further than its partners, however, since it abolished all remaining payments restrictions on residents and foreigners with respect to merchandise, service and capital transactions in the first few months of 1959. The formal restoration of full convertibility ten years after the currency reform marked the end of a chapter of German monetary policy that had begun during the currency crisis of 1931 with emergency measures to prevent withdrawals of foreign capital and at times had developed in ensuing years into an instrument of *dirigisme*.

THE DEUTSCHMARK IN THE TURMOIL OF MONETARY CRISES

Germany's external economic strength had adverse effects as well as beneficial ones. The foreign exchange surpluses, which were welcome at first as a contribution to the accumulation of an appropriate stock of currency reserves, became a potential source of inflation from the late 1950s onwards. This confronted the German monetary authorities with the question: should external equilibrium be achieved by 'adjustment through inflation' in Germany or by upvaluation of the Deutschmark against the currencies of countries with faster rates of inflation? The expectation that countries with persistent balance-of-payments deficits would themselves contribute to better international equilibrium by devaluing their currencies was fulfilled only in the case of France in 1957–8. The conflict between domestic and external stability became even more acute as a result of the decontrol of all capital movements: a restrictive monetary policy to combat imported inflation normally attracted foreign capital into the country, so that the policy was undermined, that is, proved self-defeating.

Following lengthy efforts to cope with the stability dilemma by conventional means, the Federal Government, together with the Bundesbank, finally drew the logical conclusion in March 1961: the Deutschmark was revalued for the first time against all other currencies and the dollar parity lowered from DM 4.20 to DM 4.00 per dollar. This step formally acknowledged the priority of domestic price stability over fixity of exchange rates. This revaluation, modest though it was, gained the German monetary authorities some years of calm, mainly because at the same time a number of tendencies were also working towards stabilisation from abroad. In the first half of the 1960s the USA, in particular, was an anchor of cost and price stability in the world economy with an exceptionally low inflation rate. On the other hand, during this period prices in Germany were no longer as stable as they had been during the 1950s.

From 1968–9 onwards the external tensions increased once more, not only because of a new surge of inflation in France but also because of US balance-of-payments deficits. Germany, by contrast, had returned to fairly stable conditions after the end of the slight recession of 1966–7. The struggle to maintain the stability of the Deutschmark, or more precisely: the warding-off of imported inflation by a new revaluation of the Deutschmark, even became an issue in the Bundestag election campaign in the summer and autumn of 1969.

However, the 9 per cent revaluation of the Deutschmark in October 1969 by no means settled the stability dilemma. In spite of the revaluation, the Deutschmark was increasingly caught up in the spiral of international price rises. A temporary period of floating of the Deutschmark from May to December 1971, the suspension of the convertibility of the dollar into gold in August 1971, the international realignment of exchange rates in December 1971 (the Smithsonian Agreement) and the monetary unrest of February and March 1973 were the stages on the way to the final collapse of the Bretton Woods system of fixed exchange rates in March 1973.

THE PERIOD OF FLOATING

Upon the transition to a system of widespread floating the asymmetry of monetary adjustment processes was corrected. Under the system of fixed exchange rates the surplus countries were forced by the foreign exchange inflows to create money, while no corresponding contraction of the money stock occurred in the USA, the main deficit and reserve currency country. This asymmetry, which Bundesbank President Blessing once called the 'perfect inflation machine', was partly responsible for the world-wide inflation in the late 1960s and early 1970s. Stability-minded countries were able to withstand this inflation pressure only for a limited period.

Although Germany was inexorably dragged along by the general inflationary trend from 1970 to the beginning of 1973, it was able to detach itself from the international 'inflation convoy' from the spring of 1973 onwards. With the transition to floating, the Bundesbank largely regained control over the money supply, except when it felt obliged to purchase foreign exchange because of overriding considerations. Even under the present system of floating, the Deutschmark is not shielded from all external influences. The obligation to intervene under the European narrower margins arrangement, the so-called 'snake', still remains. The rate of the dollar, too, could not always be left to market forces alone, as too rapid and excessive exchange rate swings might lead to disruptive self-reinforcement and would make undue demands on the economy's capacity for adjustment. Even international price relationships are not completely severed under a system of floating exchange rates; moreover, floating rates cannot prevent the international transmission of cyclical fluctuations. However, they do allow more latitude for national monetary policy. Given the strains to which the world economic and monetary system was exposed during the 1970s because of the large inflation differentials between major countries and, after 1973, because of the oil-price hike, floating exchange rates were unavoidable if the world economy was to be held together without too much interference in trade and capital movements.

The changes in exchange rates were mostly in the direction indicated by price and cost differentials. This is also true of the Deutschmark, the external value of which has risen quite strongly since the exchange rate was permitted to float. Between 1972 (annual average) and the end of 1977 (US$ 1 = DM 2.1050) the weighted external value of the Deutschmark against the sixteen currencies officially quoted in Frankfurt increased by about 43 per cent, that is, by an average of 6.7 per cent a year. Against the US dollar alone the Deutschmark went up by as much as 51 per cent during that period. The increase in the five years 1973–8 was thus greater than the rise in the external value in the preceding twenty-two years from 1950 to 1972, which on a weighted average came to just over 32 per cent (or a little more than 1 ¼ per cent a year). The strong appreciation in those few years at times resulted in substantial burdens for the domestic economy, especially since the appreciation in some years was greater than the divergencies in cost and price movement. This applies particularly *vis-à-vis* specific currency areas, notably that of the US dollar, which comprises far more markets than the USA alone. When considering these appreciation rates, however, it must not be forgotten that in part they merely represented an inevitable correction of the previous undervaluation of the Deutschmark, which had facilitated exports and impeded imports. The change-over to more realistic exchange rates triggered off protracted and far-reaching (but in the last analysis unavoidable) adjustments in the field of exports, and also among the industries that have to compete with imports. The new pattern of exchange rates has certainly weakened the competitiveness of the German economy, but it does not seem to have seriously endangered it.

The marked tendency of the Deutschmark to appreciate reflects not only the inflation differential and Germany's surpluses on current

133

Figure 6.1   Movement of (a) the external and (b) domestic value of
the Deutschmark, 1950–78

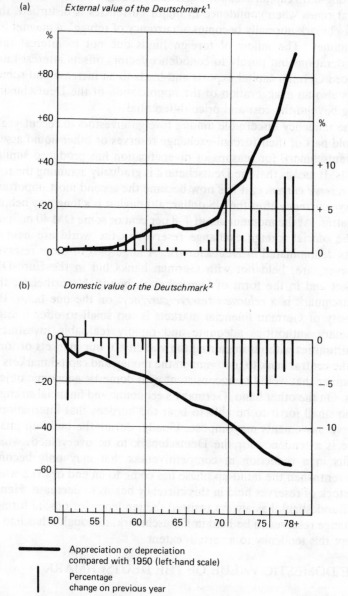

(a)   External value of the Deutschmark[1]

(b)   Domestic value of the Deutschmark[2]

⎯⎯⎯   Appreciation or depreciation
           compared with 1950 (left-hand scale)

| Percentage
     change on previous year

[1]Against the sixteen currencies at present officially quoted in Frankfurt.
[2]As measured by the reciprocal value of the cost of living index.
+ January to May.

account. Judging by its 'basic balance' (that is, balance on current and long-term capital accounts) Germany should be a deficit country. But at times when confidence in major currencies is disturbed, the Deutschmark normally becomes a 'currency of refuge', a magnet for hot money. The inflow of foreign funds due not to interest rate considerations but purely to confidence factors offsets interest-rate-induced German capital exports and leads to an increase and sometimes also an exaggeration of the appreciation of the Deutschmark going beyond the cost and price differential.

The tendency discernible among foreign investors in recent years to hold part of their foreign-exchange reserves or other liquid assets in Deutschmark for reasons of diversification has produced similar results. It means that the Deutschmark is gradually assuming the role of a *reserve currency*; it has now become the second most important reserve currency after the US dollar, although it is a long way behind the latter. At the moment about 7–8 per cent or some DM 40 milliard of the official foreign exchange reserves in the world are held in assets denominated in Deutschmark. A large part of these reserves however, are, held not with German banks but in the Euro-DM market and in the form of Deutschmark bonds. Nevertheless, the Deutschmark is a *reluctant reserve currency*: on the one hand, the capacity of German financial markets is too small to offer foreign monetary authorities adequate and rapidly realisable investment opportunities without impairing the viability of our markets or forcing the central bank to intervene in the money and capital markets in a manner that would be inconsistent with domestic economic objectives. On the other hand, Germany's economic and financial strength is too small for it to be able to bear the burdens that international reserve movements may impose. Finally, during the build-up phase there is a tendency for the Deutschmark to be overvalued, which results in a reduction in competitiveness that may only become apparent when the build-up phase has come to an end or even when the stock of reserves held in this currency begins to decrease. Hence the Bundesbank has always resisted the tendency for official foreign exchange reserves to be held in Deutschmark, although it has had to accept this tendency to a certain extent.

THE DOMESTIC VALUE OF THE DEUTSCHMARK

The 'hardness' of the Deutschmark and the continuous increase in its external value were of course only possible on the basis of a better stability record of the Deutschmark compared with other currencies, all of which were less stable. Taken by itself, however, the domestic value of the Deutschmark more than halved, as measured by the cost-of-living index, between the period immediately after the currency reform and 1977. The steepest price rises in the history of the Deutschmark – apart from the period when the new price level was settling down immediately after the currency reform – took place in 1951, at the time of the Korean boom. But those price increases were in part made good: in 1953 the cost of living fell in absolute terms. Since then prices have risen continuously in waves of varying length and varying height (see Figure 6.1). During the period of world-wide inflation in the 1970s price rises reached a new peak at the end of 1973, at an annual rate of almost 8 per cent. In the meantime the inflation rate was reduced to a lower level than at any time since the beginning of the 1970s. Germany is at least moving towards price stability, which according to a widespread view would be reached at an inflation rate of 1–2 per cent a year. (See 'The extent of depreciation of money since 1950, and the prospective trend of the value of money', *Monthly Report of the Deutsche Bundesbank*, vol. 20, no. 3, March 1968, p. 3). But over the thirty-year period taken as a whole Germany's stabilisation policy has been able to achieve only relative success. Moreover, the difficulty of maintaining purchasing power has increased over time: in the 1950s, the average annual rate of price rises amounted to 1.1 per cent; in the 1960s it came to 2.4 per cent, and between 1970 and 1977 it totalled 5.3 per cent per annum.

This is not the place to analyse in detail the very complex causes of the decline in the Deutschmark's purchasing power. But it is obvious from the foregoing that external and international causes played a major part in it. This applies particularly to the undervaluation of the Deutschmark and the obligation to purchase foreign exchange during the period of fixed exchange rates; thus, the steepest rise in wage costs since the war took place in 1970, mainly no doubt because of the lack of protection against imported inflation owing to the mistaken policies of 1968 and 1969. On the other hand, the soaring of commodity prices in 1972–3 and the oil-price explosion at the end of 1973 inevitably had an impact on the German price level, even if the floating of the Deutschmark after March 1973 somewhat attenuated their influence on German prices.

However, imported inflation is not wholly to blame for the decline in the value of money. There were, and are, enough sources of home-made inflation pushing up costs and prices. One need only

136

Table 6.2 **Overall economic developments, 1950–1977**

Year	Gross national product			Industrial production[1]	Cost of living[2]	Labour force[3]	Unemployment ratio[4]	Gross wages and salaries per employees		
	at current prices	at constant prices						at current prices		at constant prices
		Total	per employed person					DM	1950 = 100	1950 = 100
	Percentage change on previous year						%			
1950	22.3	.	.	24.6	−6.3	.	11.0	2 910	100	100
1951	10.4	10.4	7.9	18.5	7.8	1.9	10.4	3 390	116	108
1952	14.2	8.9	6.9	6.4	2.0	1.5	9.5	3 660	125	114
1953	7.8	8.2	5.4	10.3	−1.7	1.4	8.4	3 870	133	123
1954	7.4	7.4	4.7	11.5	0.1	2.3	7.6	4 070	140	129
1955	14.4	12.0	7.9	14.9	1.7	2.2	5.6	4 400	151	137
1956	10.5	7.3	4.7	8.0	2.6	1.7	4.4	4 750	163	144
1957	9.0	5.7	3.6	5.7	2.0	1.6	3.7	4 990	171	149
1958	7.2	3.7	2.9	3.1	2.2	0.8	3.7	5 330	183	155
1959	8.8	7.3	6.0	7.4	1.0	0.2	2.6	5 620	193	162

1960	11.7	9.0	7.3	11.4	1.4	0.7	1.3	6 150	211	175
1961	9.4	4.9	3.5	6.4	2.2	1.0	0.8	6 780	232	189
1962	8.8	4.4	4.0	4.3	3.0	0.3	0.7	7 400	254	200
1963	6.0	3.0	2.8	3.5	2.9	0.3	0.8	7 850	269	206
1964	9.8	6.6	6.6	7.9	2.4	0.0	0.8	8 560	294	220
1965	9.2	5.5	5.0	5.1	3.1	0.4	0.7	9 340	320	232
1966	6.4	2.5	2.9	1.3	3.7	-0.3	0.7	10 010	344	240
1967	1.3	-0.1	3.2	-2.8	1.7	-2.1	2.1	10 350	355	244
1968	8.4	6.5	6.4	9.3	1.6	-0.4	1.5	10 990	377	255
1969	11.7	7.9	6.3	12.9	1.9	0.9	0.9	12 000	412	274
1970	13.6	5.9	4.6	5.9	3.4	1.1	0.7	13 770	473	304
1971	11.3	3.3	3.1	1.6	5.3	0.3	0.8	15 390	528	323
1972	9.4	3.6	3.9	4.5	5.5	0.0	1.1	16 770	575	333
1973	11.2	4.9	4.7	6.2	6.9	0.3	1.2	18 780	645	349
1974	7.3	0.4	2.3	-2.0	7.0	-0.7	2.6	20 930	718	363
1975	4.4	-2.5	1.0	-6.2	6.0	-1.5	4.7	22 430	770	367
1976	9.1	5.7	6.7	6.9	4.5	-0.9	4.6	23 990	823	376
1977	6.2	2.4	2.9	2.9	3.9	-0.6	4.5	25 650	880	387

[1] Including construction; adjusted for working-day variations.
[2] Until end-1962 cost-of-living index for a 4-person employee household in the middle income range, from 1963 cost-of-living index for all households, calculated on the original base.
[3] Annual average.
[4] Unemployed persons as a percentage of the dependent labour force.

Table 6.3 Movement of interest rates and monetary developments 1950–1977

	Interest rates					Money stock and lending				
										of which Bank lending to domestic enterprises and individuals
Year	Discount rate	Lombard rate[1]	Three-month funds	Credits in current account[2]	Long-term interest rate[3]	Central bank money stock[4]	Currency in circulation and sight deposits (M1)	Money and quasi-money balances (M2)	Bank lending to domestic non-banks, total[5]	
	% per annum; annual average					Percentage change during year				
1950	4.4	5.4	4.9	8.9	.	.	10.7	22.1	.	.
1951	6.0	7.0	7.1	10.5	.	.	15.1	20.0	17.0	28.2
1952	5.2	6.2	6.4	9.7	.	.	10.3	16.6	17.7	29.3
1953	3.7	4.7	4.3	8.2	.	.	8.9	14.2	19.6	25.6
1954	3.2	4.2	3.8	7.9	.	.	12.9	8.0	20.1	23.1
1955	3.2	4.2	4.2	7.9	6.1	.	10.4	7.9	17.5	21.8
1956	4.8	5.8	6.2	9.3	6.3	.	7.7	11.5	11.3	13.7
1957	4.4	5.4	5.0	8.9	7.1	.	11.3	15.3	9.7	11.0
1958	3.3	4.3	3.6	7.8	6.5	.	12.6	10.0	11.1	11.7
1959	3.0	4.0	3.2	7.5	5.8	.	11.0	10.2	13.8	15.1

1960	4.4	5.4	5.1	8.9	6.3	9.7	7.2	7.5	11.6	14.3
1961	3.2	4.2	3.6	7.7	5.9	10.9	14.7	13.2	14.9	15.9
1962	3.0	4.0	3.4	7.5	6.0	8.5	7.9	7.7	11.9	13.4
1963	3.0	4.0	4.0	7.5	6.1	7.9	7.0	6.7	11.7	12.1
1964	3.0	4.0	4.1	7.5	6.2	8.5	8.0	6.8	11.8	12.2
1965	3.7	4.7	5.1	8.2	6.8	9.1	7.6	6.1	12.0	11.9
1966	4.6	5.7	6.6	9.1	7.8	5.3	1.4	6.1	8.8	8.3
1967	3.4	4.2	4.3	7.9	7.0	6.5	10.4	12.5	9.5	6.5
1968	3.0	3.5	3.8	7.6	6.7	9.6	6.3	14.2	10.5	10.3
1969	4.5	5.7	5.8	8.5	7.0	9.5	6.4	10.2	12.7	15.3
1970	6.9	9.0	9.4	11.1	8.2	6.7	8.7	10.5	10.7	11.3
1971	5.1	6.5	7.1	10.0	8.2	12.2	12.2	14.4	13.1	13.8
1972	3.4	4.6	5.6	8.7	8.2	13.1	14.4	16.9	14.5	15.9
1973	6.2	8.2	12.1	12.1	9.5	7.6	1.8	13.7	9.9	9.6
1974	6.9	8.9	9.9	13.6	10.6	6.4	10.8	5.1	7.9	6.5
1975	4.5	5.7	5.0	10.3	8.7	10.0	13.5	-0.1	10.5	4.6
1976	3.5	4.5	4.2	8.4	8.0	8.3	3.8	6.8	10.1	9.4
1977	3.5	4.2	4.4	8.0	6.4	9.8	11.3	11.2	9.5	9.0

[1] Lombard loans were not generally granted to the banks at the lombard rate between June 1, 1973 and July 3, 1974.
[2] Until March 1967 the officially fixed maximum rates, thereafter the rates for credits of less than DM 1 million according to the Bundesbank's interest rate surveys.
[3] Yield on fully taxed bonds outstanding.
[4] Currency in circulation and required minimum reserves on domestic liabilities (at constant reserve ratios, base: January 1974); seasonally adjusted.
[5] Bundesbank and the banks.

point to the excessive – and still growing – demands of the welfare state and other public expenditure on the gross national product and to the associated contraction of the productive part of the economy. Temporary overheating on the German labour market also gave a strong boost to cost inflation. On the other hand, offsetting productivity increases became less pronounced in the course of time, and in recent years the cost of environmental protection measures has gone up.

Formerly it was thought that creeping inflation, such as was observed at times even in the 1950s and 1960s, was a price that had to be paid for growth and a high level of employment. This belittling of inflation has been contradicted by actual experience, for countries with higher inflation rates have often had not lower, but higher unemployment rates than the more stable countries. Inflation has frequently resulted in low real growth and in unemployment, the reason being that it increasingly turns productive forces to unproductive but seemingly inflation-proof uses, disorganises national economies, reduces their competitiveness and obliges economic policy to pursue a course of 'stop and go' on balance-of-payments grounds. Above all, however, inflation turns very quickly into *wage-cost* inflation today; expansion of demand accompanied by stable wage costs (which Keynes had in mind in his economic policy prescriptions) no longer takes place nowadays, even in the presence of unemployment.

MONETARY POLICY AND MONETARY STABILITY

In section 3 of the Bundesbank Act the Bundesbank is assigned the duty of 'safeguarding the currency'. Under section 12 of that Act the Bundesbank is required to support the economic policy of the Federal Government, but within the framework of its (primary) duty of safeguarding the currency. Of course, this cannot be interpreted to mean that stability of the value of money could be the sole guiding principle of monetary policy, quite independently of overall economic conditions. The Bundesbank has paid due attention to other objectives as well in recent decades, for example, balance-of-payments equilibrium or the restoration of economic equilibrium. But in the interplay of forces that affect economic activity and the currency – namely the government, parliament, management and labour – it has always regarded its function of safeguarding monetary stability as its pre-eminent task. At all events, it is not allowed to neglect monetary stability deliberately in favour of other economic policy objectives, such as growth, full employment or external equilibrium.

Conflicts over this division of responsibility have not arisen as the Federal Government and the Bundesbank have been in agreement about the necessity of a stability-orientated monetary policy. Particularly at the height of the inflation in the 1970s a clear distribution of parts emerged. The main task entrusted to the Bundesbank was that of restoring monetary stability step by step. Fiscal policy, by contrast, was to devote its attention to cyclical and structural weaknesses. However, already in its monetary growth target for 1975 the Bundesbank not only aimed at a further reduction in the rate of inflation but also took account of the necessity for combating the recession, since it explained its monetary targets as follows:

The Deutsche Bundesbank will conduct monetary policy in such a way that the rate of price rises will progressively be diminished while at the same time the requisite monetary margin will be granted for the envisaged real growth of the economy.

In spite of a relatively expansionary monetary policy the envisaged real growth was not achieved immediately, however, as the depressive influence exercised by the world economy was at first too strong; but thanks to the joint efforts of fiscal and monetary policy the low point of the recession was passed in the summer of 1975 and the 1976 recovery was initiated.

For the monetary policy of the Bundesbank the suspension of the obligation to purchase dollars in the spring of 1973 represented a profound change in basic monetary conditions. It released the Bundesbank from the necessity to create central bank money involuntarily via purchases of foreign exchange, that is, monetary policy was better protected against external influences. Since the Bundesbank's monetary policy instruments were now biting again, it was only logical for it to pay more attention than before to the control of the money stock. In December 1974 the Bundesbank for the first time announced a quantitative target for its policy: a growth of 8 per cent in the central bank money stock during the course of 1975. It was the first central bank to publish such a *quantitative monetary target*. Before long a number of other central banks followed suit with monetary growth targets of one kind or another.

This new form of publicly-announced quantitative monetary policy was intended to act as a guide to the business community, management and labour and the government and as an instrument for the internal monitoring of monetary policy. It was quite deliberately introduced as an experiment. The Bundesbank is still in the process of gaining experience with this new instrument.

One thing became clear: this instrument does not give a perfect recipe for any given situation. In 1976 and 1977 the Bundesbank allowed the monetary growth target to be overshot slightly without counteracting this by restrictive measures. In this case a conflict arose between what seemed necessary in the light of the monetary indicators and what was required in cyclical terms. In the winter of 1977–8 the Bundesbank temporarily tolerated an even larger overshooting, caused partly by its substantial foreign exchange purchases and partly by changes in the cash-holding habits of the public. When the foreign exchange markets are in turmoil, the central bank cannot expose the economy to the erratic movements resulting from speculation-induced exchange rate fluctuations without taking countermeasures. The central bank is also under an obligation to ensure a certain *steadiness of the basic monetary conditions* in the economy; this includes the prevention of sharp jumps in interest rates. As regards the foreign exchange interventions in the winter of 1977–8, the simultaneous appreciation of the Deutschmark acted as a brake on domestic price rises. Thus foreign exchange interventions that are accompanied by an (unavoidable) upward movement of the Deutschmark must be judged differently, in terms of stabilisation policy, from foreign exchange interventions under a system of fixed exchange rates.

Experience with quantitative monetary policy has shown that it must be regarded as a *medium-term strategy*. In the short run there can also be tactical considerations that are influenced either by cyclical or by exchange policy factors. The essential point is that the central bank must not lose sight of its target of stabilising the value of money. To be sure, other problems and objectives of economic policy may be given due attention. But there must never be any doubt that the safeguarding of the value of money remains the paramount aim of central bank policy.

This thirty-year history of the Deutschmark has shown us that monetary stability is a matter of key importance, not only economically but also socially – indeed, in political terms as well. These thirty years witnessed some successes in stabilisation policy, at least as compared with other countries. But they also saw failures. The chief lesson to be learned from them is that the maintenance or restoration of monetary stability requires constant effort, indeed a constant struggle to ward off threats and dangers coming from both within Germany and from abroad.

POSTSCRIPT (MAY 1983)

In the essay which I wrote in June 1978 to commemorate the thirtieth anniversary of the Deutschmark, I could describe German monetary policy only in very broad lines. I touched briefly on a few topical problems, such as the transition to money-supply targets and the problems with strongly floating exchange rates. It is perhaps worthwhile to enlarge upon these two subjects with the benefit of hindsight.

Pragmatic monetarism

There are several features which have distinguished German monetarism from other, in particular Anglo-Saxon, kinds of monetarism:

1. From the very beginning, we have considered the money-supply target as only an *intermediate goal*. The aim was to keep total monetary demand on a predetermined – and as steady as possible – track, with a return to price stability as the ultimate goal. In choosing the most appropriate definition of money supply, we had to reject M_1, the narrow definition preferred by most German monetarists, since our investigation had shown that M_1 was subject to very sharp jumps – or in other terms: that the public demand for M_1, or its 'velocity', was very volatile over time-periods which are relevant for practical policy. Thus we chose a broad-based definition, namely the central bank money stock, which is under the direct influence of the central bank and is in some ways akin to the monetary base. Experience to this day has confirmed our misgivings about M_1. We were confronted from the very beginning with the problem of correctly forecasting the velocity of money (that is, the relationship between the stock of money and total demand). We inevitably made mistakes in these forecasts, but not of such a devastating magnitude as the Americans experienced in 1982. The difficulty of correctly forecasting velocity was one of several reasons which led us at the end of 1978 to set our money-supply target within a rather broad range (the 'target

corridor'), at the beginning at 6–9 per cent, gradually bein▪
lowered to the present 4–7 per cent.

2. We have never believed that it would make sense, or that it woul▪
even be technically possible, to keep the money volume precisel▪
on track from month to month or from quarter to quarter. Quanti▪
tative monetary targetry can only be used as a *medium-term*
strategy. To let interest rates jump in such inordinate ways as the▪
did in the USA in 1980 and 1981 – with the prime rate oscillatin▪
between 10 and 21 per cent – in the futile attempt to keep mone▪
supply on track from month to month has always seemed to u▪
senseless, very costly (risk premium on interest rates) and coun▪
terproductive (confusing signals to the economy). Our experienc▪
has shown that one can achieve money supply targets over th▪
medium term with much less volatility of interest rates (an▪
consequently of exchange rates).

3. We have never believed that monetary control by itself is ▪
cure-all or a magic incantation, which guarantees success irrespe▪
tive of what is happening in fiscal policy or on the wage front, o▪
with the exchange rate. When publishing our monetary targets w▪
have always emphasised in our communiqués that the desire▪
effects could only be reached if the other participants in th▪
economic process, in particular fiscal policy and the 'social par▪
ners' in their price and wage policy, fell into line. This is a far cr▪
from the euphoric slogan of leading monetarists in the presen▪
American administration, namely: 'control the money supply an▪
everything else falls into place'.

4. Although in our view the fight against inflation must alway▪
remain the primary concern of monetary policy, the central ban▪
cannot completely disregard the cyclical (or 'conjunctural') stat▪
of the economy, nor the trend of the payments balance on curre▪
account and of the exchange rate. When issuing its annual mone▪
ary targets, the German central bank has usually explained und▪
what domestic and exchange rate conditions it would attempt ▪
keep the money supply more in the upper or in the lower part ▪
its target corridor.

Taking all this together, German money-supply policy has from th▪
beginning – that is, since 1974 – evolved in a rather pragmat▪
manner, and avowedly so. The end-result, measured in terms ▪
relative price stability, has been better than that of the more do▪
matic Anglo-Saxon monetarisms. To me it came as no surprise that bo▪

in Britain and in the USA since 1982 the monetary authorities have also moved in the direction of a more pragmatic monetarism: for instance, by taking not only one, but several definitions of money into account, by no longer trying to keep on track over very short periods, by paying regard to the changing velocity of money, and by looking at exchange-rate movements as an indicator.

The role of exchange-rate trends – a two-dimensional monetary policy

Events since 1978 have shown that for medium-sized countries like West Germany, Britain, etc. the *exchange-rate trend* can be a very important influence on domestic price stability and can also constitute an indicator or guide for monetary policy.

In the case of the Deutschmark, the large exchange-rate movements had had one time a stabilising and at other times a destabilising influence. In 1978, for instance, the Deutschmark became overvalued against the dollar and many other currencies. This improved the terms of trade for West Germany. Import prices declined in 1978 by 3.7 per cent on average. Thus in 1978 Germany achieved the lowest inflation rate of the 1970s, much lower than in the last few years of the fixed rate system (1978: consumer prices + 2.7 per cent; GNP deflator + 3.8 per cent). In 1980–1 the combined effect of rising commodity (especially oil) prices together with a rising dollar exchange rate sent Germany's import prices soaring: by an average of 15 per cent in 1980, and by a peak year-on-year rate of 20 per cent in August 1981. This led to our peak inflation rate in the 1980s of 6.7 per cent year-on-year.

In both periods this had a big impact on German monetary policy. In 1977–8 the central bank intervened heavily in the dollar market in order to smooth wild speculative exaggerations. As a consequence, it had to acquiesce in a temporary overshooting of its monetary target – in 1978 the money supply rose by 11 per cent, against a target of 8 per cent. Total monetary demand did not exceed the target. But the speculative acquisition of Deutschmarks by foreigners, advance payments on German exports, and a large increase in Deutschmark notes hoarded in neighbouring countries led to a sharp decline in the velocity of money (or rather: the relationship between the stock of money to total monetary demand). In the following year 1979, Germany successfully absorbed and neutralised the surplus liquidity created in 1978.

In April 1978, I wrote in an article in our leading newspaper:

> The Bundesbank can tolerate a temporary overshooting of its target at the moment because, first, no signs of any strong demand expansion are visible, and second, the present excessive appreciation of the Deutschmark is not only dampening economic activity and the velocity of money, but also directly restraining price rises.

And I concluded:

> Monetary policy cannot be considered in isolation but only in conjunction with simultaneous exchange-rate developments. A strongly upward-floating exchange rate, with its dampening effects on demand and prices, must be regarded as an *additional dimension* of overall monetary policy . . . Foreign-exchange interventions under a system of upward-floating exchange rates must therefore be assessed differently from interventions under a system of stable rates, in which the exchange rate does not, by itself, act as a price- and demand-curbing counterweight.

This conclusion seemed to me so important that I incorporated it into the survey over the thirty years of the Deutschmark.

The recent report of the experts of the Group of Five (*Jurgensen Report*), which was published in April 1983, has not paid adequate regard to this great difference between intervention *per se*, and intervention combined with a strong appreciation of the currency.

7 The Anguish of Central Banking*

Arthur F. Burns

The international monetary system, which has been in almost constant turmoil during the 1970s, benefited towards the end of the decade from several developments. Under the amended Articles of Agreement, the International Monetary Fund can exercise firm surveillance over the exchange-rate policies of its members, and is therefore now in a position to move the nations of the world toward a rule of law in international monetary affairs. Another promising development was the establishment of the European Monetary System with the aim of maintaining relatively stable exchange rates within the Common Market.

A third positive development was recognition by the USA that the persisting deficits in its international current account would have to be eliminated, and that in the meantime decisive intervention to protect the external value of the dollar could well be needed. The conventional theory that a depreciating currency was beneficial to a nation's foreign trade and to its over-all economic activity had lost its appeal within the American government. The officials concerned with economic policy had learned that whatever merit may in some circumstances attach to this theory, it was a dangerous guide for a country whose currency was still the centrepiece of the international monetary system. 'Benign neglect' of the external value of the dollar came to an end dramatically, and I would hope irrevocably, last November.

This and other constructive developments suggested earlier in 1979 that a closer approach to international equilibrium was under way and calm returned for a while to foreign exchange markets. But uneasiness about the monetary system, particularly about the future

* This chapter originated as the 1979 Per Jacobsson Lecture, given in Belgrade on 30 September 1979, and published in the same year by the Per Jacobsson Foundation, IMF, Washington.

of the dollar, has continued and in fact intensified this summer. There were ample reasons for concern – among them, the political convulsions in Iran, the enormous new increases in oil prices by OPEC, the narrowing at times of interest-rate differentials between New York and foreign money-market centres, and the limited progress in developing an effective energy policy in the USA. While all these factors contributed to nervousness, what was most disturbing to foreign exchange markets was the re-acceleration of inflation in the USA and in much of the rest of the world. Even Germany and Switzerland no longer qualified as islands of stability.

This unhappy development was one more indication, if any were needed, that the current instability in international finance was largely a consequence of the chronic inflation of the times and that stability would not return to the international monetary system until reasonably good control over inflationary forces had been achieved in the major industrial nations – and especially in the USA. This critical consideration at once raised serious questions: why was the worldwide disease of inflation proving so stubborn? Why was it not yielding to the various efforts of the affected nations, including some determined efforts, to bring it to an end? Why, in particular, had central bankers, whose main business one might suppose was to fight inflation, been so ineffective in dealing with this worldwide problem?

To me, as a former central banker, the last of these questions was especially intriguing. One of the time-honoured functions of a central bank is to protect the integrity of its nation's currency, both domestically and internationally. In monetary policy central bankers have a potent means for fostering stability of the general price level. By training, if not also by temperament, they are inclined to lay great stress on price stability, and their abhorrence of inflation is continually reinforced by contacts with one another and with like-minded members of the private financial community. And yet, despite their antipathy to inflation and the powerful weapons they could wield against it, central bankers had failed so utterly in this mission. In this paradox lies the anguish of central banking.

My aim here is to consider the causes of this paradox and its implications for the future. Much of what I say will inevitably reflect lessons that I learned during my service as Chairman of the Federal Reserve Board over an eight-year period that ended in March 1978. I shall focus mainly, although not exclusively, on the USA. That is the area that I know best, and I also believe the American experience – despite some unique aspects – is fairly representative of that of other

ndustrial countries. The developing nations have their own charac-
eristic sources and patterns of inflation. Never the less, in our
nterdependent world, economic conditions in the USA and other
ndustrial countries are bound to have a significant bearing on the
ortunes of developing countries.

3y way of introduction, I might note that during much of the period
since the end of the Second World War, over-all economic developments were, in the main, satisfactory. By pre-war standards, recessions were brief and mild through the mid-1960s, both in the
JSA and in other industrial countries; world trade expanded rapidly
under a beneficent regime of stable exchange rates; and living standards rose impressively throughout the developed world. In most
ndustrial countries inflationary pressures were troublesome from
ime to time – as in the immediate post-war years, during the Korean
hostilities, and for a couple of years after the mid-1950s. These
pressures were more substantial in some countries than in the USA,
but in none did inflation appear to be out of control.

From 1958 through 1964, the USA enjoyed a remarkable degree of
price stability. During that stretch of six years, the wholesale price
index remained virtually unchanged and the consumer price index
rose at an annual rate of only a little more than 1 per cent. And then
the inflation that has ever since been plaguing the American economy
got under way. Average wholesale prices rose at an annual rate of 2
per cent from 1964 to 1968, 4 per cent from 1968 to 1972, and 10 per
cent from 1972 to 1978. This pattern of accelerating price increases
was found in other countries also, although rates of increase varied
widely, and in most industrial nations the acceleration began later –
typically in 1969 or 1970.

Analyses of the inflation that the United States experienced from
1964 to 1979 frequently proceed in three stages. First are considered
the factors that launched inflation in the mid-1960s, particularly the
governmental fine-tuning inspired by the New Economics and the
loose financing of the war in Vietnam. Next are considered the
factors that led to subsequent strengthening of inflationary forces,
including further policy errors, the devaluations of the dollar in 1971
and 1973, the worldwide economic boom of 1972–3, the crop failures
and resulting surge in world food prices in 1973–4, the extraordinary
increases in oil prices that became effective in 1974, and the sharp
deceleration of productivity growth from the late 1960s onward. Fi-

nally, attention is turned to the process whereby protracted experienc
with inflation has led to widespread expectations that it will continue i
the future, so that inflation has acquired a momentum of its own.

I have no quarrel with analyses of this type. They are distinctl
helpful in explaining the American inflation and, with changes her
and there, that in other nations also. At the same time, I believe tha
such analyses overlook a more fundamental factor: the persister
inflationary bias that has emerged from the philosophic and politic;
currents that have been transforming economic life in the USA an
elsewhere since the 1930s. The essence of the unique inflation of ou
times and the reason central bankers have been ineffective in dealin
with it can be understood only in terms of those currents of though
and the political environment they created.

Historically, Americans have had deep faith in the concept (
progress – in the idea that it was realistic to expect to better one
own lot and that of one's family in the course of a lifetime. During th
greater part of America's history, government intervention in ecoi
omic life was only peripheral. Personal progress was generally viewe
as a reward for personal effort – assisted, perhaps, by goo
fortune. Provision for bad times or other contingencies of life wa
deemed prudent, but that was a private responsibility. The Amer
can's way through life lay along the road of self-reliance; only i
extremity did he look to government or his neighbours for economi
assistance.

This tradition of individualism was shattered by the cataclysmi
events of the 1930s and 1940s. The breakdown of economic orde
during the Great Depression was unprecedented in its scale an
scope, and it strained the precept of self-reliance beyond th
breaking-point. With one-quarter of the labour force unemployec
personal courage and moral stamina could guarantee neither a jo
nor a livelihood. Succour finally came through a political idea tha
was novel to a majority of the American people but compellin
none the less – namely, that the Federal government had a far large
responsibility in the economic sphere than it had hitherto assumed

Under the New Deal the Federal government undertook extensiv
projects of public construction and offered work relief as well. It gav
direct relief to the needy – a function previously performed only b
local authorities or private charity. It established unemploymen
insurance and old-age pensions. It took steps to raise wages an
prices with a view to fostering economic recovery. And beyond thes
innovative actions, the Federal government greatly extended th

range of its regulatory activities. It intervened massively in the securities market, in banking, in the public utilities industry, in the housing market, and in the farm sector; and it gave labour unions broad new rights and powers. Together, these and other New Deal measures laid the foundations of an activist government – a government responsible not only for relieving suffering and insuring against economic adversity, but also for limiting 'harmful' competition, subsidising 'worthwhile' activities, and redressing unequal balances of market power. In less than a decade the government became a leading actor on the economic stage.

Just as Americans were persuaded during the depression that the Federal government should help the unemployed, so they were taught by the experience of the Second World War to look to government to prevent unemployment in the first place. Under the compulsions of war, the government had demonstrated that it could assure gainful employment for every willing hand. It therefore seemed reasonable (and not only to followers of Keynes) to expect government to do the same in a time of peace. In 1944, when President Roosevelt set forth the basis of his post-war domestic programme in an 'Economic Bill of Rights' he put 'the right to a useful and remunerative job' at the head of the list. With the war ended, the Employment Act of 1946 explicitly proclaimed the Federal government's responsibility to promote 'maximum employment,' and this came to mean 'full employment' as a matter of law as well as popular usage.

Armed with the Employment Act, the government sought to demonstrate that it could combat unemployment with preventive as well as curative measures. In fact, the period from The Second World War to the mid-1960s was marked not only by a dampening of the business cycle but also by persistent increases in the prosperity of American families. On the one side, rising incomes, reflecting substantial gains in labour productivity, made possible rising consumption, greater leisure, and better provision for retirement. On the other side, a steady stream of new and often improved consumer goods tended to sustain the growth of aggregate demand. The extensive development of consumer-credit institutions made it easier for people to acquire automobiles, household appliances, and other goods and services, the desire for which was continually being whetted by alluring advertisements and the illustrations of potential life-styles broadcast by television and the movies. The seemingly inexorable rise in living standards for the bulk of the population was reflected in upward trends in the proportion of families that owned their own home, that owned a summer home, that possessed one two and even three automobiles, that had telephones, that owned television sets, clothes washers, and food freezers; also in the propor tion of the population that had graduated from high school and from college, that travelled abroad, that owned corporate stock, that carried life insurance, and so on.

This experience of economic progress strengthened the public' expectations of progress. What had once been a quiet persona feeling that the long future would be better than the past, particularl' for one's children, was transformed during the post-war years into an articulate and widespread expectation of steady improvement in living standards – indeed, to a feeling of entitlement to annua increases in real income.

But the rapid rise in national affluence did not create a mood o contentment. On the contrary, the 1960s were years of social turmoi in the USA, as they were in other industrial democracies. In part, th unrest reflected discontent by blacks and other minorities with pre vailing conditions of social discrimination and economic deprivatio – a discontent that erupted during the hot summers of the middl 1960s in burning and looting. In part, the social unrest reflecte growing feelings of injustice by or on behalf of other groups – th poor, the aged, the physically handicapped, ethnics, farmers, blue collar workers, women, and so forth. In part, the unrest reflected growing rejection by middle-class youth of prevailing institutions an cultural values. In part, it reflected the more or less sudden recogni tion by broad segments of the population that the economic reform of the New Deal and the more recent rise in national affluence ha left untouched problems in various areas of American life – socia political, economic, and environmental. And interacting with a these sources of social disturbance were the heightening tension associated with the Vietnam War.

In the innocence of the day, many Americans came to believe tha all the new or newly-discovered ills of society should be addresse promptly by the Federal government. And in the innocence of th day, the administration in office attempted to respond to the growin demands for social and economic reform while waging war i Vietnam on a rising scale. Under the rubric of the New Economics, more activist policy was adopted for the purpose of increasing th rate of economic growth and reducing the level of unemploymen Under the rubrics of the New Frontier and the Great Society broad-scale efforts were made to stitch up open seams in the fabric of affluence – inadequate or unequal education, housing, medical care, nutrition. Under the rubrics of civil rights and citizen participation, minorities and other disadvantaged groups were given political weapons to maintain, consolidate, and extend their gains.

The interplay of governmental action and private demands had an internal dynamic that led to their concurrent escalation. When the government undertook in the mid-1960s to address such 'unfinished tasks' as reducing frictional unemployment, eliminating poverty, widening the benefits of prosperity, and improving the quality of life, it awakened new ranges of expectation and demand. Once it was established that the key function of government was to solve problems and relieve hardships – not only for society at large but also for troubled industries, regions, occupations, or social groups – a great and growing body of problems and hardships became candidates for governmental solution. New techniques for bringing pressure on Congress – and also on the state legislatures and other elected officials – were developed, refined, and exploited. Congress responded by pouring out a broad stream of measures that involved government spending, special tax relief, or regulations mandating private spending. Every demonstration of a successful tactic in securing rights, establishing entitlements, or extracting other benefits from government led to new applications of that tactic. Various groups found a powerful ally in the federal courts, which repeatedly struck down legislative or administrative limitations on access to government benefits. Even government employees, particularly at the state and municipal levels, discovered the pecuniary rewards of shedding genteel notions of public service and pressing economic demands with a strident militancy.

Many results of this interaction of government and citizen activism proved wholesome. Their cumulative effect, however, was to impart a strong inflationary bias to the American economy. The proliferation of government programmes led to progressively higher tax burdens on both individuals and corporations. Even so, the willingness of government to levy taxes fell distinctly short of its propensity to spend. Since 1950 the federal budget has been in balance in only five years. Since 1970 a deficit has occurred in every year. Not only that, but the deficits have been mounting in size. Budget deficits have thus become a chronic condition of federal finance; they have been incurred when business conditions were poor and also when business was booming. But when the government runs a budget deficit, it

pumps more money into the pocketbooks of people than it withdraws
from their pocketbooks; the demand for goods and services therefore
tends to increase all around. That is the way the inflation that has
been raging since the mid-1960s first started and later kept being
nourished.

The pursuit of costly social reforms often went hand in hand with
the pursuit of full employment. In fact, much of the expanding range
of government spending was prompted by the commitment to full
employment. Inflation came to be widely viewed as a temporary
phenomenon – or, provided it remained mild, as an acceptable
condition. 'Maximum' or 'full' employment, after all, had become
the nation's major economic goal – not stability of the price level
That inflation ultimately brings on recession and otherwise nullifies
many of the benefits sought through social legislation was largely
ignored. Even conservative politicians and businessmen began echoing Keynesian teachings. It therefore seemed only natural to federa
officials charged with economic responsibilities to respond quickly to
any slackening of economic activity – at times, in fact, as in the early
days of 1977, to sheer illusions of such slackening – but to proceed
very slowly and cautiously in responding to evidence of increasing
pressure on the nation's resources of labour and capital. Fear o
immediate unemployment – rather than fear of current or eventua
inflation – thus came to dominate economic policy-making.

This weighting of the scales of government policy inevitably gave an
inflationary twist to the economy, and so too did the expanding role
of government regulation. Traditional ways of protecting particular
groups against competition – such as raising farm price supports
increasing minimum wages, and imposing import quotas – did no
lose their appeal as inflation kept soaring. On the contrary, all these
devices of raising costs and prices were liberally employed even in the
face of accelerating inflation during 1977 and 1978. Also troublesome
were the newer social regulations – those concerned with health
safety, and the environment – that kept multiplying during the 1970s
However laudable in purpose, much of this regulatory apparatus wa
conceived in haste and with little regard to the costs being imposed
on producers. Substantial amounts of capital that might have gone
into productivity-enhancing investments by private industry wer
thus diverted into uses mandated by the regulators. Improvements in
productivity were also slowed by the discouragement of busines
investment that resulted from the increasing burden of income and
capital gains taxes. Progress in equipping the work-force with new

lant and equipment proceeded much less rapidly during the 1970s han during the 1950s or 1960s, and this shortfall contributed to the roductivity slump and thus to the escalation of costs and prices.

Additional forces on the side of supply contributed to the inflation-ary bias. As the income maintenance programmes established by government were liberalised, incentives to work tended to diminish. Some individuals, both young and old, found it agreeable to live much of the time off unemployment insurance, food stamps, and welfare checks – perhaps supplemented by intermittent jobs in an expanding underground economy. Even enterprising and ambitious individuals who sought permanent jobs could be more leisurely or more discrimi-nating in their search when the government, besides pursuing a full employment policy, provided a protective income umbrella during jobless periods. In such an environment, employed workers could demand and often achieve longer vacations with pay and more frequent holidays and sick leave, besides enjoying coffee breaks and other social rites on the job. In such an environment, they could afford to reject a pay cut or a small wage increase when their employer pleaded serious financial difficulties. Thus the number of individuals counted as unemployed could rise even at times when job vacancies, wages, and the consumer price level were rising.

The philosophic and political currents that transformed economic life and brought on secular inflation in the USA have run strong also in other industrial countries. Rising economic expectations of people, wider citizen participation in the political arena, governmental com-mitments to full employment, liberal income maintenance pro-grammes, expanding governmental regulations, and increasingly pressing demands on government for the solution of economic and social problems – all these became common features of the industrial democracies. And just as the rapid expansion of government activi-ties in the USA was accompanied by persistent budget deficits and inflation, that too happened in other industrial countries. Indeed, other countries have often practised loose governmental finance and inflation on a more intensive scale than has the USA.

And so I finally come to the role of central bankers in the inflation-ary process. The worldwide philosophic and political trends on which I have been dwelling inevitably affected their attitudes and actions. In most countries, the central bank is an instrumentality of the executive branch of government – carrying out monetary policy according to

the wishes of the head of government or the Ministry of Finance
Some industrial democracies, to be sure, have substantially indepen
dent central banks and that is certainly the case in the USA. Viewed
in the abstract, the Federal Reserve System had the power to abor
the inflation at its incipient stage in the mid-1960s or at any later
point, and it has the power to end it today. At any time within tha
period, it could have restricted the money supply and created suf
ficient strains in financial and industrial markets to terminate inflation
with little delay. It did not do so because the Federal Reserve wa
itself caught up in the philosophic and political currents that were
transforming American life and culture.

The Employment Act prescribes that 'it is the continuing policy
and responsibility of the Federal government to . . . utilise all it
plans, functions, and resources . . . to promote maximum employ
ment'. The Federal Reserve is subject to this provision of law, and
that has limited its practical scope for restrictive actions – quite apar
from the fact that some members of the Federal Reserve family had
themselves been touched by the allurements of the New Economics
Every time the government moved to enlarge the flow of benefits to
the population at large, or to this or that group, the assumption wa
implicit that monetary policy would somehow accommodate the
action. A similar tacit assumption was embodied in every pricing
decision or wage bargain arranged by private parties or the govern
ment. The fact that such actions could in combination be wholly
incompatible with moderate rates of monetary expansion was seldom
considered by those who initiated them, despite the frequent warn
ings by the Federal Reserve that new fires of inflation were being
ignited. If the Federal Reserve then sought to create a monetary
environment that fell seriously short of accommodating the upward
pressures on prices that were being released or reinforced by govern
mental action, severe difficulties could be quickly produced in the
economy. Not only that, the Federal Reserve would be frustrating
the will of Congress to which it was responsible – a Congress that wa
intent on providing additional services to the electorate and on
assuring that jobs and incomes were maintained, particularly in the
short run.

Facing these political realities, the Federal Reserve was still willing
to step hard on the monetary brake at times – as in 1966, 1969, and
1974 – but its restrictive stance was not maintained long enough to
end inflation. By and large, monetary policy came to be governed by
the principle of undernourishing the inflationary process while still

accommodating a good part of the pressures in the marketplace. The central banks of other industrial countries, functioning as they did in a basically similar political environment, appear to have behaved in much the same fashion.

In describing as I have the anguish of central banking in a modern democracy, I do not mean to suggest that central bankers are free from responsibility for the inflation that is our common inheritance. After all, every central bank has some room for discretion, and the range is considerable in the more independent central banks. As the Federal Reserve, for example, kept testing and probing the limits of its freedom to undernourish the inflation, it repeatedly evoked violent criticism from both the Executive establishment and the Congress and therefore had to devote much of its energy to warding off legislation that could destroy any hope of ending inflation. This testing process necessarily involved political judgements, and the Federal Reserve may at times have overestimated the risks attaching to additional monetary restraint.

Any such errors of political judgement are extremely hard to identify; but I believe, in any event, that errors of economic or financial judgement have in practice been far more significant. In a rapidly changing world the opportunities for making mistakes are legion. Even facts about current conditions are often subject to misinterpretation. Statistics on unemployment in the USA provide a good example. Even before the Second World War ended, some economists were trying to determine how much frictional and structural unemployment would exist when the demand for labour and the supply of labour were in balance; in other words, the rate of unemployment that would reflect a state of full employment. Before long, a broad consensus developed that an unemployment rate of about 4 per cent corresponded to a practical condition of full employment, and that figure became enshrined in economic writing and policy-making. Conditions in labour markets, however, did not stand still. A huge influx of women and young people into the labour force, the liberalisation of unemployment insurance, the spread of welfare programmes, the progressive lifting of statutory minimum wages, the increasing proportion of families having more than one worker, and the increase of national affluence itself – all these changes in the economic and social environment served to render the conventional 4 per cent figure obsolete. The unemployment rate corresponding to full employment is now widely believed to be about 5½ or 6 per cent, and this year's report of the Council of Economic Advisers appears to concur in that judgement. But governmental policy-makers, while generally aware of what was happening in the labour market, were slow to recognise the changing meaning of unemployment statistics whether viewed as a measure of economic performance or as a measure of hardship. The Federal Reserve did not escape this lag of recognition and, once again, I believe that other central banks at times have made similar mistakes.

While misinterpretations of unemployment statistics or other current information have consequences for all public policy-making there are other problems of interpretation to which the central banker's calling is peculiarly subject. Monetary theory is a controversial area. It does not provide central bankers with decision rules that are at once firm and dependable. To be sure, every central banker has learned from the world's experience that an expanding economy requires expanding supplies of money and credit, that excessive creation of money will over the longer run cause or validate inflation, and that declining interest rates will tend to stimulate economic expansion while rising interest rates will tend to restrict it but this knowledge stops short of mathematical precision.

Partly as a result of the chronic inflation of our times, central bankers have been giving closer attention to the money supply than did their predecessors; but they continue to be seriously concerned with the behaviour of interest rates. They face difficult questions about the relative weight to be given to measures of money and interest rates in the short run and long run; about the concept or concepts of money that are most significant for policy purposes about the interpretation of such developments as the growth of Eurocurrency deposits and credits; about the length and regularity of the lags with which changes in monetary growth rates influence business activity and prices; about the likely changes in monetary velocity as a consequence of institutional innovations and business cycle developments; and so on and on – as any student of central banking and monetary theory well knows. And there are more fundamental problems about potential conflicts between domestic and international objectives, about the appropriate response to exceptional events not encompassed by theory, and about the precise relevance of any theory based on past experience to a world where behavioural patterns are continually evolving.

It is clear, therefore, that central bankers can make errors – or encounter surprises – at practically every stage of the process of making monetary policy. In some respects, their capacity to err has become larger in our age of inflation. They are accustomed, as are students of finance generally, to think of high and rising market interest rates as a restraining force on economic expansion. That rule of experience, however, tends to break down once expectations of inflation become widespread in a country. At such a time, lenders expect to be paid back in cheaper currency, and they are therefore apt to demand higher interest rates. Since borrowers have similar expectations, they are willing to comply. An 'inflation premium' thus gets built into nominal interest rates. In principle, no matter how high the nominal interest rate may be, as long as it stays below or only slightly above the inflation rate, it will very likely have perverse effects on the economy; that is, it will run up costs of doing business but do little or nothing to restrain over-all spending. In practice, since inflationary expectations, and therefore the real interest rates implied by any given nominal rate, vary among individuals, central bankers cannot be sure of the magnitude of the inflation premium that is built into nominal rates. In many countries, however, these rates have at times in recent years been so clearly below the ongoing inflation rate that one can hardly escape the impression that, however high or outrageous the nominal rates may appear to observers accustomed to judging them by a historical yardstick, they have utterly failed to accomplish the restraint that central bankers sought to achieve. In other words, inflation has often taken the sting out of interest rates – especially, as in the USA, where interest payments can be deducted for income tax purposes.

In addition to these direct effects of inflation, there are other effects that raise doubts about the meaning of particular growth rates of the monetary aggregates. I have in mind changes in financial practices that evolved in the USA during the 1960s – particularly during the bouts with tight money in 1966 and 1969 – and that culminated in an explosion of financial innovations in the 1970s.

Many of these changes were facilitated by regulatory actions or the development of new computer technology. But the driving force behind them was the incentive that sharply-rising market interest rates gave to financial institutions and their customers to change their ways of doing business. Commercial banks responded to rising rates by economising on non-interest-bearing reserves, and their customers responded by economising on non-interest-bearing demand deposits. Both banks and large corporations developed new sources of funds in the Eurodollar market and the domestic commercial paper market. Banks developed new techniques of liability management by exploiting these sources as well as the vast potential of the federal funds market and the market for negotiable certificates of deposit. Other financial institutions – including savings banks, savings and loan associations, credit unions, and money-market mutual funds – developed new transactions services in connection with customer accounts on which they paid interest. Banks fought this competition for transactions balances by offering large depositors special services that reduced the average level of balances they had to carry and by employing various ingenious means to pay interest on balances that were held in large part for transactions purposes.

Developments of these kinds have had profound consequences for the environment in which American monetary policy operates. Not long ago, the thrust of monetary restraint was conveyed more by reductions in the availability of credit – particularly residential mortgage credit – than by rising interest rates; at present, rising interest rates are the primary channel of restraint. This means that a higher level of interest rates is required to achieve any given degree of restraint – quite apart from the effects of inflation premiums that I discussed earlier. But how much higher is not clear; only time will tell. Not long ago, changes in M_1, the familiar monetary aggregate confined to currency and demand deposits, reflected reasonably well changes in the aggregate volume of transactions balances; at present, with new alternatives to bank demand deposits emerging all the time, a lower rate of growth in M_1 is required to achieve any given degree of restraint. But how much lower is not clear; only time will tell. Nor is it clear what other monetary aggregate, if any, would be more serviceable than the traditional M_1 as a monetary indicator. As a result of these effects of inflation, central banking has not only lost its moorings in interest rates; that has happened to a large extent also in the case of the monetary aggregates – certainly in the USA and perhaps in other countries as well.

There is no need to expand further on the opportunities for misjudgement that in recent years have surrounded policy-making at central banks. Some uncertainty, of course, has always characterised monetary policy, just as it has characterised policy decisions generally, whether in public or private life. It should be noted, however, that lags in recognising some of the developments I have been discussing – with respect to unemployment rates, interest rates, and growth rates of the monetary aggregates – would tend to bias policy toward monetary ease. Moreover, the emergence of an inflationary psychology in industrial countries has imparted an asymmetry to the consequences of monetary errors, even if the errors themselves occurred as often in one direction as the other.

There is a profound difference between the effects of mistaken judgements by a central bank in our age of inflation and the effects of such judgements a generation or two ago. In earlier times, when a central bank permitted excessive creation of money and credit in times of prosperity, the price level would indeed tend to rise. But the resulting inflation was confined to the expansion phase of the business cycle; it did not persist or gather force beyond that phase. Therefore, people generally took it for granted that the advance of prices would be followed by a decline once a business recession got under way. That is no longer the case.

Nowadays, businessmen, farmers, bankers, trade union leaders, factory workers, and housewives generally proceed on the expectation that inflation will continue in the future, whether economic activity is booming or receding. Once such a psychology has become dominant in a country, the influence of a central bank error that intensifies inflation may stretch out over years, even after a business recession has set in. For in our modern environment, any rise in the general price level tends to develop a momentum of its own. It stimulates higher wage demands which are accommodated by employers who feel they can recover the additional costs through higher prices; it results in labour agreements in key industries that call for substantial wage increases in later years without regard to the state of business then; and through the use of indexing formulas, it leads to automatic increases in other wages as well as in social security payments, various other pensions, welfare benefits, also in rents on many properties and in the prices of many commodities acquired under long-term contracts. On the other hand, unintended central bank effects of a restrictive type do not ramify in similar fashion. To develop any significant momentum in unwinding inflation, they would need to be both large and repetitive – a combination that can hardly occur under prevailing conditions in the industrial democracies.

If my analysis of central banking in the modern environment is anywhere near the mark, two conclusions immediately follow. First, central banks have indeed been participants in the inflationary process in which the industrial countries have been enmeshed, but their role has been subsidiary. Second, while the making of monetary

policy requires continuing scrutiny and can stand considerable im
provement, we would look in vain to technical reforms as a way o
eliminating the inflationary bias of industrial countries. What i
unique about our inflation is its stubborn persistence, not the behav
iour of central bankers. This persistence reflects the fundamenta
forces on which I dwelt earlier in this address – namely, the philo
sophic and political currents of thought that have impinged or
economic life since the Great Depression and particularly since the
mid-1960s.

My conclusion that it is illusory to expect central banks to put a
end to the inflation that now afflicts the industrial democracies doe
not mean that central banks are incapable of stabilising actions; i
simply means that their practical capacity for curbing an inflation tha
is continually driven by political forces is very limited. Historically
central banks have helped to slow down the pace of economic activity
at certain times and to stimulate economic activity at other times
They have also contributed to economic stability by serving as len
ders of last resort or even going beyond that traditional function
During the 1970s alone, the Federal Reserve moved on at least two
occasions to prevent financial crises that otherwise could easily have
occurred. I have in mind particularly the failure of the Penn Centra
Transportion Company in June 1970 and the failure of the Franklin
National Bank in October 1974. In the former case the inability o
Penn Central to refinance its outstanding commercial paper caused
consternation among holders of commercial paper generally. To
prevent a financial panic the Federal Reserve put aside its monetary
targets for a while, opened the discount window wide, and changed
its regulations so that commercial banks could raise funds in the open
market to finance firms unable to renew their maturing commercial
paper. In the Franklin National case, the Federal Reserve loaned to
that troubled international bank almost $2 milliard and while these
advances were outstanding it was possible to arrange a take-over by
another bank that protected the interests of Franklin's depositors and
customers. These actions were influenced by a feeling of responsibility for the financial system as a whole – international as well as
domestic. The central banks of some other countries, notably the
Bank of England, have likewise discharged constructively the function of serving as lenders of last resort, and the entire concept o
central bank responsibility has been both widened and clarified
through discussions in recent years at the Bank for International
Settlements.

All this and much more deserves to be noted about central banks – especially their tireless efforts to awaken the citizens of their respective countries to the economic and social dangers posed by inflation. But whatever the virtues or shortcomings of central banks may be, the fact remains that they alone will be able to cope only marginally with the inflation of our times. The persistent inflation that plagues the industrial democracies will not be vanquished – or even substantially curbed – until new currents of thought create a political environment in which the difficult adjustments required to end inflation can be undertaken.

There are some signs, as yet tenuous and inconclusive, that such a change in the intellectual and political climate of the democracies is getting under way. One of the characteristic features of a democracy is that it encourages learning from experience. Recent disturbing trends in economic and social life, particularly the persistence and acceleration of inflation, have led to much soul-searching by leaders of thought and opinion. Among economists, the Keynesian school has lost much of its erstwhile vigor, self-confidence, and influence. Economists are no longer focusing so exclusively on unemployment and governmental management of aggregate demand. They are paying more attention to the management of aggregate supply – to the need to strengthen incentives to work and innovate, to ways of stimulating saving and investment, to the importance of eliminating barriers to competition, to ways of reducing the regulatory burdens imposed on industry, and to other means of bolstering business confidence. Many economists now recognise that much of reported unemployment is voluntary, that curbing inflation and reducing involuntary unemployment are complementary rather than competitive goals, that persistent governmental deficits and excessive creation of money tend to feed the fires of inflation, that the high savings rate that usually prevails in the early stages of inflation is eventually succeeded by minimal savings, and that when this stage is reached it becomes very much harder to bring inflation under control.

The intellectual ferment in the world's democracies is having its influence not only on businessmen and investors, but also on politicians, trade-union leaders, and even housewives; for all of them have been learning from experience and from one another. In the USA, for example, people have come to feel in increasing numbers that much of the government spending sanctioned by their compassion and altruism was falling short of its objectives; that urban blight was continuing, that the quality of public schools was deteriorating, that crime and violence were increasing, that welfare cheating was still widespread, that collecting unemployment insurance was becoming a way of life for far too many – in short, that the relentless increases of government spending were not producing the social benefits expected from them and yet were adding to the taxes of hard-working people and to the already high prices they had to pay at the grocery store and everywhere else. In my judgement, such feelings of resentment and frustration are largely responsible for the conservative political trend that has developed of late in the USA. And I gather from the results of recent elections elsewhere that concern about inflation and disenchantment with socialist solutions are increasing also in other industrial countries. Fighting inflation is therefore being accorded a higher priority by policy-makers in Europe and in much of the rest of the world.

In the USA a great majority of the public now regard inflation as the Number One problem facing the country, and this judgement is accepted by both the Congress and the Executive establishment. Some steps have therefore been taken within the past year to check the rapid rise of federal spending, to lower certain taxes in the interest of encouraging business investment, and yet bring down the still large budget deficit. Pressures to augment the privileges of trade unions have been resisted by the Congress. Some government regulations – as in the case of airlines and crude oil – have been eased. And even restrictive moves by the Federal Reserve, which not long ago would have stirred anger and anxiety in government circles, have been accepted with equanimity. Symbolic of the changed political atmosphere was the announcement of an increase in the Federal Reserve discount rate on the very day in July 1979 when a sizeable decline of the nation's over-all production was being reported for the spring quarter.

The present widespread concern about inflation in the USA is an encouraging development, but no one can yet be sure how far it will go or how lasting it will prove. The changes that have thus far occurred in fiscal, monetary, and structural policies have been marginal adjustments. American policy-makers tend to see merit in a gradualist approach because it promises a return to general price stability – perhaps with a delay of five or more years but without requiring significant sacrifices on the part of workers or their employers. But the very caution that leads politically to a policy of gradualism may well lead also to its premature suspension or abandonment in actual practice. Economic life is subject to all sorts of surprises and disturbances – business recessions, labour unrest, foreign troubles, monopolistic shocks, elections, and governmental upsets. One or another such development, especially a business recession, could readily overwhelm and topple a gradualist time-table for curbing inflation. That has happened in the past and it may happen again.

If the USA and other industrial countries are to make real headway in the fight against inflation it will first be necessary to rout inflationary psychology – that is, to make people feel that inflation can be, and probably will be, brought under control. Such a change in national psychology is not likely to be accomplished by marginal adjustments of public policy. In view of the strong and widespread expectations of inflation that prevail at present, I have therefore reluctantly come to believe that fairly drastic therapy will be needed to turn inflationary psychology around.

The precise therapy that can serve a nation best is not easy to identify, and what will work well in one country may work poorly in another. In the case of the American inflation, which has become a major threat to the well-being of much of the world as well as of the American people, it would seem wise to me at this juncture of history for the government to adopt a basic programme consisting of four parts. The first of these would be a legislative revision of the federal budgetary process that would make it more difficult to run budget deficits and that would serve as the initial step toward a constitutional amendment directed to the same end. The second part would be a commitment to a comprehensive plan for dismantling regulations that have been impeding the competitive process and for modifying others that have been running up costs and prices unnecessarily. The third part would be a binding endorsement of restrictive monetary policies until the rate of inflation has become substantially lower. And the fourth part would consist of legislation scheduling reductions of business taxes in each of the next five years – the reduction to be quite small in the first two years but to become substantial in later years. This sort of tax legislation would release powerful forces to improve the nation's productivity and thereby exert downward pressure on prices; and it would also help in the more immediate future to ease the difficult adjustments forced on many businesses and their employees by the adoption of the first three parts of the suggested programme.

I wish I could close this long address by expressing confidence that a programme along the lines I have just sketched, or any other constructive and forceful programme for dealing with inflation, will be undertaken in the near future in the USA or elsewhere. That I cannot do today. I am not even sure that many of the central bankers of the world, having by now become accustomed to gradualism, would be willing to risk the painful economic adjustments that I fear are ultimately unavoidable. I would therefore not be surprised if the return to reasonable price stability in the industrial democracies and thereby to an orderly international monetary system is postponed by more false starts. But if political patience in individual countries is severely tested as that happens, the learning process will also be speeded. The conservative trend that now appears to be under way in many of the industrial democracies will then gather strength; and unless political leadership falls into irresponsible hands, the inflationary bias that has been sapping the economic and moral vitality of the democracies can finally be routed.

8 Central Banking with the Benefit of Hindsight*

Jelle Zijlstra

It is well-nigh indisputable that the present time is far from easy for central banks and their governors. Not only must they do their work under difficult circumstances but they are also subject to a degree of public and political interest which does nothing to ease their burden, let alone make it pleasurable. My intention here is to discuss this subject against a background of nearly fifteen years' experience as President of the Netherlands Bank and of a similar period as President of that remarkable institution, the Bank for International Settlements (BIS) at Basle.

First, allow me to give you some details of my career before I entered central banking; as you will see, this may be useful for a proper understanding of some of the points I wish to make. After completing my university studies, I was appointed Professor of Economics at the Free University of Amsterdam in 1948. During my studies I had observed that the academic world in general had little sympathy for central banks. Even now, this is often the case. I could give colourful examples of what I mean, but I shall refrain from doing so because I do not wish to damage the reputations of the persons concerned. However, I cannot possibly resist the temptation to give you one example. It is from an interview with Professor Galbraith, which appeared in *De Haagse Post*, 15 August 1981:

> The people who man the central banks are nice men, and in our case one woman; well spoken, well tailored and of good personal hygiene. I would be kind to them and keep them in business in a

---

*This chapter originated as the 1981 Per Jacobsson Lecture, given in Washington on 27 September 1981, and published in the same year by the Per Jacobsson Foundation, IMF, Washington.

167

minor way, but I would not for a moment rely on them. One of the mysteries of monetary policy in the US has always been how one becomes an expert in it. You can have a man in high political position in Washington, who has difficulty balancing his checkbook and keeping within his family budget. But one day the President appoints him to the Federal Reserve Board and all of a sudden he is a monetary wizard. That is a form of magic that I have long admired.

Well, I don't want to be too harsh on those people, but I certainly don't want to rely on them for the management of anything so complex as the modern economy.

To some extent the tension that exists between economics in an academic context and the actual policy pursued by the central bank is natural and understandable. After all, on the one hand we have the builders of abstract models who are not confronted daily with real problems, and on the other hand we have those persons whose overfull diaries sometimes prevent them from reflecting on the fundamental relationships that could provide solutions to some problems in the longer term. I have had experience of both these worlds. In retrospect, I am somewhat amazed at the carefree way in which the young professor of yore told his students how central banks should behave. In my present position I have several times been surprised by the unworldly suggestions that are occasionally directed at central banks by academics.

In 1952 I became a member of the Dutch cabinet: first as Minister of Economic Affairs, and later, until 1963, as Minister of Finance. In this latter function I naturally learned much about the central bank. There are specific areas of friction between the Minister of Finance and the President of the central bank which are not the result of theory versus practice but are a consequence of the division of powers between the monetary authorities; these powers are vested in part in the Ministry of Finance and in part in the central bank. I am assuming now that the central bank is to a certain extent independent of the government, whether *de jure* or *de facto* (or both). By this I mean that it has its own powers either based on statute or on the authority it has in the eyes of the public. It is clear and also inevitable that from time to time differences of opinion will arise which may lead to open conflicts and have in practice also done so. In saying this I am not thinking of the Netherlands because in that country such a situation has not yet occurred. As Minister of Finance I realised at an early stage that my office would benefit most by achieving the best possible relationship with the central bank with full recognition of its powers and authority. After all, the Finance Minister is badgered from all sides by the ministers of the spending departments, who will always conspire to spend more money than is justified by a sound financial policy. In this struggle he is inevitably alone and consequently lonely. If the relationship is good, his best ally is the central bank. A government is sorely tempted to try to solve its problems by resorting to so-called monetary financing, but without the active co-operation of the central bank this is possible only for a short period and within narrow limits. Therefore, in the world in which we live, with its deep-seated inflationary tendencies, there is an immense need for a close alliance between these two parties. I felt this at the time and I acted accordingly. It also made me bold enough, when the roles were reversed in 1967, to try and impress this philosophy upon successive Ministers of Finance.

As I have already said, I joined the Netherlands Bank in 1967, a year in which the serious problems that would give rise to grave concern at the central banks were already apparent. I intend now to examine – looking back and sometimes ahead – three problems which have engaged us so fully in past years and which will also confront us in the future:

1. the exchange rate system;
2. international reserves;
3. monetary policy in theory and practice.

First, we shall take a look at the exchange-rate system. In the 1960s the existing international monetary system was subjected to increasing pressure. Fixed exchange rates, which could only be changed when there was a so-called fundamental disequilibrium, proved to be insufficiently flexible in the increasingly severe financial climate. Nor was this all. The Bretton Woods system was based on the principle of maintaining or restoring equilibrium in the *current* accounts of the balances of payments. Movements of capital were given no or only slight attention, because it was assumed that they were relatively unimportant or that they would not really disturb balance of payments equilibrium. If need be, restrictions could and should be placed on capital movements. Last, but not least, the 1960s saw a growing disequilibrium in international payments, consequent on the deficit in the US balance of payments. The dollar became overvalued and the USA found it increasingly difficult to meet its obligations to convert the dollar (into gold). It is my firm conviction that a devaluation of the dollar combined with a substantial increase in the price of gold (as provided for in Article IV of the then Articles of Agreement of the International Monetary Fund) would have meant a real improvement of the situation. The stability of the international monetary system would have been considerably strengthened. As a result it would not have been necessary to conclude, too early, that the Bretton Woods system could not be maintained, as was done in 1973 on the eve of the great oil crisis. In other words, the shock of the oil crisis would have encountered a much more stable system. This does not mean that a system of fixed exchange rates would have been stable enough, even if it had been strengthened by the two measures I mentioned above, to survive this shock. But the resulting chaos would have been significantly less.

The discussions about the best system of exchange rates will probably never lead to a definite answer. Too much depends on the actual time and place. There is a time to peg and a time to float. However, a closer analysis is called for. In my speech to the Annual Meeting of the BIS on June 15 of this year I said, and now I quote:

> Obviously, there is no question of going back to a par value system on a worldwide basis – to mention only two obstacles, the OPEC surplus and the dispersion of inflation rates rule it out. But, if the domestic price of money is not to be disregarded, why should its external price be? Or, to put it another way, what would happen if we were to disregard both for any prolonged period? We cannot safely adopt as a principle that exchange rates should be left to their own devices. The exchange rate is too important a macroeconomic variable to be relegated to the position of a residual item, in the way that the money supply was in some countries until not so long ago. We have therefore to pursue a middle course between the Bretton Woods system of fixed exchange rates and a hands-off policy in the exchange market.

But it will not be easy to find the middle course. I hope that in the turmoil of rapidly changing conditions which seriously hamper the realisation of any new exchange-rate system, it will be possible at any rate to achieve a greater degree of consistency of views and policies. Let me give an example. After a period of what was succinctly, but not entirely accurately, termed benign neglect, the US authorities in 1978 changed direction sharply. President Carter announced a mass ive support operation for the steadily weakening dollar. As this happened fairly recently I need not go into the details. At present, the policy is again one of non-intervention on principle, and the value of the dollar has risen very sharply. Should we speak of an asymmetrical policy? Intervention when the dollar weakens, non-intervention when it strengthens? Or, expressed in slightly malicious terms, does the philosophy behind the policy depend on the circumstances? How should others respond? My own answer is a paraphrase of Walter Bagehot: 'rates of exchange will not manage themselves,' or 'rates of exchange are too important to be left alone'.

The principle contained in that answer is explicitly recognised in the Bretton Woods type arrangements which exist within the European Monetary System (EMS) for fixed but adjustable rates of exchange, with narrow margins of permitted market fluctuations between the currencies of the participating countries. These arrangements have, in my view, provided a useful zone of relative exchange-rate stability in Europe and I very much hope that they will continue to do so. For that to be possible, two main conditions will have to be fulfilled: first, there must be sufficient harmonisation of economic policies within the EMS to allow a reasonable degree of exchange-rate stability; and second, changes in exchange rates, when these become necessary, must be made more promptly than was sometimes the case in the Bretton Woods system. To sum up what I believe about the application of my exchange-rate philosophy under our current arrangements, I would say the following: we need sufficient management of floating rates to avoid movements of currencies that are erratic or completely unrelated to fundamentals; and we also need, within the EMS system, sufficient flexibility to maintain a realistic structure of rates between participating currencies.

Central banks play very different roles under different exchange-rate systems. Our life was relatively simple under the Bretton Woods system of fixed parities. The rates were fixed or they were changed by government decision, often on the advice of the central banks. Within the Group of Ten and Switzerland, our activities at the time were especially the organisation of support for currencies under threat. Charles Coombs was the ideal salesman in such support credits. How shocked and sad we are today that he is no longer amidst us.

Yes, we were experts at gathering millions in a very short time. In this respect, some of us remember the slightly chaotic Group of Ten conference of Bonn in 1968. Ministers who were unable to reach agreement about anything far into the night, and the central bankers who in a single hour succeeded in organising large-scale support operations for the pound sterling and the French franc. For the rest, they were ignored. It is a pity that there are no newsreels showing the frustrated and irritated central bank governors roaming through the rooms and passages.

Under a system of floating rates, especially one of 'clean floating,' the task of the central bank is also easy. The work is done by Mr Market. However, it is not as simple as that as I shall show when I discuss monetary policy. The control of the money supply, as well as the levels of the exchange rates and of interest rates, influence each other in such a way that one cannot afford to ignore any one of them. We are willy-nilly caught up in a triangle with the points called money supply, exchange rates, and interest rates. The life of a central banker has truly become more difficult.

In the period I am discussing, it was not only exchange rates but also the problem of international reserves which played a major role. It will be remembered that the Bretton Woods system, besides providing fixed exchange rates based on gold parities, was also a system in which the ultimate reserve asset was gold. It is true that in practice it was mainly the dollar which constituted the actual reserve asset, but because of its convertibility the link with gold was defined. In August 1971 all this came to an end. The Second Amendment of the Articles of Agreement of the IMF, which became effective in 1978, settled the problem in a basically different manner. Gold and reserve currencies would gradually have to make way for the SDR. How far have we progressed in that direction? At present, the principal gold-holding central banks refuse to give more than a moment's thought to parting with their gold reserves and thus effect a *de facto* demonetisation, either by selling gold in the market against foreign exchange or by placing it in a – not yet existing – substitution account within the IMF against the receipt of SDRs. The dollar has remained the most important reserve currency, although some room has had to be made for other currencies, such as the Deutschmark and the Swiss franc. Their joint role as reserve currencies has not been reduced in favour of the SDR, as provided for by the Articles of Agreement of the IMF. What has happened to gold? During the period described here, gold was often at the centre of attention. It would be interesting to repeat here in detail the many different statements about gold made at the various international meetings since 1971. I shall refrain from doing so, but I should like to touch briefly upon those aspects of the history of monetary gold which would seem to be significant for future developments. It all started at that remarkable gathering of the participants in the gold pool in Washington on 16–17 March 1968, which led to the end of the gold pool. The result was a two-tier system, providing for a separate development of the gold price in the free market as distinct from a fixed price for monetary gold, then $35 per troy ounce. The communiqué of that meeting included the following sentence: 'They no longer feel it necessary to buy gold from the market'. During the meeting this sentence had been the subject of heated discussion. Some of the participants, including myself, opposed it, as we felt it could be interpreted as an undertaking that the central banks would never again make market purchases of gold. Thus, the combined holdings of monetary gold would have to be regarded as fixed, serving merely as an instrument of settlement among the monetary authorities. Newly-produced gold could then be sold on the free market only. The counter-argument which was advanced, stressed that the sentence could be most useful as it would have a calming effect on price movements in the free market and would, hence, check speculation. It was this argument which finally swayed the opponents. However, no sooner had the communiqué been issued than the first interpretation was widely accepted. Yes, indeed, so it was stated, the central banks had decided never again to buy gold from the market. Interested parties and especially the US authorities kept a close watch to check whether the central banks adhered strictly to this supposed undertaking.

All this is now far behind us. Step by step, not always painlessly, the freedom of central banks to effect transactions in gold, whether among themselves or in the free market, has been restored. The present Articles of Agreement of the IMF merely forbid a new official gold price. How times have changed may be illustrated by the example of the monetary mobilisation of part of the gold-holdings of the central banks participating in the EMS. How times have changed may also be illustrated by the Act signed by President Carter on 7 October 1980, approving an increase in the US quota in the IMF and including the provision that the Secretary of the Treasury should establish and chair a commission which should conduct a study to assess and make recommendations with regard to the policy of the US government concerning the role of gold in domestic and international monetary systems and should transmit to the Congress a report containing its findings and recommendations not later than one year after the date of enactment of this Act. At least, gold was no longer a dirty word.

Nevertheless, the present position cannot be termed satisfactory. The central banks of the principal countries hold vast reserves of gold. The Netherlands Bank, for instance, has gold-holdings which, at current market prices, account for 66 per cent of its total reserves. It is most frustrating that, sales in the market against foreign exchange apart, there is no systematic manner in which this reserve component can be used. I feel that it is necessary for us, within the Group of Ten and Switzerland, to consider ways to regulate the price of gold, admittedly within fairly broad limits, so as to create conditions permitting gold sales and purchases between central banks as an instrument for a more rational management and deployment of their reserves. On the occasion of the annual meeting of the IMF in Belgrade in 1979 this was brought up, but regrettably, insufficient agreement could be reached to make even a modest start with regulating the gold price in the free market. It is my firm conviction that relatively small-scale interventions, though not forestalling the subsequent explosion of the gold price, would at least have reduced it to more manageable proportions. Now that the turbulent emotions seem to have quietened down, we would be wise to reflect anew and without prejudice on these subjects.

Finally, I should like to give some attention to the SDR, the pivot of a new international monetary system. All of us are supposed to want the new system and are thus under a moral obligation to further its realisation to the best of our ability. However, those taking part in the many discussions which are devoted to the SDR do not, in my opinion, always evince an adequate insight into the problems we will face if the SDR is actually to become the pivot of a new international monetary system. Such a new system requires that two conditions be met. First, greater exchange-rate stability is essential. If exchange rates are left to be dictated by market forces, reserves are basically unnecessary. In the fullness of time the SDR will have to be the full-fledged instrument of settlement. If no settlements take place, or if this is done erratically or unsystematically, there is no need for a fundamental instrument of settlement. Second, and in connection with the first condition, convertibility will have to be restored. In an orderly international monetary system, in which the SDR is given the role formerly played by gold, major currencies, including the dollar, must be convertible into SDRs. Whoever truly wishes to make the SDR the pivot of a reformed international monetary system and yet refuses to accept convertibility into SDRs deceives others and perhaps even himself.

All this is not of course feasible at present, so that the role of the SDR will continue to be a marginal one for some time to come, even though its significance as a unit of account is on the increase. This also means that there will be no substitution account in the near future and that the allocation of SDRs will have to remain limited.

We now come to my third subject, namely monetary policy in theory and practice. When, in 1967, I entered the world of central bankers, monetarism had not yet become a political slogan. Of course, Milton Friedman was not unknown. His monumental work, *A Monetary History of the United States*,[1] was rightly renowned, and not only in academic circles. His lecture in 1970 on the monetary counter-revolution was an exceedingly lucid exposition of what is now termed monetarism.[2] But it was only as a result of the inflationary waves of the 1970s that monetarism broke out of the confines of the world of the professors and spilled over into politics. Ministers of Finance, heads of government, and even heads of state must cudgel their weary brains over the secrets of M_1 to M_x, the monetary base, and the money multiplier. In passing, it is interesting to note that something comparable happened to Keynesianism which was widely taught as an economic theory at all universities after 1936 but did not become the basis of the economic and financial policy of nearly all the important countries until after the end of the Second World War.

In examining the many problems involved here, it is necessary to be aware of the fact that monetarism, like Keynesianism, has many variations and nuances. Some stylisation, perhaps even simplification, is necessary to provide a typecasting of what I should like to term the typical monetarist. My typical monetarist's creed has three articles:

1. a politico-economic or, in other words, an ideological one;
2. an analytical one;
3. one on the techniques of monetary policy.

I shall examine each of these briefly. Our monetarist is convinced that the public sector is relatively unstable and that the private sector is relatively stable. The instability of the public sector is related to the fact that it is much too large in most countries, as well as that politicians frequently make irrational decisions based on insufficient knowledge of complex social and financial problems, whereas private sector behaviour is, in principle, ruled by rational expectations and rational reactions to the impulses from the market economy.

In the typical monetarist's analysis, the control of the money supply is both necessary and sufficient for an effective macro-economic control of the national economy. Naturally, this instrument may not be perfect but it is by far the most efficient instrument we have at our disposal.

Finally, in order to control the money supply the use of the so-called monetary base is necessary and sufficient. It makes it possible to control the money supply continuously and with the required precision.

To a central banker, the three aforementioned points vary in importance and each carries a different weight: the view one takes of the relative stability or instability of the public and the private sector is often rooted in the individual's economic philosophy. Phrased differently, this view is ideologically flavoured. My own opinion is that a great deal depends on the concrete circumstances of time and place. In the 1930s the private sector was undoubtedly comparatively unstable and it is not surprising, then, that traditional Keynesianism is based on the relative instability of the private sector, which needs to be corrected by government measures; consequently, this line of argument assumes a relatively stable public sector, which must support the shaky private sector and save it from collapsing. In present times, this is no longer quite so. In many countries the public sector is overburdened and in danger of being crushed by a multitude of tasks and responsibilities. As a result, the possibilities of using the public sector to stabilise the entire economy have become substantially smaller. An added factor is that in the immediate post-war years the private sector showed a high degree of resilience, even in the face of heavy external shocks. Ideological bias aside, the purely pragmatic conclusion is warranted that the balance between stability and insta-bility within the public and the private sectors, respectively, has shown a distinct shift since the 1930s.

The second article of the typical monetarist's creed brings us closer to the central banker's job. We are concerned here with analysis, leading to the thesis that for controlling the economy as far as possible the monetary policy instrument is both necessary and suf-ficient. All other instruments, fiscal policy in particular, are erratic and have a procyclical and, hence, destabilising effect. In this view, wage and price policies are doomed to fail. It is solely the control of the money supply by the monetary authorities, in the form of inflexible monetary expansion targets published in advance, which is capable of stabilising the private sector and of preventing or eliminating inflation. This is demonstrated with the aid of that famous equation $MV = PT$. In the longer term, the volume of transactions (T) is governed by non-monetary factors, the velocity of circulation (V) is, likewise in the somewhat longer term, stable, so that the level of price (P) varies in proportion to changes in the money supply (M). If governments are sensible enough to keep or reduce the growth of the public sector within acceptable limits, adequate macroeconomic control of the economy is feasible. This line of reasoning is further strengthened by the theory of rational expectations. Those in charge of the public sector, the politicians, often act irrationally and unpredictably. Those taking part in the economic process in the private sector are guided by rational expectations, especially as regards inflation. They have learned to see through the money illusion. Firm standards for the growth of the money supply aimed at preventing or eliminating inflation dissipate inflationary expectations and thus constitute, by themselves, an essential contribution to the fight against inflation.

As to this major issue in past and present discussions, I should like to give a brief outline of my own views before we come to the technique of monetary policy.

In my opinion, as an instrument for adequately guiding the economy, control of the money supply is necessary but not sufficient. Fiscal policy plus wage and price developments cannot be dispensed with or ignored. In theory, but in theory alone, it can be maintained that control of the money supply is sufficient. Any borrowing requirement can be covered by non-monetary means, provided that one is prepared to accept any interest-rate level and any degree of crowding out of private investment. Any discrepancy between wages and productivity can always be eliminated by sufficient stagnation of output and employment. But, let me repeat, this is pure theory. There is a size of the borrowing requirement and there is a degree of discrepancy between productivity and nominal wages which simply precludes any possibility of conducting an effective monetary policy. The reverse, of course, is also true.

The foregoing can also be phrased in a different fashion. Monetary policy, fiscal policy, and wage movements commensurate with productivity are each other's constraints. In this framework, an effective monetary policy aimed at controlling the money supply is necessary but not sufficient.

Finally, in addition to the ideological and the analytical problems, there remains the technique of monetary control, which is one of the most relevant issues for central bankers. In the reasoning of our monetarist, the money supply can be adequately controlled by controlling the monetary base, which consists of the banks' credit balances with the central bank and the banknotes held by the public. Both these items appear on the liabilities side of the central bank's balance sheet and both can therefore be controlled by the central bank. This possibility of control flows from the assumed predictability and stability of the money multiplier, which relates the money supply to the counterbalancing free and required reserves held by the banks with the central bank. It is, furthermore, assumed that there is a workable definition of the money supply. In the monetary literature we often come across the term of narrow money, M_1, consisting of banknotes and demand deposits. But its use is not strictly necessary. In monetary policy practice in the USA, for example, various measures of the money supply are distinguished (M_{1a}, M_{1b}, M_2, M_3 . . . M_x), each with its individual money multiplier. In the UK a relatively broad definition of the money supply is employed, M_3, which also includes savings deposits with the banks. Before going on let me briefly summarise the various elements of the monetarist creed.

Our true-blue monetarist believes:
1. that the central bank is able to control the monetary base;
2. that the money supply is thus controlled through a stable money multiplier;
3. that the level of prices is thus controlled assuming a stable velocity of circulation;
4. that the private sector is thus adequately stabilised;
5. that, if the size of the public sector is kept within certain limits, a reasonable degree of macroeconomic control is thereby ensured.

The many discussions about monetarism centre not least on the techniques used. They have become political issues and have even made their way to the lofty heights of the summit meetings of the political leaders of the world. Do not we, central bankers, at times stand somewhat helplessly on the sidelines? Have the central bankers among themselves come to a consensus as to the best, the most adequate monetary techniques? Let me briefly dwell upon this point.

It would appear to me that there is at any rate a large measure of agreement about one important aspect. Monetary policy is, by its very nature, a policy as to quantity. In the past many central banks pursued a policy directed toward one or more interest rates so as to achieve or maintain a certain interest-rate level. The resulting money supply was accepted as a dependent variable. It is clear that such a policy cannot be expected to produce that money supply which must be considered proper from the point of view of the stability of the economy and of the maintenance of the value of money. This does not mean, that in pursuing a policy aimed at controlling the money supply, interest rates can be neglected – I will come to that later. The questions now before us are these: in what manner can the money supply be controlled by the central bank and what are the pros and cons?

The customary variants of a policy aimed at controlling the money supply fall, roughly speaking, into two main categories, namely, direct and indirect methods. Under the direct method, some sort of ceiling is imposed upon the activities of the banking system so as to ensure that money-creating lending operations remain within the limits set. Not all central banks have the powers to do this. In the Netherlands and in France, for instance, the central banks have these powers. Under the indirect method, the central bank seeks to control the money supply by controlling other variables which are assumed to bear a sufficiently fixed relationship to the money supply. Here the interest-rate level is of major significance as an essential part of the transmission mechanism which maintains or restores the relationship. The so-called monetary base method is the principal example of the techniques in question. I will analyse briefly the most-frequently used monetary technique with the aid of the variant employed in the Netherlands, where we have for many years had at our disposal the instrument of credit ceilings, known in French as *encadrement du crédit*. If the expansion of the money supply threatens to assume unduly large proportions, the Netherlands Bank can impose restrictions on the volume of lending by the banking system. In the past, this power was exercised repeatedly; the last restrictions were imposed as from 1977. They were suspended recently, as the banks' lending had remained below the prescribed ceiling for a sufficiently long period. The system works as follows: a certain maximum percentage increase is fixed for the total assets of the banking system, except for short-term paper issued by the public authorities (an exception which may be cancelled in the future). However, **long-term** funds raised or received by the banks, or in other words, genuine savings may be used for lending without restriction. The room allowed for the expansion of lending is thus increased by the amount of such long-term funds. Expressed differently, lending by the banking system is restricted to the extent that it is money-creating, and is not restricted to the extent that it is financed from long-term funds. The result is that any demand for credit over and above the volume allowable from a monetary point of view is shifted to the capital market and may thus push up capital market rates. Experience has shown that the monetary instrument employed by the Netherlands Bank results in fairly effective control of the money supply and is attended by a distinct effect on long-term interest rates.

An additional instrument of the central bank in the Netherlands is aimed at controlling the liquidity of the banks – money-market policy. Whereas for other central banks this is *the* instrument for attempting to control the money supply, this is not the case in the Netherlands. The Netherlands Bank controls the liquidity of the banking system in such a manner that short-term interest rates are in normal proportion to long-term rates, due attention being given to the exchange rate. This policy is implemented with the aid of semi-permanent borrowing quotas available to the banks, complemented, where necessary, by an open market policy. This means that, in exceptional circumstances only, and especially in the event of heavy speculation against the guilder, a tightening of money-market policy will cause short-term interest rates to rise temporarily to well above capital market rates.

Put differently, the basic monetary policy designed to control the money supply effects this control on a medium-term basis, influences long-term interest rates, and thus also, of course, contributes to achieving over-all equilibrium on the balance of payments. The money-market policy is a short-term and complementary one, it avoids whenever possible major fluctuations in short-term interest rates and hence also tries to prevent exchange-rate movements which are not a reflection of the underlying position and development of the balance of payments.

Does this technique of monetary policy merely have advantages and no drawbacks? It has one major drawback. The allowable credit expansion for each individual bank must be based on figures from the past. If credit restrictions of this kind are continued for too long, they tend to have stifling effects on competition, counter to the fundamentals of the market economy. Consequently, a number of years of such restrictions must be followed by a sufficient number of years without them. It will be clear that in times of persistent inflation, such a break is far from easy to effect.

The monetary policy pursued in the USA aims at controlling the money supply by regulating the liquidity of the banking system. I need not go into details about the precise technique used. Let me just say that it is based on an assumed stability of the relationships between the various components of the money supply (M_1, M_2 . . . M_x) and their respective required reserves. This cannot but lead, as it has proved to do in practice, to wide fluctuations in short-term interest rates and at times to very large differences between short-term and long-term rates. This may also cause substantial exchange-rate movements. This monetary policy has been subject to severe criticism. To a certain extent this is understandable. A monetary policy which gives rise to prime rates of 20 per cent at a rate of inflation of around 10 per cent, which pushes up the exchange rate to a level far out of line with the underlying balance-of-payments position, and which thus has serious dislocating effects internationally, simply asks to be called into question, apart even from the preoccupation with weekly money-supply figures which it calls forth and the destabilising expectations thus arising with regard to interest rates in the money and capital markets (in this context, Alexandre Lamfalussy uses the term pig cycle effect, known from economic theory).[3] I find it hard to believe that this technique of monetary policy is the best conceivable one. Yet, this criticism needs to be qualified. The fact that in the USA the fight against inflation is waged with consistency and a strong sense of purpose deserves our warm approval. It is only with regard to the monetary techniques used that doubt is possible, but even this doubt must be seen against the background of the frequent failure of the critics to suggest suitable alternatives.

I outline these two types of monetary policy to illustrate the point that, as far as the question of the optimum policy for an effective control of the money supply is concerned, we as central bankers unfortunately have to speak of unfinished business. I also encountered this in the circle of the countries participating in the EMS. A multitude of instruments, differing from one country to the next, makes a harmonisation of policies extremely difficult. However, here we are in an area at the heart of central banking. In this very area we are under criticism from political and academic quarters, and increasingly so in my opinion. In the future, we shall have to intensify our discussions on this subject, for instance in Basle, so as to reach greater clarity on this issue, if only to save our hides.

After the Second World War, the central banker's life was, com
paratively speaking, fairly simple. Fixed rates of exchange, the ab
sence of inflation or at most a very low rate of inflation, smal
public-sector deficits in many countries, and often trade unions oper
to reason. Under such conditions, controlling the money supply is a
relatively simple matter. However, somewhere in the mid-1960s and
in subsequent years, many of these comfortable certainties disap
peared, the storm broke, and we have not come out of it unscathed
We are now facing the formidable challenge to regain in the last two
decades of this century some of what we lost on our way. By trial and
error we will have to find our route. Where should it lead? To
renewed stability of exchange rates and to the breaking of the
backbone of inflation also through an appropriate monetary policy
The central banks are faced with a difficult task. In performing that
task, they will not invariably receive support from the world o
politics and politicians. In his brilliant Per Jacobsson lecture of 1979
The Anguish of Central Banking, Arthur Burns was candid on thi
subject;[4] after complaining that the government is so often busy 'to
enlarge the flow of benefits to the population at large, or to this or
that group' (page 156), he described why it was so difficult politically
for the Federal Reserve System to keep the money supply under
control (page 156):

> If the Federal Reserve then sought to create a monetary environ-
> ment that fell seriously short of accommodating the upward press-
> ures on prices that were being released or reinforced by
> governmental action, severe difficulties could be quickly produced
> in the economy. Not only that, the Federal Reserve would be
> frustrating the will of Congress to which it was responsible – a
> Congress that was intent on providing additional services to the
> electorate and on assuring that jobs and incomes were maintained,
> particularly in the short run.

No, life is not going to be easy for central bankers in the last two
decades of the twentieth century. But however difficult it may prove
to be, we central bankers should remain intent on what I see as our
primary task – irrespective of the many differences in our statutory
positions – to be the guardians of the integrity of money.

Notes

1. M. Friedman and A. J. Schwartz, *A Monetary History of the United States, 1867–1970* (Princeton: Princeton University Press, 1963).
2. M. Friedman, *Counter-revolution in Monetary Theory* (Westminster: The Institute of Economic Affairs, 1970).
3. A. Lamfalussy, *Observation de règles ou politique discrétionnaire: Essai sur la politique monétaire dans un milieu inflationniste* (Bâle: Banque de Règlements Internationaux, 1981).
4. A. F. Burns, 'The Anguish of Central Banking' (Chapter 7 of this volume).

Part III
The Central Bank and
Commercial Banks

9 Banks and Economic Policy*

Reinhard Kamitz

The scale of this subject requires a choice. I shall therefore tackle only two basic themes: first, some aspects of economic policy that are of special interest to the private banking sector; and, second, those relating to external economic relations.

I shall briefly look at the way in which banks have changed over the years and, without going into great detail, describe how banking has evolved into its present form, in which ordinary banking operations – deposit-taking and lending – are supplemented by the creation of credit and how all kinds of new institutions have developed. I am referring to the enormous range of credit operations undertaken by commercial banks, investment banks, savings banks, building societies and many other credit institutions, as well as the leading international institutions such as the World Bank and the Regional Development Banks. It must be remembered, moreover, that this enormous expansion is far from having reached its final stages. It is part of a general evolution in which every change in economic life requires the banking sector to adjust.

Prior to the First World War an eminent Austrian banker, when asked how his investments were faring and what criteria he employed in his business, replied that in his opinion there were two kinds of loan, one that permitted a banker to sleep well and the other that allowed him to eat well. This naturalistic picture can no longer be considered a true likeness, of course, but one none the less has the impression that today some loans permit bankers both to sleep and to eat well and the rest permit neither one nor the other.

In this connection it is worth clarifying once and for all that the banker is an entrepreneur like any other. He occupies a special

*Originally published as 'Banken und Wirtschatspolitik', in *Verhandlungen des X. Deutschen Bankiertages, München, 14, und 15. Oktober 1963* (Frankfurt a.M.: F. Knapp, 1964), this is a translation of the Italian version 'Banche e politica economica' published by the Associazione Bancaria Italiana in *Bancaria*, 1963, pp. 1354-60.

position in the economy, but his task is in every way comparable with that of other entrepreneurs – to match supply and demand in the market (in his case that for money and capital). The fact that other entrepreneurs produce or distribute goods does not change the characteristic feature of the performance of their economic role one iota.

This reality needs to be constantly borne in mind since there is an increasing tendency to minimise the merits of banks. This is often accompanied, moreover, by an underestimation of the activity of the banking sector. The margin of profit on raising and lending funds is rightly considered important in an economy, but it is often suggested that it should be kept as small as possible. This view is sustained by leading figures who are also frequently to be heard discoursing on other sectors of the economy. I am referring in particular to commerce, which is not highly respected in this age of planning and government control.

The private banker none the less finds himself in the market like any other entrepreneur with the task of exploiting the opportunities that the market itself provides. In fulfilling this task, he, like any other entrepreneur, takes on a risk which could drive him out of the market. That the banker deals with a special good – money – makes no difference at all to the substance of his work. The fact that this good comes from another bank, that is, from the central bank, is a special feature that necessarily results in the banker and his business falling within the sphere of the central bank itself. The due reward for the risk the banker takes is the corresponding entrepreneurial profit, just as for every other entrepreneur operating in the market. The private banker – indeed all bankers – need to be seen as performing the economic function not just of disbursing credit but also of providing advice and assistance to other firms.

In the economy there are entrepreneurs with excellent technical qualifications and a flair for judging the suitability of production formulas, reorganisation plans, etc. Sometimes, however, they lack a commercial outlook. It is at this point that banks are called upon to perform their most important role, that of educating these entrepreneurs in the various concrete aspects of running a business and thus putting their genius back on the rails of reality. In addition, bankers have always been pioneers in promoting economic growth. They have always been and still are especially well-qualified for this role, since their detachment from events in industry and commerce enables them to make an objective assessment of opportunities and to judge prospective developments.

My purpose in saying this is not to sing the banking profession's praises, but to highlight these features because there is a tendency today for the typically entrepreneurial nature of banking to be overlooked. This is not for lack of outstanding personalities among bankers or because their willingness to run risks has diminished; rather it is because economic policy is, and will have to remain, on a course that is ill-suited to the traditional business of bankers.

Since the end of the Second World War the concept of the welfare state has grown into the dominant factor. Everything that has helped man to develop through the struggle to live and the risks associated with that struggle threatens slowly to disappear into the sense of fulfilment settling over the welfare citizen, who would rather shift all his risks on to the state. If we could live in Cockaigne where nothing in life involves risk and virtually everything can be reduced to material vegetation, there would be no problem. Reality, however, is very different. Nobody frees us of our worries about life or spiritual and cultural development; no welfare state or public institution can shoulder our responsibility for the future.

At this point I should like to raise an issue that is close to my heart in view of my experience as Minister of Finance, and which I find perhaps even more worrying today in my role as an observer. Throughout the free world the public sector's share of GDP has grown enormously since 1945. This implies a growing influence of the public sector on every aspect of economic and social life. The process can be linked to the philosophy of the welfare state and is fuelled and reinforced by the increasing tax burdens which governments impose on their citizens. Even when no new taxes are introduced, the progressiveness of the major direct taxes leads, as a result of persistent monetary depreciation, to citizens having to pay more taxes. In addition to direct taxes there is, of course, a whole series of indirect taxes. I have always sought to ensure that the problem of taxation was not viewed exclusively in terms of direct taxation. The total tax burden which a country has to bear must be considered. Indirect taxes tend to increase prices via production costs while direct taxes tend to reduce profits and sometimes to cause prices to rise as well.

I made three substantial cuts in direct taxes in Austria and was sharply criticised by many political opponents on each occasion. The results none the less demonstrated that cuts in an excessively heavy fiscal burden do not lead to a reduction in fiscal revenues but to an increase. As far as raising fiscal revenues is concerned, a flourishing economy is obviously much more effective than high tax rates. The impulse and stimulus imparted to economic expansion by reducing an excessively heavy fiscal burden can therefore be expected to produce an increase in government revenues.

Unfortunately, the trend towards increasingly heavy fiscal burdens is now considered by many, and sometimes even by entrepreneurs themselves, as an irreversible fact of life. Reference is frequently made to the enlarged role of the public sector as justifying the drift towards collectivism. It is forgotten, however, that the regular increase in fiscal burdens not only results in the public sector's share of GDP expanding, but also causes GDP to be smaller than it would have been with lower taxes. High taxes have an anti-economic effect on entrepreneurs. When profits fall, there is less investment and less desire to produce. Many projects are shelved because they are too risky or are undertaken only with certain public sector guarantees. A cumulative process thus gets under way that swells the sphere of the public sector, continually eroding the scope for free enterprise.

There is confirmation of this state of affairs every day and its damping effect on the spirit of free enterprise is unfortunately not appreciated by many. At present, it is claimed in economic discussion that countries should raise taxes one way or another in order to reduce purchasing power and thus curb inflationary pressures. This proposal, however, fails to take account of the fact that fiscal measures are a broken reed today as far as reducing purchasing power is concerned. Except in countries like Switzerland, which is unique in Europe today, it is no longer possible to sterilise increases in incomes in this way, since the corresponding amount gets spent anyhow through one channel or another. Other premises therefore need to be adopted to make experience conform to the new reality and avoid erroneous conclusions.

We thus live in an age in which uninterrupted expansion of the public sector is accepted with a varying degree of passivity by those who are burdened by it. Short-sightedness often leads to the belief that the level of tax rates is only a question of equity. There is a tendency to ignore the importance of profit in economic life, and not only for entrepreneurial initiative but above all for the formation of capital. I therefore approved of the brave decision by the USA to cut taxes by $11 milliard in 1963.

What impact does the spread of the public sector have on the position of bankers in the economy? An increasingly large volume of funds flows to the economy through the public channel. The private sector, or that part of the economy influenced by entrepreneurial activity, tends to shrink. The traditional function of the banker, linked to purely economic situations and based on the assessment of firms in their economic environment, is whittled away as the influence of the public sector grows, as the banker loses his freedom of action, which was a key feature of his profession. The banker's greater skill in judging economic and financial affairs, his assessment of events and the scope for him to operate in his own field of business are increasingly circumscribed. In part the growth of the public sector is completely autonomous, so that a yardstick with which to measure its performance is lacking. Indeed, this growth can be viewed in many different ways, but nobody can foresee how committees or directors-general will decide. In this field there is no room left for the activity of the banker, as there used to be in the past.

The area within which banks operate becomes smaller and the scope for them to assist diminishes accordingly. Initiative is squeezed out. The public sector decides, for example, which branches of the economy are to be developed and consequently provides subsidies or takes other action to achieve the planned development directly. In these conditions the banker's contribution is reduced to credit inter-mediation and better accounting management. The private banker's creative role, intuition of new opportunities, pioneering spirit and belief in progress are all tightly fenced in today. Risk, which normally goes hand-in-glove with all private economic activity and which is the characteristic feature of every entrepreneurial activity, is consider-ably attenuated by government intervention.

The debate regarding entrepreneurial profit and the profit in general that bankers earn as entrepreneurs is well-known. The idea is increasingly gaining ground that entrepreneurs have a right to a recompense, but much less so to a profit. In other words, the idea is to recompense the entrepreneur for his organisational rather than his entrepreneurial activity. But as risk is steadily reduced, even the conditions for making entrepreneurial profits cease to exist, since such profits are the reward for risk-taking. When the expansion of the various sectors of the economy is determined by the government or when it is decided which sectors are to be promoted and which sectors allowed to grow, there is a big reduction in the risk associated with the performance of these sectors. That is, when the attitude of the government towards certain sectors is known, major unexpected developments become unlikely. In these circumstances, credit institutions are reduced to acting as money and capital merchants. This, of course, involves a much smaller risk than the banker, who trusted his judgement and his independent assessment of economic affairs, used to take.

The shift in the maturity structure of credit from the short and medium term to the long term can be linked in part to the change in the economic situation produced by the increase in the influence of the public sector. Analogously, the fact that savings banks now operate as virtually fully-fledged banking institutions and have diverged from their original aims is due in part to the modern welfare state having redistributed income very widely and to most of these incomes having flowed into savings banks, thus greatly strengthening their position in the money and capital markets.

All these developments need to be carefully followed and should lead us to take stock of our position. They have not come about by chance. When I was a student, the problem of competition between savings banks and commercial banks did not exist. At that time, however, the welfare state concept was not yet in fashion and there was no problem of over-taxation. We must therefore be quite clear in our own minds that the problems facing us today are due to an intervening change in the economic, social and political climate.

The second of the two important themes I mentioned at the beginning of this chapter concerns the problems associated with the international monetary order. Let me try to summarise the question briefly. Up to the First World War there was a monetary order based on the gold standard. A key feature of this system was that deviations from equilibrium were corrected automatically. When, for example, a country recorded a balance-of-payments deficit, there was an outflow of gold. This entailed a reduction in the volume of means of payment in circulation and hence brought pressure to bear on the level of prices and wages. This helped to restore competitiveness and create the conditions for the elimination of the external deficit. Adjustment occurred indirectly as a result of restrictive measures and, especially, as a consequence of reduced employment.

I am not in favour of a return to this system, but merely wish to remind you that it existed. After the Second World War a new international monetary order was established on the basis of the Bretton Woods agreements. Key features of this order were: mutually agreed exchange rates between the members of the IMF, the obligation to make contributions to the Fund, and the possibility of obtaining Fund loans in the event of balance-of-payments deficits.

Every time man intervenes to modify the automatic mechanisms of economic relations, something new and unexpected occurs. For example, when a government fixes a price for bread as the maximum, it notoriously disappears from the market and is only to be found on the black market. To prevent this, the government has to introduce a new set of regulations, that is, rationing. Abandoning the market price thus entails other measures, and this holds true for the international monetary system. The monetary order established in 1946 has not remained unchanged, but has evolved quite considerably in recent years. It is still too early to say whether this evolution has been appropriate and advantageous. It has none the less been a consequence of the changes that have occurred in conditions and cannot but be considered a necessary consequence. One aspect of the evolution is that surplus countries make their currencies available to deficit countries through 'swap' agreements or the purchase of short-term government securities denominated in the deficit country's currency. Furthermore, the Basle agreements have brought significant co-ordination of monetary policies, especially as regards those for gold and foreign exchange. Today we are faced with the possibility of a further evolution of this monetary order. At its last annual meeting last October the IMF decided to study this issue and I foresee that there will soon be a new spate of discussion. Commercial banks are necessarily an integral part of international monetary relations. When, for example, a country's central bank restricts credit to prevent the economy from overheating, completely free monetary and capital flows may lead banks to obtain funds from abroad, thus diminishing or even nullifying the effects of the central bank's action. Since there is a propensity today to find a scapegoat for everything, the finger is pointed at the banks for having pursued their private profit rather than the national interest at a time when the whole country was faced with monetary problems.

Even though I represent a central bank myself, I am forced to admit that commercial bankers' behaviour can hardly be expected to be in conflict with their natural tendency to make profits.

If a banker is able to obtain money abroad for certain projects, this form of fund-raising cannot simply be prevented with special bans. If the authorities wish to stop such funds from flowing in, they must take other kinds of steps, which I shall briefly discuss.

Insofar as banks play a key role in the economy, they appear to have a great deal of responsibility for the success of monetary policy. I myself am firmly convinced that the apparent conflict between the behaviour of banks and the objectives of the central bank is due to the present international order. What is needed is closer international co-operation and co-ordination on the major problems of financial and monetary policy with the aim of preventing excessive balance-of-payments surpluses and deficits. The abandonment of automatic mechanisms in international monetary affairs makes adequate alternative measures indispensable. Today's international monetary order is undoubtedly excellent, but it has to be continually adapted as conditions change. One such adaptation should be to prevent the difficulties we are currently experiencing at the national level from arising by having recourse to international co-operation. Action taken exclusively at the national level is unlikely to eliminate the conflicts between bankers' profit-seeking propensity and central bankers' policy objectives. I do not believe that the importance of central banks has diminished to any great extent; indeed, in the last few years it appears to have grown again as a result of the various forms of co-operation set up in the field of international monetary relations. Central banks still have plenty of scope for effective operations to regulate their domestic markets; they will none the less need to seek a valuable supplement to their domestic activity in international co-operation.

Lest there be any misunderstanding, I should like to add that the system whereby banks currently come to gentlemen's agreements regarding credit policy is undoubtedly to be judged positively. I none the less believe that such systems have their limits, and that it is dangerous to go beyond them. We are living, unfortunately, in a world in which great care is taken to remove the symptoms of thing we do not like. Among the medicines used for this purpose I would include 'swaps' and other such agreements designed to restore the balance of the international monetary situation. In the long run the problem cannot be resolved in this way. It is the causes of imbalance that need to be eliminated, and this can only be done through international co-operation.

Countries will, of course, continue to record balance-of-payments surpluses and deficits. But it has to be admitted that the size of those found today creates a serious disequilibrating factor.

The banker, therefore, also has a role to play in the vast network of monetary relations woven between a country's policies and its monet ary and financial dealings with the rest of the world. He finds himself cast as a protagonist, even though in appearance he may be unable to contribute to the solution of problems. In the disbursement of credit he is bound to follow the course that appears advantageous in terms of the interests of banking. None the less, insofar as the banker plays a part in international monetary relations, he also has a duty to co-operate and contribute to their orderly development.

Hence, even though the position of the banker in economic affairs means that his business activity is unlikely to make a decisive contribution to the solution of international monetary problems (except in the case of gentlemen's agreements) and even though it does not allow him to fend off the danger of a further advance of collectivism in the country's political and social fabric, he none the less has a major task and a major responsibility.

Bankers are not just passive executors. In their typical function they are active agents. The instruments available to realise this potential are few, but there are men of outstanding ability. The day that these men recognise the problems and dangers that are looming and wish to avoid a situation in which private entrepreneurs would no longer exist and everything would be decided by bureaucracies and committees, they and all the other bankers will have to rise above their daily problems and, armed with their spirit and the voice of their organisations, oppose the excessive growth of public action in the economy and formulate constructive proposals able to offer a new configuration of international monetary relations. This will be necessary if we wish to live in a system that not only maintains free enterprise but also offers the advantages of unrestricted social, cultural and scientific development together with the possibility for everybody to decide his own destiny.

We are living in a period marked by the elimination of restrictions on trade and capital movements, by progress towards complete convertibility. This advance towards freedom should give us a sense of optimism. Our task is to use all the means at our disposal to prevent any backsliding. Monetary order is itself a condition for progress along this path. As bankers and participants in the world of economic enterprise, it is our duty to co-operate in the promotion of this advance. Bankers are required to perform this function in view of their position, experience and ability. Better than any others they can discern the basic differences between our world and that on the other side of the Iron Curtain together with the advantages that our social and political system offers for spiritual development.

All man's efforts are bounded by the limits of the human mind. If we consider a moment how long it took for man to acquire certain notions that appear obvious today, we are spontaneously led to ask whether we have become extremely modest or excessively presumptuous. It is none the less always the task of man to pursue an end – to aim at something better. In this connection I wish to call on bankers to recognise the existence of the dangers I have described and to fight them with all their might. If bankers were able to proclaim with Tibullus, *Est nobis, voluisse satis*, we would be on the right road and probably stand a chance of establishing the principles in which we believe.

10 The Banking Act 1979*

Lord O'Brien of Lothbury

The UK is, so far as I know, the only country in the world which has for centuries had a highly developed banking system not comprehensively regulated under a Banking Act. Naturally this does not mean that regulation has been entirely absent. On the contrary, the Bank of England has for many years exercised a very effective control by informal means with the potential backing since 1946 of the provisions of the Bank of England Act. In addition, banks and related financial institutions have been subject to the provisions of various statutory requirements, notably those of the Moneylenders Acts, the Protection of Depositors Act, the Exchange Control Act and, more recently, the Consumer Credit Act. The passing of our first Banking Act in 1979 was therefore a highly noteworthy landmark in our banking history.

The freedom which banks enjoy in the UK and the understanding and sympathy with which they are regulated by the Bank of England are the envy of the world. Many of our admirers may well be puzzled as to why at so late an hour we should have needed a Banking Act, and some may even be apprehensive about the possible change in climate for banks operating in the UK which it may portend.

THE EARLIER YEARS

It is a truism to say that we live in a changing world. This is inevitably so in all spheres of human activity and particularly so after a war which convulsed the whole globe like none before it. For some years after 1945 it seemed that the world of banking had been less dis-

*This chapter was originally presented by Lord O' Brien under the same title as the 1979 Ernest Sykes Memorial Lecture at the Institute of Bankers in London on 20 November 1979, and published in the same year by the Institute of Bankers, London.

turbed than many other aspects of life. Interest rates remained low and monetary policy was virtually non-existent, banished from the thoughts of policy-makers by fears of post-war recession and the return of high unemployment such as had so embittered the pre-war years.

In the event things turned out very differently. After the pump had been primed by Marshall Aid and the international financial system had been effectively stabilised and regulated by Bretton Woods, there was a great expansion of world trade. Confidence grew and internal demand grew with it, bringing inflation and the revival of monetary policy as one of the essential weapons with which to fight it.

In the UK from 1957 onwards the fight against excessive internal demand and the balance-of-payments crises which it brought in its train required repeated crash programmes of internal restraint. These always included a fierce quantitative and qualitative restriction of clearing-bank advances. I well remember the complaints of the clearing banks, not at the restrictions in themselves, but because the many hire-purchase finance houses were free of them and thus able to do the very business denied to the banks. The net was cast wider in later years, but the process of disintermediation, as our American friends call it, had begun. As the years passed it spread and gave birth to many financial institutions on the fringe of the banking system proper, which were to cause much trouble in the mid-1970s. The Radcliffe Committee on the working of the monetary system in its report of August 1959 noted the emergence of such peripheral financial institutions, but did not consider that at that time any special measures to control them were justified. They might have thought differently if they could have foreseen the future growth of such institutions and the way in which their weaknesses were shown up by the severe blows to confidence in general, produced by sudden and over-violent changes in government economic policy.

Long before the fringe banking crisis broke upon us in 1974 the Bank of England foresaw the dangers of disintermediation, which increasingly ossified the banking system proper while leaving peripheral financial institutions to grow and multiply in comparative freedom. One of the main objects of the radical changes introduced by Competition and Credit Control was to arrest and gradually reverse these unhealthy developments. It was a tragedy that this necessarily delicate process of readjustment was totally upset by a notably imprudent expansion of the economy, followed by the inevitable harsh restraint.

However, to return to earlier years, not long after the changes in domestic financial institutions which I have described began to develop, other far more important changes began to take place in the banking world proper. These were brought about by the growth of the new international capital markets based principally on the Eurodollar and, to a lesser extent, on some other currencies traded in outside the bounds of their domestic origin and at rates of interest not tied to their domestic market but established internationally. As these markets grew, so it became necessary for banks who wished to do business in them to become more international in character. This has now reached such a pitch that there is hardly a leading bank in the world which does not gain a substantial part of its profits from business done outside its own country of origin. At least one US bank derives more than three-quarters of its profits from international business.

These developments do nothing to ease the task of domestic regulatory authorities. In addition to this, the British authorities have a special problem arising from the very attractiveness of the environment for banking business which they have created. There is, indeed, no more attractive centre in the world from which to do international business. As a result the influx of foreign banks to London during the 1960s and 1970s has been enormous, so that they now far outnumber our domestic banks.

Because of these domestic and international developments, the banking system which the Bank of England is required to regulate is vastly more diverse than the cosy little banking community that existed before the war.

EEC OBJECTIVES

But the changes do not end there. Since 1973 we have been members of the European Economic Community. Whatever the political outcome of this union may eventually be, the harmonisation of economic policy is already an acknowledged objective. This entails harmonisation in many subsidiary fields of which banking is one. There are many aspects to banking harmonisation, but only the harmonisation of regulation, I think, has a place in this chapter. Indeed, it is central to my theme because, whatever other consideration may have led our authorities to produce a Banking Act, the inescapable need for it arises from the requirements of banking harmonisation within the Community. In short, all Community banks are required to be officially licensed before they can do banking business.

This requirement is embodied in the First Banking Directive issued by the EEC Commission in Brussels, with the approval of the Ministerial Council, in 1977. Since the formulation of this Directive had a crucial bearing on the shape of our Banking Act perhaps I may briefly recall its history. The six original member-countries of the Community all regulate their banks by statutes of considerable weightiness and detail, in a tradition very foreign to our own. When we came on the scene a draft of the First Banking Directive was already in being. It required detailed harmonisation on a statutory basis, and would have run completely counter to our informal methods in the UK. After much discussion in Brussels an alternative approach was secured, more in line with the British tradition of bank supervision. This achievement was in no small measure due to the efforts of the British Bankers' Association. Thus the Directive as approved sets out a list of principles which must be adhered to, while leaving it to each regulatory authority to use such methods of doing so as suit it best. The only new requirement, so far as the UK is concerned, is that banks and similar financial institutions must be officially licensed. Hence the need for a Banking Act.

Thus it was our European Community obligations which were primarily responsible for the Banking Act 1979, but the story by no means ends there. The pressure and need for such an Act arose at least as much from the trauma of the fringe banking crisis and from the lessons it taught us all. In particular, it drew attention to the lack of adequate supervision and control of such fringe institutions, and to the considerable public confusion about what were and were not banks. Other considerations pointed in the same direction, notably the increasing tendency of banks to operate internationally instead of simply in their own domestic markets.

So in many respects the time was ripe for some departure from the UK's long-standing informal style of bank regulation. Even without the need to satisfy EEC requirements, the UK authorities were convinced that some statutory reinforcement of existing controls was necessary. Indeed, I think it fair to say that our authorities regarded the domestic reasons for the strengthening of control as having the greater importance and urgency. Certainly these considerations dictated the two-tier structure established by the Banking Act. The banks in general readily accepted the need for change. The questions occupying everybody's mind over the many months of discussion which preceded the preparation of the draft bill, concerned the nature and scope of the new statutory controls and who should be responsible for enforcing them.

THE BANK'S ROLE AS REGULATOR

I do not think I am flattering the Bank of England unduly when I say that I am sure the whole banking system was most anxious that the Bank's traditional function as regulator of the system should in no material respect be impaired. It is not always easy when one is on the inside looking out to assess correctly the image that one presents. Nevertheless, after many years of experience I judge that the Bank is highly respected for its meticulous enforcement of official policy, for the fair and even-handed way in which it carries out these responsibilities and for the sympathy and understanding which it nevertheless evinces in all its dealings with the banking community. The best evidence of this is perhaps provided by foreign bankers working in the London market. On countless occasions they have expressed to me their boundless admiration for the excellence of the relations between our central bank and the banking system, and have contrasted them to our advantage with those existing in many countries abroad – frequently including their own.

Needless to say the Bank was equally anxious to retain its traditional role, realising full well how much would be lost if it were to become a mere post-office between Whitehall and Westminster on the one hand, and the banking system on the other.

But even assuming that this very proper and legitimate aspiration was accepted by all concerned, it was not one that could be easily achieved. Statutes are passed by parliament to whom the appropriate ministers are answerable and they must be briefed and supported by civil servants. This necessarily establishes a line of responsibility, which is not easily broken to leave responsibility and the right of action to some other body. Yet this is very largely what the Banking Act does, subject to minimal involvement of HM Treasury and of the Chancellor of the Exchequer. In all important respects the position of the Bank of England is preserved, and indeed is now specifically reinforced by law. I believe that the banking community has every reason to be grateful to the Governor of the Bank for securing such a satisfactory result. It gives the assurance that the essence of our long-standing arrangements will remain, with benefit to all recognised banks and licensed financial institutions in the UK.

It is now more than six years since I ceased to be Governor of the Bank of England, so I have made no contribution at all to the official thinking on which the Banking Act was based. But since the Act seems to me to be on the whole a pretty satisfactory piece of legislation, I would like to tell you why I approve of its division between recognised banks and licensed deposit takers.

In all branches of business activity I am firmly in favour of encouragement being given to new blood, and much against the erection of insuperable barriers against its entry into any business, trade or profession. Equally, I do not believe that any good comes of giving a too-easy run to those who have not sufficiently demonstrated their fitness for the business in hand. This applies particularly in some spheres of which most would agree that medicine must be one of the most important. For my part I would put banking alongside medicine. Banking failures may not kill, but they certainly destroy and, as we have seen so many times in the past, the repercussive effects of one bank failure can be devastating. So I would be much opposed to any easy entry into the community of recognised banks. I believe that the central bank ought to have ample opportunity to assess the integrity, performance and financial soundness of those who aspire to this status, and have the assurance that the market as a whole is satisfied that they are worthy of it. In the past too many of the aspiring deposit-taking institutions grew up too fast, with over-exalted ideas of their place in the world, and considerable impatience with the caution and conservatism of the long-standing banker. We need brilliant bankers and we need cautious bankers, but above all we need sound bankers. I believe the new Act will help the Bank of England to see that this last requirement is met.

THE BANKING ACT

Which brings me to the Act itself. Although it runs to over seventy pages, it is a slim affair compared with most such Acts around the world. This is because, mercifully, it is not designed to regulate and control in detail every aspect of the business of banking.

The main purposes of the Act are:

1. to prevent any bank or other financial institution, whether existing or newly formed, from accepting deposits without obtaining authority to do so from the Bank of England;
2. to lay down the criteria which must be satisfied if such authority is to be received and retained;
3. to provide statutory authority for the supervision by the Bank of England of the activities of all such institutions;
4. to control the use of banking names and descriptions limiting them in the main to recognised banks;
5. to provide a measure of protection for depositors in licensed institutions through the medium of a Depositors' Protection Scheme.

A substantial number of institutions which do take deposits are specifically excluded from the requirements of the Banking Act. The Bank of England itself does not require a licence, nor do local authorities, the Giro, the National Savings Bank or the trustee savings banks. In one way or another these institutions are all held not to be subject to the same risks as prevail in the private sector. The building societies also are excluded from the terms of the Act. They, of course, are massive takers of deposits which are not without risk, but the building societies are covered by separate legislation, and are already controlled by the Chief Registrar of Friendly Societies. Insurance companies are also exempted being covered by other legislation.

As I said earlier, the Banking Act provides for two forms of authorisation for deposit-taking institutions, namely those of: (i) recognised bank; or (ii) licensed deposit taker. This division is not required by the EEC banking directive, but has been devised to enable the Bank of England to limit the use of banking names and descriptions, and to retain for recognised banks the informal type of supervision which it has hitherto exercised over them, while applying more rigorous controls over licensed deposit takers.

The new Act was brought into operation from October 1979 and the relevant institutions which are already taking deposits must apply to the Bank of England, before April 1980, for recognition or a licence enabling them to continue to do so after that date. Meanwhile, pending a decision on their application, they may continue to accept deposits as heretofore. It is now illegal for any new institution to start up in business to take deposits, without first being licensed by the Bank of England to do so.

All who gain a Bank of England licence are equally free to take deposits, and all may provide as many banking services as they wish. Some licensed deposit-takers may well be content to remain as such, with no aspirations to become recognised banks. Others will want to achieve this status as soon as possible. Whichever road a particular institution takes, the choice is theirs, but the ultimate decision to authorise belongs to the Bank of England, subject to the appeal provisions enshrined in the Banking Act.

RECOGNITION

Those who seek either a licence or recognition have to satisfy the appropriate criteria, which are set out in the Act. The minimum conditions are that the applicant must satisfy the Bank of England as to its solvency and as to the competence of its management. In addition, an applicant for recognised status must normally demonstrate that it provides a wide range of banking services and can satisfy the Bank as to its standing and reputation in the financial community. Much of this will be familiar to you because such considerations have long guided the Bank before reinforcement by statute was thought of.

The kinds of banking service required of a recognised bank are set out in the Act. They are five in number being:

1. the acceptance of deposits;
2. the making of loans;
3. foreign exchange;
4. the provision of bill finance and the handling of documentation for foreign trade;
5. investment management and corporate finance.

This is a far cry from the traditional legal view of what constitutes a bank, the essential ingredient of which was, if Paget's 'Law of Banking' is any guide, that current-account and cheque-cashing facilities must be available.

Having listed the five basic banking services, the Act then goes on to give the Bank of England discretion to excuse the provision of one or two of the last three of them. Thus it might be possible to obtain recognition just by taking deposits, making loans and providing one other of the five basic services. Finally it is possible to qualify for recognition, not by providing the five services but by demonstrating that, as the Act puts it, a 'highly specialised banking service' is provided. However, it is understood that this provision would be used only in the case of discount houses. So the hurdles for the would-be recognised bank may all be of the same height but their construction can apparently differ widely. It will be interesting to see how these requirements are interpreted in practice.

Perhaps at this point I may summarise by saying that in future all deposit-takers will require a Bank of England authority, all successful applicants for which may associate their deposit-taking with as wide a range of banking services as they think fit. Those, however, who aspire to recognised status must satisfy the more stringent conditions which I have described.

In future, only recognised banks will enjoy the unqualified right to use in their name the words 'bank', 'banking' and 'banker', or any of their derivatives, or in any way describe themselves as a bank or indicate that they are a bank. Unfortunately, the distinction thus made between recognised banks and the rest, could not be made as clean cut as one might have wished. Since licensed deposit-takers may offer any range of banking services they like, it was deemed unreasonable to prevent them from saying so. They may consequently use the expression 'banking services' but only in specified circumstances and with appropriate safeguards. Moreover any concern which has to call itself a 'bank' or a 'banker' in order to be able to assert that it is complying with, or taking advantage of, any other provision of law or custom, international agreement or commercial practice, is not prevented from doing so by the Banking Act, regardless of whether the concern is a recognised bank or not.

There is another exception which generated a good deal of heat while the prospective Act was in passage. This concerns foreign banks having a branch in the UK. It was decided that, even in those cases where such a bank received only a licence as a deposit-taker, it should nevertheless be allowed to use the banking name under which it traded in its own country. This appeared to many to be leaving wide open the very door through which many foreign banks, with high-sounding names and dubious origins, had entered this country in

recent years. The official answer to such objections was that so far as
EEC banks are concerned we have no choice, being bound by the
First Banking Directive, and that there was no justification for
discriminating between foreign countries for this purpose. Furthermore there are obvious difficulties in requiring a branch of a foreign
bank to describe itself with a name different from that of its parent.
The solution to a real problem has been to require that the words
'licensed deposit-taker' shall appear alongside such names and in
letters of equal prominence. I appreciate the difficulty but I cannot
say that I am entirely happy about the solution. At least the Bank of
England now has undoubted supervisory authority over all such
licencees, and no doubt will successfully prevent abuse.

STATUTORY POWERS OF CONTROL

In fact, under the Act the Bank of England is given statutory powers
of control over licensed institutions which do not extend to recognised banks. For example, strange as it may seem, the Act does not
give the Bank powers to obtain information from recognised banks.
The answer no doubt is that those banks have with good grace for
many years been supplying the Bank with all the information it
needs. Thus help has been afforded on the basis of mutual understanding and co-operation, the fruits of which might well be impaired
by any hint of coercion. Having so long profited from this informal
approach, I would expect the Bank to do their best to apply it to the
wider range of deposit-takers, even though they now have statutory
powers on which to fall back. To see those powers described in
association with words such as 'indictment', 'summary conviction',
'fine' and even 'imprisonment' conjures up a picture very different
from the one with which I grew up. I like to think that the Bank, by
and large, will not need to change its ways, and that the threats
implied by the words I have quoted will rarely, if ever, need to be put
into practice. The great improvement as compared with the past is
that the Bank's field of responsibilities is now precisely defined, and
its right and duty to exercise them can no longer be in doubt. In
discharging them the Bank is already devoting more of its resources
to the task than was previously the case. I would expect to see some
further expansion of such activities but not, I would hope, to the
extent of placing undue burdens on the banking system. It is heart-
ening to see that the Bank is evidently much concerned to develop

flexible non-statutory criteria on which to base supervision and that they have been doing this in consultation with the banks.

Before I leave the question of supervision I would like to say something about the position of foreign banks, of which there are now so many doing business in the City of London.

For the purposes of authorisation under the Banking Act, the foreign banks in the UK will be treated in precisely the same way as domestic banks. They will have to apply for a licence, or make their case for acceptance as a recognised bank. They will be treated neither more nor less favourably than their British counterparts, except that, as I have already explained, a branch will automatically be entitled to use the same name as its head office.

When it comes to supervision, however, there will be a difference. The Bank has always regarded foreign bank branches as inseparable from the parent bank for supervisory purposes. Accordingly the head office of the foreign bank and not merely the UK branch will have to apply for a licence or recognised bank status. This poses the question of how to apply the stipulated criteria to such applications which must embrace the bank as a whole, even though most of its activities occur outside UK jurisdiction. The Act resolves this problem in a rather novel, but realistic way. The Bank of England is allowed – though not obliged – to delegate some of its responsibilities to the supervisory authority of the parent bank. In forming its view of the management and solvency of a foreign bank, the Bank of England can dispense with making its own judgement and instead rely on the testimony of the overseas supervisory authority about the bank's management and financial soundness. In fact this does little more than formalise an existing reality. As banking has become more international, and as banks have more and more branched across national frontiers, so in recent years we have seen more co-operation among the various national supervisory bodies. The Act recognises this trend.

SOLVENCY

Beginning with the authorisation of the two categories of deposit-taker, I have been carried on naturally to the discussion of how each will be supervised. In so doing I have left aside the vitally important question of solvency. Whether a deposit-taker is licensed or recognised as a bank the solvency requirements set out in the Banking Act will have to be met. As in the case of the management criteria, the precise wording is different for each. New deposit-takers will need to have a minimum amount of capital and reserves before they can obtain recognition or a licence. The minimum figure is £250 000 for a licence, and normally £5m for recognition. Existing deposit-takers are subject only to the general, but much more important, requirement that their resources are at all times adequate in relation to the scale of their business. The wording of the Act is deliberately vague, to allow the judgement of what is adequate to be left to the Bank of England. It would be fruitless at this stage to speculate on how the Bank of England will interpret the solvency requirements in the Act. The important point is that the Act itself does not contain specific solvency or liquidity tests which the Bank must apply and to which all deposit-takers must conform. The Bank of England has always rejected rigid ratios applied across the board to all banks. It has recognised that different banks have different needs for capital and liquidity, depending on the structure and nature of their business. On this point the Bank of England and the banking industry have always been in close accord. It is gratifying to see that the Banking Act allows the Bank of England to continue with its traditional philosophy of supervision.

When I said that the Banking Act had been brought into operation as from 1 October 1979, I expect many of you noted with disapproval the lack of precision in that statement. It is true that most of the Act then came into force, but not all of it. The parts now operative are Part I which deals with all matters germane to the control of deposit-taking, Part III which controls advertising for deposits and the use of banking names, and almost all of Part IV which covers miscellaneous and general matters.

DEPOSIT PROTECTION SCHEME

Part II, which deals with everything concerning the Deposit Protection Scheme, cannot come into operation so soon, because the authorities first need to know how many recognised banks and licensed deposit-takers there will be to begin with. Only when they know this can they establish the deposit base of institutions required to contribute to the Deposit Protection Fund.

This is the one part of the new legislation to which the banks reacted with considerable hostility. They argued, very reasonably, that, despite the severity of the 'fringe banking' crisis, no member of the public had lost any money. They argued that the new Act itself should greatly lessen the possibility of such an emergency again arising. They pointed to their own long-standing and blameless record in relation to their own depositors. The big banks thought it unfair that they, who could not conceivably close their doors on their depositors, should have to put up most of the money to bail out depositors in frailer institutions. In addition, many banks could see no need for a cash fund rather than simple guarantees from all banks to provide up to a total specified sum in case of need.

These objections were politely listened to but not heeded. The one, very valuable, concession made in response to the banks' pleas was the Treasury's agreement that contributions to the Deposit Protection Fund should be treated as qualifying business expenses for tax purposes.

Despite the success with which it was handled, there is no doubt that the fringe banking crisis was responsible for the determination of government and civil servants to have a deposit protection scheme. They could point to similar schemes abroad, notably in the USA, and were also riding on the prevailing tide of consumerism.

The scope of the scheme, as set out in the Act, is in fact rather modest. It is intended to protect only small depositors in a failed institution by limiting compensation from the Fund to 75 per cent of the first £10 000 of any one deposit. Thus no depositor, however large, will receive more than £7500. Moreover, since the aim is to protect the general public, not professionals, no deposit placed by a bank or licensed deposit-taker will be protected at all.

The Fund, therefore, is to be financed by cash subscriptions from recognised banks and licensed deposit-takers. Contributions have been fixed by reference to each institution's deposit base to yield a total of £5–6m. The contributors are subject to further calls on them in case of need.

The National Girobank and the trustee savings banks, being outside the scope of the Banking Act, are not required to be contributors to the Deposit Protection Scheme although it is understood that the TSBs will, at the appropriate stage of their development, be brought into the scheme, and that the Girobank will be required to contribute an amount to the Treasury, equal to its contribution to the scheme if it had to make one. This also was ill-received by the banks, but in the end had to be accepted.

IN PRACTICE

By the middle of next year we shall begin to see how the Banking Act is working in practice. It has been long in preparation and the banking industry has had ample opportunity throughout to join in discussions with the Bank of England and the Treasury and to make its views known. Naturally not all sections of the industry necessarily see every aspect of the subject in the same light. Thus the final result pleases some more than others, and probably no one completely. This is in the nature of things. I think it can be claimed, however, that the process of preparing the way for the Act has been carried through in a workmanlike manner. Perhaps from the point of view of the banks matters were helped towards the end by the need to get the bill through parliament before the general election. Certainly some useful amendments, which might in other circumstances have been fought by the government, went through unopposed. The most welcome of these really had nothing to do with the subject in hand at all. That was the amendments of the Consumer Credit Act 1974 contained in section 38. A splendid piece of opportunism by Lord Seebohm in the House of Lords, where I was very glad to support him, secured this amendment which has the welcome effect of taking overdrafts further out of the scope of the Consumer Credit Act.

All in all, therefore, I feel that both the regulators and the regulated should be fairly well satisfied with our first general Banking Act. In practice it seems likely to remove uncertainty about the scope of the Bank of England's powers, and to reinforce them where they have been shown to be deficient. It should remove a good deal of confusion arising from divided responsibilities, for example, between the Bank of England and the Department of Trade. It also puts a stop to the use of recognition under Schedule 8 of the Companies Act 1948, under section 127 of the Protection of Depositors Act and under section 123 of the Companies Act 1967 as cachets of banking respectability, the limitations of which the general public did not understand. Indeed, as is right and proper, the general public should be the chief beneficiaries of the Banking Act.

Finally, the Act should benefit our banking system by ensuring good order and discipline throughout the whole range of deposit taking institutions, while not to any degree impairing that freedom to do business under the benevolent if watchful eye of our central bank on which all of us in the British banking industry set such great store.

POSTSCRIPT (MAY 1983)

It is now four years since I gave the lecture on which this chapter is based. In 1979 there were many fears among banks and deposit-takers about the effect of the new Banking Act and how it would be operated by the Bank of England. In my lecture I sought to allay some of those fears and what I say now shows, I think, that they were without foundation.

Operation of the two-tier system

Many of the qualms initially felt by licensed institutions have been eased once it was seen how the provisions of the Act have been applied in practice. It has widely come to be accepted that the distinction between the licensed and recognised sectors is more one of function than of status. This view was encouraged by a speech given by the Governor in May 1980, when he said 'the Bank would not expect the market to make crude judgements of creditworthiness based merely on the distinction between recognised banks and licensed deposit-takers'.

Another important factor in settling the concerns felt in some quarters about the two-tier system has been evidence that movement from the licensed to the recognised sectors is possible. Since the Act came into operation twenty-six licensed institutions have received recognition. In particular it has become common practice for foreign banks opening branches in London to be licensed initially until they have been able to build up their services to the level needed to qualify for recognition.

It remains true, however, that there are certain statutes in which discrimination is made between recognised and licensed institutions. An example is the Building Societies Act 1962 (as amended) which allows building societies to hold their surplus funds with recognised banks, but not with licensed deposit-takers. The Banking Act itself generally limits the use of banking names and descriptions to banks. In its operation the Banking Act has helped to maintain the integrity of the primary banking system by identifying a group of major institutions that would commonly be regarded as banks among their peers in the markets while allowing other institutions freedom to develop their business subject only to prudential constraints. By earning high reputation and standing and providing the requisite range of services such institutions have the opportunity, if they choose, to develop into banks.

Legal powers under the Act

The Act gave the Bank of England powers to obtain information, appoint investigators and petition for the winding-up of authorised institutions. In spite of these new powers, however, the Bank has continued to exercise its supervisory responsibilities as far as possible in its traditional manner, relying on personal contacts and powers of persuasion rather than legal sanctions.

The Act, however, did extend the Bank's responsibilities, so that it now finds itself supervising types of institution with which in the past it would not have had any contact. In the great majority of cases the traditional supervisory approach has continued to be successful and the Bank has taken pains to establish with all the institutions which it supervises, relationships based on mutual confidence. In a few cases, however, it has been necessary to invoke the Act's legal powers, and the Bank has successfully petitioned for the winding-up of three institutions.

Principles of supervision

The Act sets down some rather broad requirements relating to capital and liquidity to be met by licensed and recognised institutions leaving it to the Bank in the course of its supervision to develop more detailed principles. It has elaborated on its principles in a series of three papers it has published: 'The Measurement of Capital' (in September 1980), 'Foreign Currency Exposure' (in April 1981) and 'The Measurement of Liquidity' (in July 1982). These papers were prepared after extensive consultation with the banking industry.

These policy documents do not lay down any hard and fast rules or specific ratios which must be met. Rather, they describe the method of measurement which is used by the Bank and the various factors which the Bank takes into consideration when assessing the figures for individual institutions. The Bank discusses each institution's position with it in the course of regular prudential meetings and as a result determines the appropriate guidelines for each institution in the light of its particular circumstances.

Within the field of supervised institutions there is a great range of different institutions, each with its own characteristics in terms of size, business specialisation and exposure to risk. The guidelines for capital and liquidity adequacy reflect this diversity. Some institutions will require proportionately more capital and more liquidity than others. The system of measurement is applied consistently but the ratios expected of particular institutions will differ markedly.

The Bank's supervisory resources

The numbers of staff employed in the Bank's supervisory activities have grown from 77 before the Act came into force to 109 now. Over the same period the number of institutions has grown from 538 (of which 279 were recognised banks) when the Act first came into force to 592 now (of which 294 are recognised banks).

11 Why Banks Are Unpopular*

Guido Carli

We are going through a period in which the banking community has increasingly come to be regarded with hostility; this is certainly the case in my own country. Antipathy toward bankers has old roots: it is said of Schopenhauer that, on visiting the gallery where the portraits of the Fugger were hung and observing their images, he exclaimed: 'When I look at your faces I have to admit that God is not with you.' I propose to examine the reasons for the resentment which is felt toward bankers and banks in some countries.

In earlier times banking failures stimulated interest in the banks' conduct of their affairs; this has also happened recently, but to a lesser degree. One of the reasons for the doubt and suspicion, I feel, must lie in the widening involvement of the financial intermediaries both in international settlements and in domestic payments transactions. The feeling of mistrust derives from a conviction that the commercial banks have appropriated too large a share of monetary sovereignty.

I have no wish to retrace the long road toward reform of the international monetary system, but let me just recall its final objectives. These were:

- to restrict the use of the dollar as a reserve, intervention, and settlement currency;
- gradually to eliminate gold from the international monetary system and replace it with a reserve instrument created by the authorities; and
- to establish a new code of conduct for a system in which fixed and flexible rates exist side by side.

This chapter originated as the 1976 Per Jacobsson Lecture, given at Basle on 12 June 1976, and published in the same year by the Per Jacobsson Foundation, IMF, Washington.

The attempt by the EEC countries to set up a monetary zone within which interventions on the foreign exchange market were carried out in currencies other than the dollar, and settlement between central banks were made using various currencies in proportions corresponding to the composition of the debtor-country's reserves, lasted from April until June 1972. It was followed by the reinstatement of the dollar, both as an intervention currency and as an instrument for settling balances.

The resoluteness shown in pleading the need to exclude gold from the international monetary system reaped its reward. Without any fear of paradox it may be said that the result was more spectacular than expected: instead of a gradual displacement, what happened was tantamount to a total eradication by virtue of the freezing of gold held in official reserves. One exception was the mobilisation of a small quantity of the metal in the crossed deposit operation between the Deutsche Bundesbank and the Banca d'Italia in September 1974.

The freezing of gold coincided with the emergence of greater disequilibria in payments balances in the wake of the increase in the price of oil: in only a few countries had the international liquidity previously created augmented the official reserves, while those more exposed to payments deficits held gold in their reserves; the shortage of international liquidity was made up by the banks, and in large measure by the American banks through their overseas branches.

The scale of intermediation by commercial banks in the financing of the oil importers' deficits and the oil exporters' surpluses is noted by some with satisfaction: market forces, they say, made up for the indolence of the authorities. Others see it as corroboration of the evil intentions of the authors of reform, maintaining that the eradication of gold from the system and the failure to replace it with official intruments confirm a malicious design to strengthen the dominant position of the American banks.

I do not subscribe to these interpretations; on the contrary, I believe that there was a lack of clear vision as to the consequences of the attitudes adopted. Clearly, like everyone else, I too maintain that the vision was lacking in others; I shall therefore quote myself.

On 5 March 1974, I wrote in the European pages of the four major European dailies:

It would be as well to take a closer look at other aspects of the growth of the Eurodollar market. If it were to take the course described there would be an expansion, on the one hand, of the Eurobanks' sight liabilities and, on the other, of their claims in the form of lending to the oil-importing countries at maturities in the range of seven to eight years. In these circumstances transfers of funds from one bank to another and from the banking sector as a whole to the market for government securities could produce a liquidity crisis which only the intervention of a lender of last resort would be able to resolve. Under a floating exchange-rate regime, shifts of funds from the Euromarket to national markets and vice versa would be reflected in exchange-rate fluctuations which, in the absence of co-ordinated interventions by central banks, could assume such proportions as to disrupt international trade.

I do not feel it is wanting in respect toward my former fellow central bankers to say that there was an absence of co-ordinated central bank intervention. I believe that one of the reasons lies in the difficulty of reconciling the interests of countries whose exports are sensitive to exchange-rate movements in varying degrees. Those whose exports are less sensitive tend, in formulating objectives, to give priority to shielding the domestic market from the liquidity repercussions of flows of funds from abroad; they are therefore more inclined to cushion the impact of these flows on exchange-rate fluctuations.

The need for co-ordination was solemnly affirmed in November 1975 by heads of state, heads of government, and ministers meeting in a *château* near Paris. Inspired by the solemnity of the occasion, they discovered the potential of the telephone on three levels: talks between ministers, between central bank governors, and between foreign exchange dealers. The same needs were reaffirmed in the announcement in Jamaica of the new Articles of Agreement of the International Monetary Fund. Commenting on their significance, the former French Minister of Finance declared: 'It is a great presumption to attempt to institutionalise anarchy. The drafters of the new IMF Articles have shown such presumption!' I find it difficult not to concur in this judgement.

I thought it relevant to recount these experiences because I wanted to underline the fact that the international monetary system has evolved along different paths from those mapped out by the reformers: the process of international liquidity creation has indeed been divorced from gold production or changes in gold price, but it has become exclusively dependent on the supply of reserve currencies to the system and, in particular, that reserve currency which is its pivot: the US dollar.

In the five years between 1970 and 1976 total international liquidity reserves soared from US$ 93 milliard to US$ 227 milliard – an increase of US$ 135 milliard. By far the largest component was made up of currency reserves, which rose by US$ 116 milliard. The major part of the increase consisted of claims in dollars: at the end of 1975 official dollar claims on the USA stood at US$ 80 milliard and claims in dollars and other currencies on the Euromarket stood at about the same amount.

The long-term and short-term foreign indebtedness of the USA jumped from US$ 47 milliard at the end of 1970 to US$ 126 milliard at the end of 1975, and its liabilities *vis-à-vis* official institutions from US$ 24 milliard to US$ 80 milliard, of which US$ 49 milliard was toward official institutions.

The banking system played a large part in this process, contributing to the creation of international liquidity through the expansion of credit. At the end of 1972, short-term lending by the American banks amounted to US$ 16 milliard, and at the end of 1975 to US$ 50 milliard. At the end of 1973, Eurobank credits totalled US$ 132 milliard, and at the end of 1975 US$ 197 milliard. This lending represented the counterpart of deposits which flowed either into official reserves outside the USA, largely from the OPEC countries, or into the liquid asset holdings of commercial banks and individuals in the same countries.

The huge expansion of the Eurodollar market occurred in the two-year period 1974–5 in conjunction with the accumulation of surpluses by the OPEC countries; reliable estimates put the surpluses accumulated during this period at US$ 101 milliard; the share flowing to official institutions was US$ 43 milliard and the currency portion was US$ 38 milliard. The remainder went to non-official institutions and was in part placed in financial, real, and direct investments and in part held in liquid form; at the end of 1975 the portion held in the form of deposits with banks in the USA was about US$ 9 milliard, the remainder being deposited, either in dollars or in other currencies, in the Euromarket, where foreign branches of American banks were operating on an increasing scale.

The process of expansion of international financial intermediation chiefly involved the American banks: between 1972 and 1975 the total assets and liabilities of the US banks' foreign branches rose from

US$ 78 milliard to US$ 176 milliard – an increase which exceeded the rise in M_1 and M_2 in the domestic US economy over the same period. This development is plainly reflected in the balance sheets of the major banks: at 31 December 1975 total deposits in the books of the Bank of America stood at US$ 56 milliard; deposits at its foreign branches amounted to US$ 23 milliard. Some 41 per cent of earnings, against 29 per cent in the previous year, accrued from its international business activities. Total deposits in the books of Citibank amounted to US$ 45 milliard, and deposits at its foreign branches to US$ 25 milliard. The corresponding figures for Chase Manhattan were US$ 34 milliard and US$ 15 milliard respectively. Morgan Guaranty announced that in December 1975 approximately one half of its outstanding loans were through its overseas branches.

The scale of the American banks' participation would be even more striking with the inclusion of non-residents' deposits with these banks' domestic branches, figures for which are not published.

The figures recorded suggest that during this period the international monetary system shifted out of the domain of the official international institutions: the private banking system took over the functions proper to an official institution possessed of the power to finance balance-of-payments disequilibria through credit-granting and to create international liquidity. The realisation that this had come about has provoked opposite reactions within and outside the USA. In a number of countries the growing internationalisation of the big American banks serves to reinforce hostility toward multinational corporations. The presence of bank branches tied to decision-making centres in the USA rouses fears of a loss of sovereignty. Conversely, in the USA there is growing alarm that the huge expansion of operations abroad might compromise the American banks' autonomy by exposing them to the risk of withdrawals by this or that foreign depositor and insolvencies among those countries which are major debtors.

The rating of credits according to the country of the borrower and their allocation according to the presumed degree of solvency has caused controversy in Italy. The first news of this practice became public in September 1974; the rating given to Italy occasioned considerable alarm both in the country itself and abroad, and it cannot be ruled out that this added momentum to the wave of deposit withdrawals from Italian banks which broke out in the summer of that year. The Italian banks met these withdrawals by mobilising foreign claims.

Fuller details on the rating of US banks' foreign loans contained in the bank examiners' reports appeared in the press in January of this year. In Italy there were again outcries at the plot, and the American conspiracy was blamed as one of the causes of the monetary events of that month. But this should not give cause for wonder: have we not seen how in other times, in countries which had given birth to Immanuel Kant and Galileo Galilei, official explanations laid shortage, unemployment, and flights of capital at the door of the treasonous activities of the the Jews?

The assumption by the private banking system of the function of a clearing union, which according to Keynes ought to have been performed by the International Monetary Fund, inevitably brought it to the focus of the public authorities' attention. The international institutions which are appointed to finance growth and development generally adopt a country-by-country credit-rating; the private banker tends to place greatest weight on the creditworthiness of the individual borrower. It is hardly surprising, therefore, if the government inspector insists that he apply a national reliability rating, particularly in a period in which there has tended to be a shift in lending from the economically stronger to the economically weaker countries.

The Committee of Twenty met in Rome in January 1974 in a climate of anxiety. This meeting took place only a few months after announcements in Nairobi of imminent success in the reform of the international monetary system. During the meeting, an authoritative voice spoke in warning that the situation created by the quadrupling of the oil price was unmanageable. In the event, the industrial countries succeeded in mastering it sooner than anticipated. But the problems of the economically weaker countries have grown.

The rapid improvement in the industrial countries' current account payments balance found its counterpart in a deterioration of the position of the developing countries. In the five year period 1968–72 these countries' current account deficit had held steady at around US$ 6 milliard a year; in 1973 it rose to US$ 9 milliard, in 1974 to US$ 26 milliard, and in 1975 to US$ 35 milliard. In this last year the group of countries with an annual per capita income of under US$ 375 accounted for about 60 per cent of the developing countries' overall deficit. This confirms that, while preserving the oil exporters' surplus, the policies conducted by the stronger countries to reduce their deficit concentrated the negative effects on the weaker countries. It should be added that in 1975 the burden borne by these countries in servicing their foreign debt rose to some 12 per cent of the value of their exports; this total is distributed unevenly among individual countries, and for some the percentage is much higher.

With the improvement in their external position, the industrial countries have become less active as borrowers in the international capital market; to some extent their place has been taken by the developing countries. Between 1973 and 1975 the total amount of loans granted on the international capital market increased from US$ 6.3 milliard to US$ 13.2 milliard.

At the end of 1975, with the total of loans outstanding amounting to about US$ 120 milliard, the proportion accounted for by official borrowing was 56 per cent.

In 1976 it is estimated that the developing countries' deficit, including redemption and interest service on their external debt, will come to US$ 42.5 milliard. It should, however, be pointed out that this estimate is based on the assumption that restrictive measures will reduce the level of their imports; it probably also assumes an expansion of their exports, pulled along by the recovery of production in the major industrial countries, on a scale regarded by some experts as optimistic. If all IMF facilities were activated, international agencies would contribute up to US$ 28 milliard toward financing this deficit. Part of the remainder would be covered by export credits; but this would still leave a substantial amount to be met by the international banking system, and hence, chiefly by American banks.

From the situation just depicted certain conclusions may be drawn. The most important, I think, is that there is at present no international monetary system, that is, there is no official institution capable of supplying the international payments system with the liquidity required for the further expansion of trade. This function has been taken over by the private banking system, and primarily by the US banks, through operations carried out by their branches at home and abroad. The private banks have shown a greater ability than the official institutions not only to create the necessary liquidity for the development of trade but also to organise its efficient distribution.

As a result, the IMF's ability to enforce observance of rules of conduct has diminished; it should be remembered that, as originally conceived, the Fund's prescriptive powers derived from its ability to exclude refractory countries from access to conditional credit. As almost all credit is now drawn from other than official sources, the Fund's ability to lay down conditions has been correspondingly reduced. And as the function of creating international liquidity has been transferred from official institutions to private ones, so the task of supervision has passed from international bodies to national ones, whose surveillance, though keener than in the past, has none the less never reached beyond the boundaries of national interests.

Furthermore, the achievement of total independence by countries which in the past enjoyed only limited sovereignty has resulted in a greater differentiation of economic structures. The area occupied by the market economy has been narrowed, and in some countries completely replaced by government intervention. The greater the recourse to government intervention, the more difficult it becomes to achieve co-ordination on the international level. The gold standard provided for only one type of intervention, purchases and sales of gold when the exchange-rate level reached the gold points; this rule was observed by the majority of countries.

In the absence of a lender of last resort, the barrier to the private banking system taking over the function of a clearing union is the creditworthiness of the debtor-countries. As I have already said, the burden of the economically weaker countries is tending to grow; but it is doubtful whether a system based on private institutions can support it. The ability of the system to expand is consequently nearing its limits. It is possible that as these limits are approached, balance-of-payments equilibrium may have to be sought at progress-ively lower levels of economic activity – and primarily at the expense of the weaker countries. The dimension of the problems calls for greater co-operation among central monetary institutions; recent decisions are encouraging.

It may be added that there is evidence in several quarters that American multinational companies have begun a slow movement of withdrawal. This may have been prompted by a number of factors – not least the narrowing of the gap between labour costs in some of the countries in which these companies have set up subsidiaries and those in the USA. Obviously, the transition to economic systems in which the state is extending its influence is restricting the area in which multinational companies can operate and inducing some of them to move out of areas where there is a greater degree of socialism to those where there is less. On the other hand, there has been a change of attitude toward multinational companies in some of those countries where opposition to them used to be greatest. In Italy, for example, now that there are more obvious signs of the multinationals withdrawing from our market, the same political parties which not long ago regarded them with hostility are openly bewailing their departure and have even gone so far as to propose resisting it.

It is quite conceivable that the return of the multinationals within national boundaries may in time induce a reaction in banks which, for their part, had established branches abroad. A constraint would thus be set on the financing of imbalances in world trade not only by the limited credit-granting capacity of the existing institutions but also by the reduction in their number.

In short, the current withdrawal of American industrial and financial enterprises in response to hostility in countries in which nationalistic attitudes are re-emerging could further loosen the bonds which have held together the structure of the international economy in the last few years.

Evidence of the US banks' waning enthusiasm for expansion abroad can be deduced from the growing interest shown in extending merchant-banking operations. It may be, however, that this trend will increase the mistrust felt by those who fear the consequences of an excessive concentration of power in the banking system.

I have dwelt at length on the banks' role in the development of the international financial and monetary system because this role has given fresh motivation to the long-standing unpopularity of bankers. There is something schizophrenic in the fact that, while the international community proves to be incapable of governing monetary events through co-operation in international institutions, their substitution by private institutions is feared as a loss of control both by the countries of origin and by the host-countries. The unpopularity of bankers stems from the growing hiatus between the size of the problems and the inadequacy of the institutions called upon to resolve them. But the same difficulties and the same dissatisfaction are found in the role played by the banks within their own countries, where the problems and conflicts that have emerged in the last few years are no less great.

Concern at the concentration of power in the hands of the banks lies behind the appeal made by the political parties for more rigorous supervision and fuller information. One circumstance that has helped to shape this attitude is the fact that fiscal policy is formulated through the medium of parliamentary debates under the scrutiny of public opinion, whereas monetary policy is framed in secret and may in some cases come into conflict with fiscal policy. Nor does the fact that it is partly thanks to its autonomous and discreet nature that monetary policy contributes more effectively to the rare successes of

economic policy render any more acceptable this element of secrecy
which is still its distinguishing trait.

The power of the banks and the need to bring it within narrower
bounds are topics of debate in Italy within the political parties, the
trade unions, and the universities. The head of the Communist
party's planning department recently published a survey examining
the causes of the increase in the economic power of the banks; he
concluded by calling for the creation of a capital market where there
could be more direct contact between enterprises and savers and
where they would be offered a wider range of financial instruments.

In general the proposals for reform of the banking system put
forward in Italy stem from the mistaken conviction that the changes
that have occurred in Italy's financial structure are radically different
from those that have taken place in other capitalist countries; there
have been differences at times in the number of changes, but not in
their nature. The proposals to which I have referred are based on the
belief that the low ratio of shares to other financial instruments is a
feature peculiar to Italy. I have on more than one occasion drawn
attention to the fact that in 1975 in the USA, of the US$ 208 milliard
worth of funds' raised on the capital markets, barely US$ 1 milliard
was taken up in the form of shares.

Likewise, I have pointed out that of this total of US$ 208 milliard,
the government and the public sector (including the local authorities)
absorbed approximately half, which is not very different from the
proportion in Italy at the present time. But in Italy the public sector,
besides drawing from the capital market, claims further portions of
total financing both by direct recourse to bank credit and by deferring
payment for goods and services purchased; moreover, being largely
attributable to current expenditure, the Italian public sector's deficit
is less flexible than the US one.

Lastly, in the past decade all industrial countries have experienced
falling profits, a declining propensity to invest, and an increase in
financial intermediation. In a speech at a conference at Harvard
University, Henry Wallich observed:

> Corporations have financed this growth by shifting away from
> internal and toward external sources of funds, away from equity
> financing and toward debt, and from long-term debt to short-term
> debt. These trends in financing have produced financial structures
> that make additional financing difficult. It is useless to argue that if
> internal cash flow is inadequate, and if the stock market is not

receptive to equity issues, business should just continue to borrow. This advice is like Queen Marie Antoinette's 'Let them eat cake'. Where there is not enough profit, there will be no equity financing, and where there is not enough equity, there will not be much debt money available. An adequate flow of profits is the basis for debt financing, equity financing, and, of course, internal financing.

In Italy the result of the decline in profits and the deficiency of risk capital has been the transfer of firms from the private sector to the public sector, and this has happened at a time when the public sector was progressively losing its ability to measure the efficiency of its resource utilisation. Meanwhile, as in other industrial countries, there has been a growing tendency over the past decade for large groups to increase in size, partly by assimilating smaller firms, and this process, in turn, has helped to quicken the pace of expansion of the public sector. In the end it has become evident that it is not the state that rules the enterprises but the enterprises that rule the state. This is the reason why in Italy the Communist party has taken a stand against the excessive power of public enterprises. To the foreign observer it may appear paradoxical; but in a situation such as exists in Italy at present, a party whose aim is to strengthen the authority of the state must seek to encourage this by bringing the state back to the arena of its fundamental duties, and limiting the field of those which are sources of contamination.

In all countries the lack of continuity in the economic system has been an obstacle to the success of demand management policies at a time when changes in the terms of trade have been making them more necessary. Everywhere there has been a perceptible shift in the Phillips curve: the cost of maintaining a given level of employment is increasingly high rates of inflation; the cost of price stability is ever higher rates of unemployment. In these circumstances more is being required of the banking system as an organ of propagation of monetary policy, to the detriment, in some cases, of its distributive function, the importance of which, however, has been enhanced by the increasing rift between investment and saving. At the same time, enterprises' increased dependence on external financing has meant that they are more exposed to changes in the volume and cost of financing, and this has made the monetary authorities more reluctant to introduce restrictive measures, and sometime more inclined to delay changes in their policy course, so that when these measures finally come their impact is more violent. Calls for the adoption of selective policies and, with them, of compulsory planning are being heard with increasing frequency.

Parallel to that of enterprises, the financial imbalance of the public sector has been aggravated by growing demand for action in the social field and by an economic theory which argues that in conditions of underemployment of resources, deficit spending expands income and creates the savings necessary to finance itself. The conflict which has arisen in more than one case between the public administration and enterprises with regard to the distribution of household savings has obliged the authorities to sift through the instruments available to them and search for means of reconciling the different objectives; this could not leave the banking system unscathed.

Thus, in recent years the public sector's financial deficit has in many countries had profound repercussions on the structure of the credit institutions. Not only have the monetary authorities had the control of the monetary base taken out of their hands, this having become increasingly dependent on Treasury requirements, but they have been given the task of obliging the banking system to take up public securities, thereby changing the structure of the banks' balance sheets and restricting their ability to regulate flows of funds and interest rates. For their part, the banks, forced to operate as collectors of savings in order to channel them to the public sector, have lost something of their financial imagination, and this has led to an impoverishment of the productive system.

The scale of official intervention of this nature has shown that, when the authorities do not exercise coercion by making use of their power to levy taxes, they are forced to exercise it by putting pressure on the institutions that operate in the credit sector. The crowding-out of enterprises may be brought about by different means. Auctions of public securities are one way; but this is a solution that only has the appearance of being a rejection of coercion when the authorities are prepared to pay any rate of interest whatsoever. 'Underlying the problem of the banking system's ability to perform its role of distributing savings is the problem of the relation between the "fiscal" element, or the element of coercion, and the "credit" or "market" element in the financing of the public sector' (M. Monti and T. Padoa-Schioppa, 'Per un riesame del sistema creditizio italiano', in G. Carli (ed.), *La struttura del sistema creditizio italiano* (Bologna: Il Mulino, 1978) p. 88.

The changes that have occurred in the structures of industrial countries have meant that discontent, previously spread over various sectors, has come to be focused on the banking system. When growing expenditure is financed by increasing taxation, criticism is concentrated on the government; when, however, it is financed by channelling a greater amount of credit to the public sector at the expense of the private sector, the blame is directed at the banks, that is, the institutions that have to turn down private demand. Something similar happens when the contraction of profits obliges businesses to raise a larger volume of funds through long- and short-term credit.

According to the Marxist–Leninist theory, the financing of investment through capital accumulation by enterprises is a manifestation of oppression by the middle classes, which the working classes should oppose. However, the authors of the survey on the Italian banking system to which I referred earlier maintain that the greater dependence of enterprises on bank financing increases the latter's hegemony and raises problems of distribution of power similar to those raised by self-financing. Criticism is shifting from the excessive power of business to the excessive power of the banks.

Extension of the banks' realm of influence, excessive power of the public enterprises, increasing exercise by the public authorities of their power of coercion in the financial sphere; but, on the other hand we can also say increasing subordination of the banks to the political authorities, of these to the large public enterprises, and of the latter to the banks. The main feature of this chain of dependence is that the sum of the losses of power is greater than that of the gains. It is the whole system that is progressively losing its capacity to control itself, to direct its own course of development and – ultimately – to govern its own future.

In most industrial countries there seems to be a consensus on the advantages of directing economic activity according to a basic plan. Even in the USA politicians from both parties in Congress have tabled a draft law to this effect. In Italy advocates of planning say that a selective credit policy is an essential prerequisite for putting it into effect; the banks in general are reproached for not having applied a selective-credit policy; often the accusations come from those complaining that too much credit has been granted to the next man rather than to themselves. In this case the charges laid at the door of the banking system are basically due to the fact that it is required to do what is really the duty of others; it seems to me that the planning of economic activity, if it has to be, should be the responsibility of authorities who have to answer for their actions to democratically elected assemblies.

In international relations the banks of some countries are accused of promoting capital exports and those of others of doing the reverse. We are again faced with the consequences of the authorities' inability to pursue the desired goals of economic and monetary policy and an attempt to delegate the task to the banks. In periods of social and political unrest, if governments wish to continue giving priority to the objective of maintaining communication between their economies, they must accept that funds will move from countries considered to be less stable to those considered to be more stable. Compensatory intervention would certainly be possible, neutralising the effects of inflows and outflows; guidelines to this effect have been issued within the European Economic Community. But the whole body of provisions aimed at curbing outflows and inflows of capital by means of restrictions – often tried, always without success – does not reflect the ideals on which the Community is based.

During the nineteenth century, banks carried out their activities surrounded by an aura of great respect. Even then, however, irreverent voices were raised, such as that of the author of *Alice in Wonderland*, who portrays a banker's clerk thus:

> He thought he saw a banker's clerk
> Descending from the bus.
> He looked again and found it was
> A hippopotamus.
> 'If this should stay to dine', he said,
> 'There won't be much for us.'

None the less, I think that nowadays it is possible to dine with a banker without fear of his taking it all. . . .

POSTSCRIPT (JUNE 1983)

On 12 June 1976 I had the honour to deliver a lecture at the Per Jacobsson Foundation under the title: 'Why Banks are Unpopular', now reproduced here. Seven years on, I would like to comment on three statements made then. The statements are:

> . . . the international monetary system has evolved along different paths from those mapped out by the reformers: the process of international liquidity creation has indeed been divorced from gold production or changes in gold price, but it has become exclusively

dependent on the supply of reserve currencies to the system and, in particular, that reserve currency which is its pivot: the US dollar (pp. 217–18).

The banking system played a large part in this process, contributing to the creation of international liquidity through the expansion of credit (p. 218).

. . . transfers of funds from one bank to another and from the banking system as a whole to the market for government securities could produce a liquidity crisis which only the intervention of a lender of last resort would be able to resolve. Under the floating exchange-rate regime, shifts of funds from the Euromarket to national markets and vice-versa would be reflected in exchange-rate fluctuations which, in the absence of coordinated interventions by central banks could assume such proportions as to disrupt international trade (p. 217).

We solemnise this year the tenth anniversary of the floating exchange-rate system. The experience has demonstrated that:

1. the need for foreign exchange reserves has not decreased, it has increased;
2. the expansion of foreign exchange reserves occurred to a very large extent outside the control of the IMF;
3. the importance of the dollar as a reserve currency declined but the dollar still represents three-quarters of the foreign exchange reserves;
4. the extension of central banks' interventions in the foreign exchange markets has been much greater than it was under the fixed exchange-rate system;
5. the amplitude of exchange-rate swings has increased and has brought about deviations from purchasing power parities in the four major currencies covering extended periods.

The floating system had been advocated on the ground that it would release domestic policies from external constraints and would preserve free flows of goods and services. In fact, to the extent that it allows strong depreciation or strong appreciation of real exchange rates, it is imposing constraints on the freedom of policy-makers.

Countries experiencing strong appreciation of real exchange rates, that is, deterioration of international competitiveness, become fertile ground for protectionist pressures. Two reasons of the volatility of the exchange rates can be mentioned:

- the mass of mobile money ready and free to move from one currency into another is so enormously greater than it was, not only in absolute terms, but certainly also in relation to the funds of national and international monetary authorities which might be available to offset such movements;
- inflation in the main industrial countries has been much faster over the past ten years or so than during the previous twenty five. Higher rates of inflation have been accompanied by greater differences between rates in different countries.

Under such conditions a return to a fixed rate system appears neither feasible nor desirable; however, a higher degree of concerted action between the monetary authorities of the three major currency areas: USA, European Economic Community, Japan, is feasible and desirable, with a view to counteracting what they would consider unnecessary and harmful deviations from the long-run equilibrium rates. The exchange market behaves as an asset market and, as in all asset markets, exchange-rate determination is dominated by expectations and the authorities should and could correct expectations.

The counter-argument is: why should the authorities succeed where market participants failed? The answers are:

- the authorities are in possession of more information on the course of their own policies and on the techniques to reach their policy objectives;
- the authorities can and perhaps should take risks that private market participants are right to avoid.

What is required while making progress in policy convergence is an improvement of the working of the current floating system, which lacks calculability and dependability and invites economic nationalism and speculation.

12 Central Banks as Regulators and Lenders of Last Resort in an International Context: A View from the United States*

Henry C. Wallich

The term 'lender of last resort' implies a degree of specificity that goes beyond what that function can legitimately claim. I have never seen, in visits to central banks, a door marked 'lender-of-last-resort department,' nor met a vice-president in charge of such an activity.

It is true that there are situations in which the function of a central bank is properly described as lender of last resort. It is true also that a market looks to a lender of last resort, functions better when it knows that there is one, and will try to push some existing institution into that role if none has been appointed by higher authority.

At the same time, markets as well as central bankers know that it is unwise to hoist crisis signals before the condition becomes obvious. Neither market stability nor the credit standing of particular institutions have much to gain from the widespread advertising of a lender-of-last-resort operation. But since concealment is also not an acceptable policy, the part of wisdom often has been not to draw a finer line than circumstances require between what is last resort and what is not. The discussion of last-resort matters will deal for the most part with Federal Reserve activities and powers.

This chapter was originally presented as an address to the Bald Peak Conference on Key Issues in International Banking (sponsored by the Federal Reserve Bank of Boston), at Melvin Village, New Hampshire, on 6 October 1977, and was subsequently published in *Monetary Policy and Practice* (Lexington, Massachusetts: Heath, 1982).

FEDERAL RESERVE POWERS

To meet its lender-of-last-resort responsibilities, the Federal Reserve has a variety of powers that reflect, at least in some measure, the variety of cases that may call these responsibilities into action. For a generalised lack of liquidity, open-market powers and the ordinary facilities of the discount window are appropriate. A generalised lack of liquidity has been the characteristic feature of some historic crises that were met by central banks and, in line with Bagehot's rule, were dealt with by lending freely at a high rate. These crises sometimes focused on the failure or near-failure of some major firm, whereas in others there was no obvious single focus. The common denominator, however, was that firms perfectly solvent and under ordinary circumstances liquid, both banks and non-banks, were unable to obtain short-term credit at almost any price. The famous British crises of 1867 – Overend Gurney – and 1890 – Baring Brothers – as well as the US panic of 1907 were of that character. The last-named experience finally led to the creation of the Federal Reserve.

A potential crisis of this same type that was successfully forestalled by lender-of-last-resort action was the Penn Central failure in 1970. At that time it appeared that this failure might interfere with the rollover of commercial paper by certain finance companies.

The Federal Reserve assisted a shift of finance-company debt to the banks – both by granting liberalised discount-window credit to the particular banks involved (under the emergency provisions of Regulation A) and by suspending the Regulation Q ceiling on thirty- to eighty-nine-day Certificates of Deposit (CDs), enabling such banks to raise funds through the market.[1] These System initiatives provided needed reassurance to the financial community and helped to halt the general scramble of commercial-paper investors for higher-quality assets. At the height of the crisis, special System advances to facilitate transfers out of commercial paper rose to about $500m, but by early autumn these had been largely repaid.

The specialised emergency-lending powers of the Federal Reserve are appropriate particularly for the case where illiquidity focuses on a particular institution without spreading to the rest of the market. Here the Federal Reserve can supply credit to member banks for maturities of not more than four months and where the credit is secured to the Reserve Bank's satisfaction, at a rate at least one-half per cent above the discount rate if the collateral offered is not eligible for discounting at the regular rate. For others (that is, individuals partnerships, and corporations that are not member banks) the Fedeal Reserve can, in unusual and exigent circumstances, by the affirmative vote of not less than five members of the Federal Reserve Board, provide emergency credit. Rates on such credit would be set by the Board of Governors at the time credit was granted. To qualify for such credit, the party in liquidity straits must be unable to secure adequate credit from other banking institutions.

The foregoing provisions provide broad powers to deal with liquidity problems of particular institutions. It should be noted, however, that all types of discounts and advances must be secured by assets and in the manner specified in the Act and the regulations or 'to the satisfaction of the Federal Reserve Bank,' that is, to the satisfaction of the directors of the Federal Reserve Bank making the loan. The requirement that Federal Reserve credit must be secured has meant, in terms of the Board's policies to date, that Federal Reserve lending to any bank can continue only so long as that bank is solvent; the reason for the Board's view has been that collateral obtained from a bank in a state of insolvency might be exposed to legal challenge. Reasonable questions can be asked as to whether insistence on solvency, a criterion which at critical times may be very difficult to apply, really best serves the public interest. Nevertheless the following discussion rests on the policies that are in effect with regard to the solvency issue.

ILLIQUIDITY VERSUS INSOLVENCY

Power to deal with insolvency situations is in the hands of the Federal Deposit Insurance Corporation (FDIC). The FDIC, as insurer, can accept a loss. Frequently the FDIC finds it less costly to deal with an insolvency by subsidising a merger or arranging the transfer of the deposits and the sound part of the assets to another bank through a 'purchase-and-assumption' operation, rather than to pay off the insured depositors and liquidate the closed bank. Considerations relating to the welfare of the local community also apply in decisions as to whether a bank should be saved or wound up.

This dualism of functions and powers between the Federal Reserve and the FDIC is neater, to be sure, than the real world, in which illiquidity and insolvency may in some cases be separable and in other cases may merge. A bank or any other firm may be illiquid but not insolvent. Nevertheless, if illiquidity leads to a run and to the liquidation of assets at distress prices, insolvency may follow. Likewise, an institution may be insolvent but not illiquid. However, as soon as this situation is diagnosed, the bank is likely to be closed by the regulatory authorities to protect the creditors.

An institutional division of different types of rescue functions, such as exists in the USA, prevails only in a limited number of countries. Elsewhere, the central banks as lender of last resort may find it necessary to deal with the distinction between illiquidity and insolvency in a more *ad hoc* manner.

Interaction of illiquidity and insolvency as it is at present interpreted is well illustrated by the case of Franklin National Bank. While the Comptroller of the Currency had declared Franklin to be solvent, the Federal Reserve loaned Franklin, on a secured basis, up to about $1.7 milliard. When solvency could no longer be assured, Franklin, under the auspices of the FDIC, was taken over by the bank that had put in the highest bid, and the FDIC took over the Federal Reserve loan and that part of the assets not going to the merging bank.

The question is sometimes raised whether banks should be allowed to fail. That is not a meaningful issue. Even the most intensive supervision cannot make sure that no bank will ever suffer losses large enough to wipe out its capital. As far as the stockholders and management are concerned, the bank has then failed. The real question is whether the depositors and other creditors, and in a broader sense the monetary system and borrowers dependent on their banking connection, should be allowed to suffer the consequences. The answer may well have to depend on such circumstances as the availability of alternative sources of credit in particular regions or local communities. Giving too much advance assurance to management, stockholders, and depositors risks losing some of the discipline of the market on which regulators rely to some extent to keep banks 'in line.' Proponents of 100-per cent liability insurance must keep this in mind. So must lenders of last resort. In this imperfect world, perfect safety is not an ideal condition. Regulators, central bankers, and insurers would soon find the odds they have created being exploited against them. In response, they might find themselves driven to regulate and supervise bank operations to a degree inconsistent with the free flow of credit.

INTERNATIONAL ASPECTS

The growing internationalisation of banking adds new dimensions to regulatory and lender-of-last-resort responsibilities. National legislations, regulations, and supervisory practices differ widely among countries. Nobody would dream of trying to co-ordinate laws and practices internationally, but increasing regulatory co-operation is possible, and considerable progress has been made. Regulators meet regularly, under the auspices of the Bank for International Settlements (BIS) and otherwise. The result has been a better understanding of one another's problems and interests, as well as co-operative policies with respect to particular issues.

The matrix of international banking relationships has been expanded as a result not only of the growth of old-established national markets but also through the appearance of new banking centres, frequently referred to as off-shore centres. As regards regulation, practices among these centres range widely from technically competent and tight regulation and supervision to virtual non-existence of such efforts. As far as lender-of-last-resort facilities are concerned, it is, of course, very difficult and often impossible for small political entities to exert such a function.

Accordingly, bank regulators and lenders of last resort will find themselves involved in different degree in the activities of their banks abroad. In the case of the USA, the foreign activities of banks and bank holding companies are closely supervised. Bank holding companies and banks need the approval of the Federal Reserve for foreign acquisitions and branches and with regard to the nature of the activities conducted overseas. Foreign branches are examined by the Comptroller of the Currency and the Federal Reserve, except in a limited number of countries where national laws bar such access. Where regulatory and supervisory laws and institutions exist, as is the case in all countries with significant domestic banking activity, it is, of course, the national authority that is the primary regulator and supervisor within its borders. Because of the special characteristic of American bank examination, which focuses on appraising the quality of assets in a way few other supervisory systems do, reliance on local banking authorities for the direct supervision of foreign branches and subsidiaries has not yet occurred.

International banking also raises the question of lender-of-last-resort responsibility. Today, that responsibility is exercised in a framework of floating exchange rates. This eliminates one of the problems that has beset lending of last resort and that has led to probably the most spectacular failures to live up to that responsibility. I would count among those failures the unwillingness of the Reichsbank to go to the aid of its banking system in 1931 and the failure of the Federal Reserve to deal with the mass failures of

American banks during the depression of the 1930s. In both cases, the constraints of the gold standard impeded, by the lights of those days, action that might have forestalled the respective crises. I would not, today, belittle the very real concerns of those who had to make traumatic decisions in those days. The Reichsbank feared that Germany's international credit would be destroyed if it violated its 40 per cent gold-cover requirement. The Federal Reserve had no means of knowing that the Supreme Court would some day invalidate the gold clause and in that way avoid the consequences, for many borrowers, of a departure from gold. Nor would I argue that all the superior wisdom is on the side of our days. We have not done well enough in managing paper-money to be able to claim that. In any event, today we do not operate under the constraints that, forty-five years ago, helped to produce major financial failures.

The multiplicity of possibilities and national circumstances makes it obvious that no general rule can be established for a particular course of action in case of a banking crisis that was not of purely local character. The problem, if it were to arise, could be market-wide or focused on a single institution. It could be a problem of liquidity, or solvency, or of both. It could occur in a market with a strong central bank and regulatory system or in a centre where neither exists. It could focus on the home currency or on the dollar and other currencies.

The need for concerted action in such a case nevertheless was recognised by the central bankers who meet monthly at the BIS in Basle. After careful examination of the issues, the central bankers arrived at the same conclusion that I have just indicated: that detailed rules and procedures could not be laid down in advance. But since considerable concern existed at that time about the state of the Eurocurrency markets, the following statement was issued: 'The Governors . . . had an exchange of views on the problem of the lender of last resort in the Euromarkets. They recognised that it would not be practical to lay down in advance detailed rules and procedures for the provision of temporary liquidity. But they were satisfied that means are available for that purpose and will be used if and when necessary.'

This approach reflects the experience also that the Federal Reserve has had in handling its own lender-of-last-resort responsibility. There are dangers in defining and publicising specific rules for emergency assistance to troubled banks, notably the possibility of causing undue reliance on such facilities and possible relaxation of needed caution on the part of all market participants. The Federal Reserve has always avoided comprehensive statements of conditions for its assistance to member banks. Emergency assistance is inherently a process of negotiation and judgement, with a range of possible actions varying with certain circumstances and need. Therefore, a predetermined set of conditions for emergency lending would be inappropriate.

In the international field, extensive discussions of the role of host and home-country central banks for extensions of emergency assistance to subsidiary and multinational financial institutions have produced a common understanding of the problem. Co-operation among central banks is clearly necessary. No central bank can avoid some degree of responsibility for events in its market. No central bank can disinterest itself in the international activities of the banks for which it is responsible at home.

An important aspect of the close co-operation among central bankers and other regulators is being implemented through central bankers' meetings at Basle and through a regulators' committee that meets periodically at other times. There can be no question, of course, of making national legislation homogeneous. The differences are too deeply rooted for that. What is possible is to develop a close understanding of the expectations, intentions, and *modi operandi* of different countries and to make them mesh. Institutions like those under the aegis of the BIS are making this happen.

CO-OPERATION

Co-operation is particularly important where the supervisory and lender-of-last-resort responsibilities are different. Countries meet in one market increasingly frequently because of the internationalisation of banking. As far as regulation is concerned, the role of the local regulator, in most cases the central bank, under present conditions is bound to be major. The local regulator charters and supervises foreign subsidiaries and joint ventures, and, where local legislation so provides, examines them. Foreign supervisors and regulators, have different degrees of access to local offices of branches, subsidiaries, and joint ventures of banks and bank holding companies of their own countries, depending on local legislation.

Under these circumstances, the local regulatory authority inevitably has a concern with any problems of liquidity and solvency of banks under its jurisdiction. The financial resolution of both types of problems, of course, is in the first instance a concern of the parent organisation. For branches this goes without saying, since they are an integral part of a banking organisation. For wholly-owned subsidiaries, parents have historically demonstrated a strong sense of responsibility. Banks do not cast their foreign operations in the form of subsidiaries rather than branches to take advantage of limited liability. Nor would such subsidiaries be able to operate on a large scale if the market suspected that in case of trouble the parent would walk away from them. These foreign operations are cast in the form of subsidiaries rather than of branches principally because in that form they enjoy broader powers, better tax status, and greater operating flexibility.

Parents, therefore, expect to back their subsidiaries, even though ultimately that must be a business decision and, where the regulatory framework so provides, a decision of the regulatory authorities of the parents as well as, of course, of the host-country regulator. This is one of the reasons for the Federal Reserve's requirements that adequate financial data for both branches and subsidiaries abroad be kept and made available to examiners in the USA.

As far as American banks are concerned, the great bulk of foreign operations, in dollar terms, is carried out through branches. Subsidiaries typically are small relative to the size of their parents, and usually well capitalised (except in the special case of shell organisations). Minority participants, accompanied by a management interest, so-called joint ventures, are usually those of large banks, which historically have shown readiness to back their offspring, although they may want to limit their support to their own share in the venture. The Federal Reserve, in an interpretation issued in 1976 has made clear that for American banks, which by law must obtain Board approval for this as any other type of acquisition, the Board would take into account the ability of the applicant to support more than its own share in a joint venture. The Board also said that it would give great weight to the potential risks in cases where the joint venture was closely identified with its American parent by name or through managerial relationships.

EVOLVING ROLE OF THE IMF

Since this chapter has been burdened by much technical detail, I would like to conclude by taking a broader and more evolutionary look at the lender-of-last-resort problem. It has often been pointed out that the function of the International Monetary Fund in helping countries in balance-of-payments difficulties has some of the characteristics of a lender-of-last-resort operation. In time, this role of the IMF may expand. It is important to note where the similarities and the differences are likely to manifest themselves.

Central-bank lending to money markets for particular banks in crisis conditions, and IMF lending to national governments, have in common that the objective is mainly to protect the monetary system rather than to help individual banks. Neither should engage in bail-out operations for banks.

The Fund's ability to help countries with balance-of-payments problems, however, depends on the willingness of the borrowing country to meet the Fund's policy conditions. It is not an unconditional form of assistance. For that reason, banks that have lent to a country cannot take for granted that the Fund will come to that country's rescue.

An important difference between central-bank and IMF lending is that the IMF, unlike central banks, need not and should not wait for a crisis to develop. In fact, the earlier a country applies for assistance to the IMF in the upper tranches of its quota, the sooner a set of policies will be in place that should help the country overcome its difficulties. In that sense, the IMF need not be a lender of last resort.

The IMF role in imposing conditionality and guiding the policies of the borrowing country finds a counterpart in the regulatory activities of central banks. Good national policies, like sound banking policies, should reduce greatly, if not altogether eliminate, the need for lender-of-last-resort activity.

Still another difference between the lending of the IMF and the classical lender-of-last-resort operation may be noted: the Fund's normal technique is not to lend freely at a high rate, but to pay out limited funds on a phased basis after a showing that performance criteria are being met.

These differences reflect, of course, the inherent distinction between a country borrower and a money market or single bank. A country is inherently a stronger debtor, not because it controls a printing press but because adequate policies will make it possible to pay except perhaps temporarily in the direst of circumstances. A country cannot go out of business in the manner of a bank or other business enterprise. Solvency is represented by the existence of the political will to deal with economic difficulties.

Given the great potentialities of the IMF's role, its further strengthening is obviously desirable. This is currently underwa[ ] through the proposed Witteveen facility, and through quota increase[ ] already decided and still to be decided. More adequate resources wi[ ] enable the Fund not only to meet better such needs as may arise bu[ ] also to be more effective in influencing the policies of borrowin[ ] countries and in that manner enhance the willingness-to-lend of th[ ] private market. In that sense, too, the activities of the Fund coul[ ] come to constitute a parallel to those of national lenders of las[ ] resort: to create conditions of confidence in which the private marke[ ] can again function adequately.

POSTSCRIPT (MAY 1983)

This Chapter on central banks as regulators and lenders of last resor[ ] in an international context is a commentary, in part, on the statemen[ ] of 10 September 1974, that the central bankers who meet monthly a[ ] the BIS in Basle made in response to concerns prevailing at the tim[ ] about the state of the Eurocurrency markets:

> The governors . . . had an exchange of views on the problem of th[ ]
> lender of last resort in the Euromarkets. They recognised that [ ]
> would not be practical to lay down in advance detailed rules an[ ]
> procedures for the provision of temporary liquidity. But they wer[ ]
> satisfied that means were available for that purpose and will b[ ]
> used when necessary.

That statement had given rise to occasional questions of the kin[ ] that, as the governors indicated, could not be answered in advance[ ] The chapter examines some of the reasons why detailed rules an[ ] procedures for the provision of temporary liquidity cannot be pr[ ] vided. It also notes that extensive discussions of the roles of host- an[ ] home-country central banks have produced a common understandin[ ] of the problem. It points out that the host authorities have a[ ] inevitable concern for the liquidity and solvency of all bankin[ ] operations in their jurisdiction, whatever the organisational form [ ] such operations. At the same time, the financial resolution of prob[ ] lems occurring at internationally active banking institutions is, in th[ ] first instance, the concern of the parent commercial bank. It co[ ] cludes that co-operation among central banks is clearly necessar[ ] and that no central bank can avoid some degree of responsibility f[ ] events in its market nor disinterest itself in the international activities of the banks for which it is responsible at home.

It should be noted that the nature of co-operation and of sharing roles among central banks in a lender-of-last-resort situation is not necessarily identical with that laid down in some detail for supervisory matters in the 'Concordat' adopted in 1975 by the central bank governors meeting in Basle. The Concordat deals with allocation of supervisory responsibility among national regulators of branches, subsidiaries, and joint ventures of international banks. It reflects the principle that, as far as possible, no banking institution or part thereof anywhere in the world should remain unsupervised. The lender-of-last-resort function, which potentially involves the commitment of substantial amounts of money, differs from the regulatory function. It is quite generally a central-bank function, whereas the supervisory function in some countries is at least partly in the hands of a government agency other than the central bank.

The question who should initiate action in case of a liquidity problem affecting a part of an internationally-active banking organisation is in some respects similar, however, to the question of allocation of supervisory responsibility. Some sharing of responsibility between host and parent central bank is to be anticipated and the principle of parental responsibility is likely to play a role. In addition, the allocation of supervisory and lender-of-last-resort functions is essentially unrelated to the currency in which the operations of a bank in a particular jurisdiction are primarily conducted.

Some of the broader issues of lender-of-last-resort activity are also examined. Among others, it treats the role of the IMF as a lender to countries and discusses some of the similarities and differences between that role and the lender-of-last-resort function. Recently, central banks have supplemented the IMF's role by supplying bridging finance to certain developing countries in payments difficulties. While differing from support to banks provided under usual lender-of-last-resort arrangements, such assistance has some characteristics in common with conventional procedures. In the light of experience gained in these operations, the statement of the central bankers that a precise procedure cannot be laid down in advance seems to stand up well.

Since this chapter was written, international financial activity has vastly expanded in both volume and scope. International banking operations, in particular, have been extended into new markets and embraced by banks previously mainly domestic in character. The pace of change in international banking activity has further re emphasised the impracticality of fixed rules and procedures governing liquidity assistance from central banks.

Note

1. Under section 201.2(e) of Regulation A: 'Federal Reserve credit i available to assist member banks in unusual and exigent circumstance such as may result from national, regional, or local difficulties, or from exceptional circumstances involving only a particular member bank.'

Part IV
The International
Dimensions of Central
Banking

Part IV

13 The International Capital Market and the International Monetary System*

Erik Hoffmeyer

In this chapter I shall discuss three main problems. The first concerns the breakdown of the Bretton Woods system – the fixed-rate system or adjustable-peg system. In order to understand the forces now at work, I think it is necessary to have a clear notion of why the old system was abandoned.

The second concerns the structure of the present system including the basic features of monetary integration and the exchange rate system. It goes without saying that the offshore monetary system (I use offshore in the broad sense including all monetary transactions outside the country of the currency) will be discussed in some detail as its role is often misinterpreted.

The third deals with the problem of stability, which, of course, is essential for the functioning of the system and thereby its chance of survival, which then again leads to the question of a possible strengthening of the system or the establishment of a substitute.

WHY WAS THE BRETTON WOODS SYSTEM ABANDONED?

It is a well-known fact that the Bretton Woods system was based on the philosophy that the mistakes of the 1930s should be avoided. During the Great Depression economic warfare was characterised by

*This chapter was originally presented under the same title as a comment to the 1978 Per Jacobsson Lecture, given in Washington, on 25 September 1978, and was published in the same year by the Per Jacobsson Foundation, IMF, Washington.

restrictions on trade and payments and so-called competitive devaluations. It was therefore decided that restrictions on goods and services should be abolished, thereby liberalising the transactions on current account of the balance of payments.

On the other hand, the references to capital movements were meagre. In the two main plans leading to the Bretton Woods system the Keynes Plan and the White Plan, some discussion actually took place on the role of capital movements. The general idea was that some sort of restriction on capital movements was necessary. On this point Keynes especially was very clear: 'It is widely held that control of capital movements, both inward and outward, should be a permanent feature of the postwar system.' However, it was left to the individual countries to decide about capital movements.

In the final version of the Fund's Articles of Agreement, capital movements were only mentioned briefly in Article VI:

> A member may not use the Fund's resources to meet a large or sustained outflow of capital . . . and the Fund may request a member to exercise controls to prevent such use of the resources of the Fund.

Finally, regarding controls of capital transfers:

> Members may exercise such controls as are necessary to regulate international capital movements, but no member may exercise these controls in a manner which will restrict payments for current transactions or which will unduly delay transfers of funds in settlement of commitments.

In order to avoid competitive devaluations and apart from certain transitory rules, a country was allowed to change its exchange rate only if the International Monetary Fund agreed that its balance of payments was in fundamental disequilibrium. This concept, however, was never defined; but it was clearly unnecessary to do so.

The pressure for adjustment had been an old issue in international economic discussions, that is how strong should the pressure be on surplus or creditor countries compared with deficit or debtor countries. The Keynes Plan took a very clear position on that by proposing that the pressure should not be applied only to deficit countries but equally to surplus countries. Eventually, only the famous scarce currency clause was left, according to which the Fund was allowed to impose limitations on the use of a currency which had become scarce because of a country having a constant balance-of-payments surplus.

After the war, the USA took a strong leadership role in building an international trade and payments system based on market forces. This however, was, not done primarily via the IMF but via a special aid programme to Western Europe and the establishment of the Organisation for European Economic Co-operation (OEEC) – later the Organisation for Economic Co-operation and Development (OECD).

In a way there were two phases in this liberalising process. The first phase was the most difficult. It concerned the liberalisation of goods and services, which included a lot of bargaining among the participating countries, but eventually it gathered momentum and, to all intents and purposes, it was brought to a successful conclusion by the introduction of convertibility at the end of 1958. Production had been integrated among the member-states in such a way that market forces in principle determined the location, magnitude, and trade of production. By historical standards this was indeed an impressive achievement obtained in less than ten years.

The second phase concerned the liberalisation of capital movements, first and foremost, credit connected with trade and direct investments, whereas portfolio capital movements were not included among the obligatory commitments. The liberalisation of capital movements was far less dramatic than for goods and services. To a large extent it was a natural consequence that free trade gradually included trade credit. The two phases overlapped, but the impact of freer capital movements was felt particularly in the 1960s. It implied a far-reaching monetary integration among the member-states, which meant that the degree of national monetary independence was drastically curtailed.

It became quickly perceptible in a country like my own. If we wanted to restrict monetary policy by reducing the money supply and increasing interest rates, a large part of the effect was offset by private sector borrowing abroad. Similarly, it was obvious that the market mechanism put stronger and stronger pressure on exchange rates that were not credible.

The exchange crises became bigger and bigger in the late 1960s, and much to the chagrin of many central bankers, politicians got more and more involved in the negotiations to solve the crises. I only have to mention March 1968 (the dissolution of the gold pool and the partial abolition of the convertibility of the dollar into gold), August

1971 (the final termination of the dollar–gold convertibility), and December 1971 (the Smithsonian Agreement).

In particular the last-named event may be considered as a rear-guard battle to save the Bretton Woods system of fixed rates. It was hailed as a historical event, because it was the first time in monetary history that a comprehensive exchange-rate adjustment had been negotiated. But, in little more than one year, the system was abandoned.

Whereas the trade integration process ended with convertibility of currencies, the monetary integration process ended with the abandonment of the fixed-rate system.

Having participated in some of the negotiations and read and listened to reports of other meetings, I do not find it reasonable to argue that it was a deliberate decision taken by the authorities to abandon the old system. I would rather say that market forces were too strong to be handled by the authorities. It was a struggle between politicians and the market forces – let loose by the politicians – and the market forces won.

It was quite clear that the authorities were not willing to adjust exchange rates sufficiently – with the advantage of hindsight, the size of adjustments in the Smithsonian Agreement could have been doubled – and they did not have the imagination to foresee the amount of exchange market intervention that was necessary to defend the decisions taken. This is one example of authorities underestimating the severity of realities.

Consequently, my contention is that the unwillingness of authorities to adjust to realities was the main factor causing the breakdown of the Bretton Woods system and that monetary integration based on market forces was instrumental in this respect.

Many seem to feel some nostalgia toward the old system. I do not. I think it is far too dangerous to have a system that is as unstable as the old one. The instability came mainly from the confrontation between the market-oriented trade and monetary integration on the one hand and the unwillingness of authorities to undertake the necessary adjustments on the other hand. You cannot play a game with different rules for the various participants.

THE STRUCTURE OF THE PRESENT SYSTEM

I have put so much weight on the confrontation between monetary integration and the exchange-rate system that it seems natural to follow the same pattern when describing the present structure.

Whereas there is a fairly high common degree of freedom for capital movements in the dominant countries – in particular regarding credit connected with current account transactions and direct investments – there are substantial differences regarding portfolio capital movements. Some countries have restrictions on inward movements in order to avoid becoming reserve countries (the Federal Republic of Germany, Switzerland, and Japan) and to try to maintain monetary independence. Other countries have restrictions on outgoing movements in order to prevent reserve losses and possible capital flight (for example, the UK, France, Italy, and the Scandinavian countries). The USA has, since January 1974, reintroduced freedom for capital movements in both directions. Finally, here are the so-called offshore markets which essentially are money and capital markets where transactions are conducted in currencies other than the currency of the country concerned. The largest market is the much debated Eurodollar market with dollar-borrowing and lending outside the USA.

The offshore markets are characterised by very few, if any, restrictions, much to the dismay of many authorities. The function and role of these markets has created much confusion during the past fifteen years, although quite a number of important studies have been published.

There is an increasing tendency to stress the line of presentation which has recently been given by Professor R. Aliber in a very clear way. I shall give a brief outline of this kind of reasoning. As regards long-term capital transactions, throughout history it has been quite usual for loans to be expressed in a currency unit that is external to the national system. Such transactions do not present special problems for the analysis of monetary integration.

However, things are different regarding banking operations. If a bank receives a deposit in a foreign currency, for example, a bank in London receives a dollar deposit, this deposit is ordinarily treated as an external affair by the local monetary authorities and similarly by the US monetary authorities. It is a monetary transaction in no-man's land and therefore suspect from the point of view of national monetary authorities. But, if a bank has a demand-deposit or a time-deposit obligation, it is necessary at the same time to be certain that cash can be provided if necessary. This means that deposits with offshore banks must, in the end, have a relation to the money base in the country of issue.

There has been a long and animated discussion about the money multiplier of the offshore banking systems. This is probably not a

relevant question any more than you can ask for a separate mone
multiplier for banks on Fifth Avenue in New York, or in the souther
part of California.

Insofar as reserves held voluntarily by offshore banks are propor
tionally less than required reserves in the USA, the composite mone
multiplier becomes fractionally larger than the national US mone
multiplier. What is more important is that these markets work a
catalysts for international monetary integration. This role of th
market was underlined two years ago by Helmut Mayer of the Ban
for International Settlements (BIS) in an article which clearly demon
strated how significant a part of the gross figures of the Eurocurrenc
market was accounted for by inter-bank positions. Only a tiny frac
tion of the net size estimated by the BIS would have to be added t
the narrowly defined world money stock (M_1) and about 25 per cer
to the other world monetary aggregates, making up a very small pa
of the total world money supply. This, however, is not equivalent t
reducing the role of the Eurocurrency market to this small percen
age, but to stressing the nature of the market as an important channe
for money and capital flows.

This integration of national and international capital markets ha
important implications for the effects of policy actions in the sens
that whenever there are restrictions of some sort or another, thes
will tend to be offset if possible by the unregulated offshore markets

This point is very clearly illustrated by the development of th
Eurodollar market, which took place in the light of restrictions o
international capital movements and the ceiling on the rate of intere
(Regulation Q) in the USA. The introduction of the Interest Equal
zation Tax in 1963 and the Foreign Direct Investment Program i
1965, as well as the curtailing of the US commercial banks' shor
term lending in 1965, gave a strong impetus to the development o
the Eurodollar market. The market developed in countries like th
UK which had the fewest restrictions on international banking tran
actions.

There is no mystery. It is simply a consequence of a law that is ju
as important as Gresham's, namely, that financial transactions ten
to take place where restrictions are least. I think it is a gener
experience in the international financial system that transactions ma
originate from national or offshore institutions. The effects are iden
ical and substitution is easy.

My main point is that the monetary integration which developed the 1960s and was instrumental in changing the fixed exchange-rate system is still dominating the exchange markets and that the offshore markets make this dominance stronger. The road from the Smithsonian Agreement to general floating will undoubtedly become a central issue in future analysis of international monetary problems.

From an official point of view it has proved to be impossible to negotiate a so-called symmetrical system. Leading non-US countries wanted the USA to undertake a commitment to make the dollar convertible into another asset, for example, SDRs, implying that the USA had in effect the same obligations as other countries. This would obviously have diminished the role of the dollar as a reserve currency. The US answer was that symmetry must include not only a convertibility commitment but also a commitment to adjust either the exchange-rate or internal economic policy if certain economic indicators, such as reserve positions, showed signs of disequilibrium.

It was the old unsettled issue of the degree of pressure on surplus countries (now the Federal Republic of Germany and Japan) versus pressure on deficit countries, which now, more often than not, include the USA. As might be expected, it was impossible to negotiate such a treaty and future historians may well express doubts as to the sincerity of the wish to reach a successful conclusion to the negotiations.

Be that as it may, the outcome was a system of more or less managed floating among the most important currencies, whereas small countries, for well-known reasons, as a rule chose to link their currencies to one of the major currencies, the SDR, or some other composite unit. It is not necessary in this connection to go into detail about the degree of management of the floating system, the willingness to intervene, the need for reserves, and the degree of monetary independence. This is dealt with in the Fund's Annual Report.

I think the major point is that the impact of market forces is such that we now have a more symmetrical system in the sense that pressures through exchange-rate adjustment concern deficit and surplus countries equally. On the other hand, the symmetry does not apply to economic policy. Recent developments have shown that deflationary policies in many deficit countries have not been accompanied by correspondingly expansionary policies in surplus countries. I know very well that it is widely felt that the dollar, as the leading reserve currency, is in a special position and that pressure for economic adjustment is not so strong as on other currencies.

I wonder, however, whether this is true to the same extent as before. In the old days under the fixed-rate system with little pressure on surplus countries, the USA could finance a deficit without difficulties; but today things are different. Neither the USA, nor Japan, nor the Federal Republic of Germany have an obligation to intervene in the exchange markets, and US monetary policy cannot any longer be independent of the exchange rate of the dollar. As has been demonstrated recently, market reactions are quite strong, and the decline of the dollar is so big, that it is safe to say that benign neglect belongs to the past. At any rate, the word 'benign' should be omitted, because neglect is costly as has been proved by recent US monetary policy measures.

Even though we have a mixed system regarding both the degree of monetary integration and the degree of management of floating, I think that the present system is more coherent than the old one. But this does not necessarily mean that it fulfils the necessary stability conditions.

PROBLEMS OF STABILITY

It is extremely difficult to present a satisfactory analysis of the stability of the present system. One often has a feeling that it should be lawyers rather than economists who present the arguments. The criteria used are subjective, the concepts are unclear, and the statistical material is unreliable. Nevertheless, it is necessary to evaluate the performance of the present system in this respect.

What are the tasks assigned to the system? The system must be flexible in order to absorb shocks but, at the same time, it must support forces that work for stable development. There are particularly three aspects. The first concerns financing. Deficits should be financed but not so easily that the adjustment process is not set in motion. The second concerns the role played by exchange rates. The adjustment process should be influenced by changes in exchange rates but not so much that too-strong demands for protection (surplus countries) or too-strong inflationary pressures (deficit countries) are generated. The third concerns economic policy actions. Pressure should be exerted via movements of exchange rates or foreign exchange reserves on political authorities to change economic policies but neither deflation nor inflation should be created. Let us take these three aspects one after another.

Table 13.1 **Current account balance of payments of selected countries,
1974–8** *(in milliards of US dollars)*

	1974	1975	1976	1977	1978	Total
OPEC	61	29	39	34	19	182
OECD, hard-core surplus countries[1]	8	8	14	18	29	77
OECD deficit countries	–41	–14	–39	–50	–46	–190
Non-oil developing countries	–24	–40	–27	–27	–38	–156
Other	–10	–18	–13	–11	–10	– 62

[1]The Belgian–Luxembourg Economic Union, the Federal Republic of Germany, Japan, the Netherlands, and Switzerland.

Financing the deficits

The role of capital movements has been discussed extensively in the economic literature. Some have analysed so-called autonomous capital movements from one country to another and the economic mechanisms that determine the real absorption or transfer of resources between two areas. Others have been more interested in the fact that differences in economic performance – growth and inflation – create deficits and surpluses between countries and consequently a need for counterbalancing finance. The basic problem here is more political in the sense that financing is necessary in order to keep the system flexible; but there should be pressure on authorities to introduce corrective policy measures. This raises the big issue of the degree of conditionality of international lending.

The system should be shockproof but not so flexible that it is instrumental in creating instability. It can also be formulated very simply that it should neither be too difficult nor too easy to borrow. Irrespective of how it is formulated, it does not lend itself to precise interpretation.

In the period 1973–8 the international payments system has certainly been exposed to shocks: first and foremost the oil price increase in 1973 and later, large discrepancies in growth and inflation rates. Figures for the current account of the balance of payments for certain groups of countries are given in Table 13.1.

It appears that the accumulated surpluses of these country groups over the five-year period have been approximately $260 milliard and the deficits approximately $410 milliard. The discrepancy between surpluses of $260 milliard and deficits of $410 milliard represents quite a substantial margin of error, even though it is small compared with the total trade flows. On the other hand, the amounts are enormous compared with the resources that are available under the facilities of the IMF or the abandoned OECD Financial Support Fund.

In the years 1974–7 the total identified net external lending in domestic as well as foreign currencies of banks in the Group of Ten countries, Switzerland, and foreign branches of US banks amounted to $230 milliard. In the same period registered Eurobonds and foreign issues of bonds totalled $95 milliard, that is, international bank lending and bond issues added to $325 milliard. In comparison, the net lending from the International Monetary Fund came to only $16 milliard (gross lending $23 milliard). For the present discussion, this is the relevant issue because here again we have a confrontation between the market mechanism and the authorities.

It is a plain truth that deficits of this order of magnitude could not have been financed via official channels, either national or international. Had it not been for private market financing, we would probably have been in a much more serious recession than the present one. I would not dare to assess the consequences of the alternative.

It has been a remarkable feature of recent lending that not only the industrial countries but also several larger non-oil developing countries have obtained access to the private capital markets and, indeed, to such an extent that these countries as a group have been able to build up their international reserves quite significantly, by almost $30 milliard from the beginning of 1976 to mid-1978. The credit available under the existing development aid organisations did not correspond to the increased financing requirements of these countries.

For the developing countries, however, it can be argued that it would be desirable to have an increased share of official credits carrying a longer maturity and a higher grant element than is obtainable in private credits. Most observers have a positive attitude toward the private international capital market, but many contend that it has crowded out official channels, including the IMF, to such an extent that the degree of conditionality is too low. In other words, it is too easy to borrow, which tends to maintain balance-of-payments disequilibrium and inflationary conditions.

It is very hard to establish criteria to form an opinion on this but we have seen quite a number of policy adjustments to reduce deficits on current account of countries that had no difficulties in borrowing internationally. Over the past years, the UK, France, and some smaller European countries could be mentioned. The reason has been that there are widespread political anxieties about becoming too dependent on foreign loans, and, at the same time, domestic considerations regarding inflation have played a significant role.

Besides the self-imposed adjustment by the borrowing countries, the market itself also exerts discipline. During recent years we have witnessed several situations where the private banks have denied countries access to the market and subjected the countries to the conditional borrowing of the International Monetary Fund as a prerequisite for obtaining further private credits. The question is whether the private banks are able to perform this role satisfactorily. With the knowledge I have of the conditions imposed by the market I have no serious doubts about discipline.

There are, however, serious differences of opinion in this field and many participants in the discussion have favoured some kind of regulation of the private capital market. In particular, there has been much interest in proposals about regulating the offshore markets, especially the Eurodollar market. The debate has been kept alive for many years, but must definitely be considered a blind alley.

There are, in principle, two ways in which authorities could gain control of offshore transactions. One way is to reach agreement among countries where offshore transactions take place. This would mean not only the Group of Ten countries but also the newcomers – Bahamas, Barbados, Grand Cayman, Singapore, etc. It seems, however, highly unlikely that agreement could be reached. And what would happen if some commercial banks hired a satellite and conducted bookkeeping there? Another method is to bring transactions under the control of authorities in the country of issue, for example, dollar transactions under the control of the US Federal Reserve.

However, in order that such control is not circumvented, far-reaching restrictions on payments are required with the consequence of curtailing not only the Eurodollar market but also the use of the dollar as an international currency.

Exchange-rate movements

Exchange-rate movements have an impact on relative prices of goods and services and consequently on the balance of current account. In addition, they influence the relative attractiveness of national and foreign assets and consequently the portfolio composition. These are two markets, and an equilibrium rate of exchange in one market may not necessarily be the equilibrium rate in the other market. Furthermore, short-run equilibrium rates may not be identical with long-run equilibrium rates. To complicate matters further, a vicious circle may develop in the sense that, for example, a deficit country with a higher-than-average inflation rate may experience a decline in the value of its currency, which, in turn, causes more inflation. Again, it is not possible by objective criteria to determine the degree of stability in the system.

Do market forces overshoot when exchange rates are determined, or do they hit equilibrium levels more or less accurately?

I do not consider it useful on this occasion to deal with the theoretically highly complicated interrelationships between the current account aspect (flows) versus portfolio (stock) approach, the role and determinants of expectations influencing the relation between spot and forward rates, and the interaction between exchange-rate movements and internal demand. I would like to express an opinion on the stability of the system in a more general way.

Many measures have been proposed in the current debate in order to evaluate exchange-rate movements. A common approach is to select a base period with the implicit assumption that this period represents a state of equilibrium and then correct exchange-rate movements for differences in price or cost behaviour. There are admittedly many non-price factors that affect competitiveness, for instance, product adaptability and delivery conditions. Furthermore, the balance of payments is influenced to a large extent by differences in growth rates. This means that exchange rates corrected for purchasing power differences or real effective exchange rates only give part of the answer and in several cases obviously unreasonable ones, such as when the USA and Japan are compared.

In order to illustrate my point, the calculations in Table 13.2 may be useful. Real effective exchange rates have been calculated with second quarter 1973 as basis, using unit manufacturing costs, export prices of manufactures, and consumer prices. It is a bewildering picture with particularly large discrepancies between export price and consumer price corrected exchange rates.

It can be said that exchange rates in general have moved in the right direction; but it is difficult on the basis of these calculations to judge about overshooting or interaction between exchange rate and price behaviour.

Table 13.2 **Changes in real effective exchange rates, second quarter 1973 to fourth quarter 1974**

(%)

	Adjusted for		
	Unit manufacturing costs	Export prices of manufactures	Consumer prices
USA	− 9	½	− 7½
Japan	17	−3	25½
Germany, Federal Republic	− 1½	−4	−½
Switzerland	9½	5	17
UK	0	2	− 3

A more simplistic attitude is to illustrate on the one hand the degree of floating measured by the amount of official intervention and, on the other hand, the magnitude of exchange-rate movements over short periods. The idea is that adjustment takes time and big changes over a short period can most often be considered a sign of instability, especially if the exchange rate moves in an opposite direction within a few weeks or months.

During the five years of floating, we have experienced a dramatic increase in official intervention in the exchange markets. In the first three years interventions were modest compared with the imbalance in the international economy. From early 1977 to mid-1978, official dollar intervention was in the order of magnitude of $50 milliard. The major part has been undertaken by the UK and Japan, whereas Italy, France, and the Federal Republic of Germany have bought lesser amounts of dollars. In spite of that, exchange-rate stability does not seem to have improved. But, in the absence of intervention, exchange-rate instability would probably have been more pronounced.

Exchange-rate movements have been very large since the beginning of widespread floating. For instance, three currencies – the yen, the Deutschmark, and the Swiss franc – appreciated *vis-à-vis* the US dollar by 45, 47, and 105 per cent, respectively, from March 1973 to mid-August 1978. The movements have not been smooth. In several shorter periods exchange rates have fluctuated widely in both directions. The recent exchange-rate movements have been especially abrupt, for instance, the yen appreciated 25 per cent and the Swiss franc 27 per cent in terms of the US dollar in the three months from the end of May to mid-August 1978.

It is hard to avoid the conclusion that, in spite of periods of massive intervention, there are examples of serious instability created by market forces.

Perhaps the most useful criterion for evaluating the stability performance of the system is to examine whether it has been satisfactory from a political point of view. Recent developments have demonstrated the fragility of the system. The numerous periods of instability have created demands for restrictions, trade disruptions, and investment uncertainty, just to mention some of the severe consequences.

It seems worth considering whether the exchange-rate changes during the past year and a half have not carried too large a part of the adjustment burden. Once more the experience has been that exchange-rate movements cannot do the work alone, but must be accompanied by appropriate economic policy.

Economic policy reactions

When authorities want to influence markets there is often a three-step process: declarations, market intervention, and economic policy measures.

There is sufficient experience to show that declarations, which are the easiest way out, are not impressive. Declarations are not taken at face value, to say the least. Market interventions have greater effect but, as has been shown above, instability cannot be prevented by intervention alone.

The obvious conclusion is that economic policy measures are necessary in order to convince market forces. This is an old experience and therefore not surprising, but nevertheless, one of the important truths that has to be learned by every new generation of authorities.

The IMF, which has a special educational role, has recently introduced a new concept 'the underlying balance-of-payments position' to illustrate this. An endeavour is made to show what would happen to the balance of payments of the industrial countries, if price competitiveness were maintained and a stipulated growth pattern achieved.

If such scenarios – to use a modern word – are analysed, the dire consequences of not taking policy actions become clear and, very often, seemingly unrealistic exchange rates become justified in the sense that market forces anticipate the lack of economic policy response, for example, the movements of the yen and the Deutschmark *vis-à-vis* the US dollar.

This again brings us back to the confrontation between market forces and the authorities. The authorities are always reluctant to react, which means that the stimulus from the markets may grow very strong, as has indeed been the case lately.

To some extent this awkward relation may turn into a highly dangerous race, where the authorities react to last year's market stimulus not being aware that new stimuli have superseded the previous one. An example of this is the deflationary effects of profit squeezes in countries with revaluing currencies like the Federal Republic of Germany, Japan, and Switzerland.

The inevitable conclusion is that a floating rate system does not relieve authorities of harmonising economic policy. This statement should probably be strengthened in the direction that the present floating rate system cannot be maintained unless the important countries take more seriously the obligation to harmonise economic policy.

CONCLUDING REMARKS

I have chosen the confrontation between market forces and authorities as the strategic relation in the development of the international monetary system over the thirty years up to 1978.

It was a political decision of fundamental importance to let market forces play a dominating role in the OECD area. Free market forces do not necessarily lead to optimal conditions, and there are, furthermore, many departures from the system in all countries. Nevertheless, it cannot be denied that this system has been one of the major forces behind the strong economic growth during this period.

Market forces in the form of what I have called monetary integration were let loose by the political authorities in the 1960s and some readers may feel that I have described the ensuing process as a repetition of the sorcerer's apprentice.

That was not my intention; but I think it is necessary to understand that market forces are not necessarily creating long-run equilibrium, that there are extremely complicated and delicate relationships between market forces and economic policy performance, and that it is highly dangerous to ignore them. This is particularly important when we look into the future.

We have been through a period of unprecedented growth and easy expansion until the beginning of the 1970s.

We have not experienced economic equilibrium in the past and we cannot expect it in the future. Economic equilibrium exists only in

260   *International Capital Market and Monetary System*

textbooks. But tensions in the economic system are now becoming more serious.

Let me just mention three points:

- The monetary hegemony of the USA is declining, which points in the direction of a multiple key currency system as was the case in the late nineteenth century. This will probably increase instability.
- The difficulties in combining full employment with reasonable price stability are increasingly creating serious political problems in all countries.
- The structural changes in the location of production between the old and the new industrial countries require changes of a very large order of magnitude.

Faced with these problems it is vitally important to understand the different significance of declarations, intervention, and economic policy measures. The Bretton Woods system collapsed because leading countries relied too much on declarations and intervention, but were too reluctant to apply economic policy measures. The old system was superseded by managed floating, but there is still too strong an inclination to try the easy way out by relying on declarations and intervention, which are weak instruments against market forces. The core of the problem is that exchange-rate movements should produce economic policy reactions. There is no short-cut road to stability. This is just as true of the present system of managed floating as it was of the pegged-rate system. In my opinion, this also implies that it is misleading to put a great stake on IMF surveillance over exchange-rate policy because such surveillance will probably not provoke economic policy reactions. The reason why I stress this so strongly is that the alternative to the present system is not a fixed-rate system but a return to a world of restrictions.

POSTSCRIPT (MARCH 1983)

This article was written between the first and the second oil shock; it was written after the breakdown of the Bretton Woods system but before the country risk problem became really severe.

There is a tendency among economists to disregard authorities in economic models and there is a tendency among politicians to put the blame for undesired developments on some kind of market-based conspiracy, such as speculation against currencies.

Both attitudes are deficient.

In order to understand what has happened in the international economic system I chose the confrontation between market forces and authorities as the dominant theme.

The line of reasoning is very simple. Goods and services were liberalised in the 1950s and capital movements in the 1960s. This meant that monetary integration became a dominant feature of the international system including the offshore credit markets, for example, the much-debated Eurodollar market. Monetary integration means that authorities have to undertake economic policy measures in order to secure stable conditions – declarations and market intervention are not sufficient.

My main findings are as follows:

- the Bretton Woods system broke down because authorities underestimated the severity of realities;
- the offshore markets are dependent on the national monetary systems and cannot be said to be the cause of instability;
- managed floating does not relieve authorities of the obligation to take economic policy actions in order to secure stability, which means that the transition from a fixed-rate system to floating does not change basic conditions.

Today with five more years of experience I do not think that I would have to revise my basic reasoning concerning the obligations of authorities when they have allowed a market system to develop.

14 The European Monetary System and Italian Participation

Paolo Baffi

THE EXCHANGE-RATE MECHANISM

In late 1977 and early 1978 the attempts to ensure greater exchange-rate stability between the EEC currencies were put on a new footing. The decline of the monetary Snake into a Deutschmark area, which meant that the Community had been without a clear exchange-rate policy for some time, justified renewed efforts in this field.

The Copenhagen meeting of EEC heads of state and government in April 1978 gave new impetus to the technical studies and political meetings designed to promote agreement on a common EEC policy for exchange rates and the mechanism to be used for that purpose.

The Council of Finance Ministers entrusted the EEC Governors' Committee and the Monetary Committee with the formulation of proposals and three schemes were put forward.

The first, sometimes called the 'boa' by the press, basically involved an enlargement of the existing Snake, though it provided some flexibility for the currencies that were floating at the time.

The second scheme foresaw exchange commitments being made with reference to a weighted exchange-rate index instead of a grid of bilateral nominal parities. The index to be used could be based alternatively on: (i) effective exchange rates, that is, weighted by each country's trade distribution; (ii) the European Unit of Account (EUA), the 'basket' of European currencies; or (iii) a weighted average of the Snake (or, more simply, of the Deutschmark) and the US dollar.

*'Il sistema monetario europeo e la partecipazione dell'Italia', Hearing of the Italian Senate Finance and Treasury Committee (26 October 1978), *Thema*, no. 2, 1978, pp. 7–19.

The third scheme envisaged the fixing of reference zones for the three currencies that float independently. Each zone was to be fixed in one of the ways described above. This approach differs from the other two by not involving explicit intervention commitments but only automatic consultations in the event of divergence from the goals set and a general undertaking not to take measures that would cause the exchange rate to move out of the reference zone.

All three approaches involved, either explicitly or implicitly, a common policy towards the US dollar as the most important external currency. It was also unanimously recognised that for any exchange-rate mechanism to work and promote the Community's economic objectives there would have to be a convergence of underlying economic conditions and therefore active co-ordination of national economic policies. The Community exchange system was none the less seen as making a contribution, albeit small, to this convergence through the 'announcement' and disciplinary effects on economic agents of fixing exchange rates. To reconcile the positive effects of a Community exchange system with diversified economic situations and policies, which, moreover, can only come into line towards the end of the process, all three proposals foresaw the need for simple procedures that would not give rise to controversies about changing the reference framework adopted.

At their meeting on 19 June 1978 the EEC Finance Ministers opted for a system that would;

(i)   permit all the EEC currencies to participate;
(ii) entail symmetrical obligations for surplus and deficit countries;
(iii) enable the Snake to be incorporated;
(iv) embody formal obligations to intervene in exchange markets and well-defined economic policy commitments;
(v)   help to reduce the divergences between the economies of the member countries but not prevent exchange rates from reflecting the real disparities that would remain;
(vi) not damage third currencies but rather seek greater stability between them and the European currency bloc.

At the end of its meeting at Bremen in July 1978 the European Council issued a press communiqué with an annex describing the projected European Monetary System in greater detail. The most important points in the Bremen Annex as regards the design of the exchange-rate system were:

1. the European Monetary System (EMS) was to be at least as strict as the Snake;
2. the European Currency Unit (ECU) was to be at the centre of the system;
3. in the initial stages of its operation member-countries that were not then participating in the Snake would be able to opt for wider margins around parity;
4. in principle, interventions made necessary by the system were to be made in Community currencies;
5. participating countries were to co-ordinate their exchange-rate policies towards third countries.

The apparently clear indications of the Bremen Annex soon gave way to various interpretations among the groups of experts entrusted with the detailed formulation of the guidelines laid down by the heads of state and government.

The first interpretation, supported by the Germans and the Dutch, was that the ECU was to be used only at the start of the system's operation to determine the bilateral parities between the EEC currencies, the so-called grid of bilateral exchange rates. According to this view, the latter would then serve as the basis for the system since the fluctuation margins would be fixed with reference to bilateral rates and not to the weighted average represented by the EUA. In practice the mechanics of the system would have been identical to that of the Snake and the EUA would have played a purely fictitious part in the exchange-rate system.

The interpretation at the opposite extreme was upheld by the French. The injunction that the ECU should be at the centre of the system was taken to mean that not only parities but also fluctuation margins were to be fixed with reference to the basket of currencies making up the ECU.

These different interpretations stemmed from two totally different concepts. The Germans saw the exchange-rate mechanism as requiring only the currency at its upper limit (the appreciating currency) and the currency at its lower limit (the depreciating currency) to intervene – with no possible distinction between them – to maintain their mutual exchange rates within the margins set. This formal symmetry is accompanied, however, by an asymmetrical situation in practice since the effect on the strong-currency country is a rise in its international reserves and a corresponding increase in its domestic liquidity. The weak-currency country, by contrast, suffers the more serious effect of a fall in its international reserves and a corresponding decrease in its domestic liquidity. Historical evidence of this basic asymmetry is to be found in the fact that creditor countries have been able to withstand the effects of exchange-market interventions much more easily than debtor countries, for which the drain on reserves, potentially until they are exhausted, is an insurmountable obstacle to their remaining in the system. Experience with the Snake, which has always sloughed off weak currencies (the French franc twice, the lira, the pound sterling and the Swedish crown once each) without ever shedding a strong currency, is further proof of this asymmetry.

According to the French interpretation of the Bremen Annex, making the ECU the real pivot of the system would have permitted the problem of asymmetrical burdens to be overcome by determining which currency was diverging most from the average of EEC currencies (that is, the ECU) and imposing on this country most of the burden of intervention to meet its exchange-rate commitments with both exchange-market sales or purchases and domestic economic-policy measures.

The groups of experts finally agreed on a 'functional compromise' between the two extreme positions. This took account, on the one hand, of the desirability of keeping the function of 'divergence indicator' that the ECU could play and, on the other, of the serious technical difficulties that rendered any system based exclusively on the ECU extremely inflexible. The difficulties can be summarised as follows:

1. the possibility of establishing different margins of fluctuation for different countries conflicted with the provision in the Bremen Annex for wider margins for the non-Snake currencies;
2. changing parities defined in ECU would have been a very laborious process since the decision by one country to change its parity would have entailed the recalculation of those of all the other countries;
3. a currency's abandonment of the EMS while remaining in the EUA would have created virtually insurmountable difficulties for the working of the system;
4. only the adoption of rather complicated technical devices, which the market would not have easily understood, would have made it possible to get round the problem of currencies having different weights in the EUA, made equal to the new ECU in the Bremen Communiqué;

5. the very nature of unilateral intervention obligations would have meant that if the divergent country intervened in Community currencies it would inevitably push the country whose currency it used into an 'involuntary' creditor (debtor) position.

The 'functional compromise' sought to unite the advantages of the exchange-rate grid in terms of the simplicity of the ensuing exchange-rate mechanism with the usefulness of the ECU as an indicator of divergence. With some reservations on the part of the British, the meeting of the Council of Finance Ministers in September 1978 judged the 'functional compromise' approach to be a valid starting-point for detailed technical studies leading to the drafting of an agreement.

These studies none the less revealed the existence of unresolved differences of interpretation regarding the significance of 'divergence' in relation to the ECU. A minimalist view, held by the Germans and the Dutch, wanted the signalling of divergence – the so-called ECU alarm – to trigger nothing more than consultations without any obligation to intervene, either in the exchange market or in domestic policy. This approach was opposed by a more meaningful interpretation, put forward by the Italians and the British, whereby the divergent country, especially if this were a strong-currency country, would be required to take positive adjustment measures, in principle involving both exchange and domestic policy. In order to enforce these requirements, it was considered advisable to envisage some 'financial penalty' for countries that continued to diverge.

There was also a median view on this issue, advocated principally by the Belgians and the French. This approach took the 'ECU alarm' as implying a presumption that countries would undertake market intervention as well as being obliged to enter into consultations leading to action aimed at overcoming the situation of divergence. When it met in October, the ECOFIN Council again chose the median solution and required the groups of experts to formulate a proposal along those lines.

THE ITALIAN POSITION

In this difficult iterative process leading to the definition of a European Monetary System the Italian position was designed to promote the construction of an exchange-rate system that could be adapted to the special conditions in Italy and which, without imposing unjustified burdens, would make a useful contribution to the convergence of the Italian economy with the prevalent conditions in the rest of the Community. At the same time Italy was well aware of the Community's requirements and of the need to furnish Europe with a common policy on exchange rates. To achieve this goal, it was essential to construct a solid, and hence realistic, system. An exchange-rate regime can produce positive effects if it is credible and if economic agents are convinced of its durability. After the collapse of the Bretton Woods system and the decline of the Snake into a Deutschmark area, another failure in this field would have jeopardised the use of a similar instrument for a long time to come. Thus, construction of a system virtually doomed to failure would have damaged the economy of the Community in two ways: the collapse of the system would have created tensions and consequent losses of reserves and exchange-rate policy would have been discarded almost definitively from among the instruments available at the Community level.

With these aims in mind, Italy has continuously sought to reconcile the need for strictness that an exchange-rate system must embody if it is to perform its stabilising action effectively, with the reality of a Community with pronounced disparities and, in particular, with the needs associated with the transition phase Italy has entered. To try to satisfy these partly conflicting requirements, an extremely cautious attitude was adopted in the first phase of the negotiations since there was as yet no proof of the will which was, at least apparently, to be shown at Bremen, to create a new system that would be different from the Snake, which Italy had abandoned in 1973 and could have rejoined whenever it wished.

The Italian attitude was reflected in the proposal for an exchange-rate system based on effective exchange rates, initially without any obligation to intervene. Acceptance of compulsory intervention was subordinated to improvements not only in domestic costs and prices and the balance of payments but also in the medium-term prospects for the Italian economy.

The gradual emergence of an apparently broad and unambiguous intention on the part of our European partners to build a really new European Monetary System with greater financial solidarity increased Italy's willingness to discuss more demanding exchange-rate systems. The Italian authorities were also encouraged to take this decision by the persistence of the improvement in the domestic economy and above all by the progress that the medium-term plan envisaged.

The changed Community attitude and Italy's willingness to consider more binding agreements were reflected both at the Council of Finance Ministers held on 19 June and even more strongly at Bremen. Within the framework laid down by the heads of state and government Italy immediately proposed and upheld an interpretation whereby:

1. the principle that the new system was to be as strict as the Snake should be interpreted in an economic and not a mechanical sense;
2. a range of margins was needed that would be compatible with inflation and interest-rate differentials, and hence with the forward rates existing between the currencies of the EEC countries, and that would simplify rate changes without allowing easy profits from speculation;
3. countries were to be allowed to change their central rates in a simple manner if they could show that a serious effort to adjust had been made. On a recent occasion I indicated that evidence of this effort could be the acceptance of a temporary downturn in the rate of growth, a relatively high level of interest rates or an initial convergence of the rate of inflation;
4. the asymmetry inherent in the ECU owing to the different weights of currencies was not to be·allowed to have iniquitous effects on the working of the system or to grow worse.

The technical studies made at the time clearly showed that precisely these conditions, which we considered to be fundamental, were the most difficult to satisfy in a system based exclusively on the ECU. For this reason we supported the compromise solution put forward by the Belgians, since it appeared to offer the possibility of combining the operational advantages of the grid with the important innovation provided by the ECU as the means of identifying the divergent currency. We believed that our position, held in common with the British, was a logical interpretation of the spirit of the 'Bremen Annex' and responded to the needs of the Community over and above our own. We proposed that the ascertainment of divergence in relation to the ECU should trigger not only consultations leading to economic policy guidelines but also obligations extending beyond exchange-market intervention and regulation. We also suggested that the required strictness of the system, which had to be compatible with the flexibility I indicated earlier as being necessary, could be achieved by fixing the ECU divergence threshold within both the general and the Snake bilateral margins, so that the threshold would normally be reached before either of these and thus allow reasonable scope for action between the ECU alarm going off and the general margins being reached. The latter were, of course, to be wider than those of the Snake, which, in accordance with the Bremen Annex, was to be left intact as a special exchange-rate agreement within the more general arrangement provided by the European Monetary System.

At the present moment we are endeavouring to discover how much scope there is for Italy's needs, and for what we believe to be the true interests of the Community to which we belong, in a system based on the choice made by the Council of Finance Ministers in October, when the Council entrusted experts in the field with the task of ascertaining whether it would be possible to bring the extreme interpretations of the compromise proposal into the orbit of the Franco-Belgian interpretation.

Recent events in exchange markets strengthen our case in the current technical negotiations. During the month of October, notwithstanding a virtually unchanged effective exchange rate (-1 per cent), the lira fell by more than 6 per cent against the Deutschmark while rising 3.3 per cent against the dollar. These variations occurred in the almost total absence of intervention by the Bank of Italy. The two pounds recorded a pattern very similar to that of the lira, while the French franc depreciated 4 per cent against the Deutschmark.

Such large exchange-rate movements confirm the basic soundness of plans designed to ensure greater monetary and exchange-rate stability but, simultaneously, they make it clear that we must seek formulas leading to the construction of a system with sufficient flexibility to be workable, credible and lasting.

THE EUROPEAN MONETARY FUND (EMF) AND THE EXTENSION OF SHORT-TERM SWAP AGREEMENTS (IN THE 'TRANSITION PHASE')

The desirability of creating an EMF to support the Community Exchange Agreements was affirmed in the technical annex to the communiqué drafted after the Bremen summit.

The setting up of the Fund none the less raises legal and political problems that cannot be solved in a few months. It has therefore been agreed that the technical analysis of the issue should proceed in two stages: it is, of course, necessary to define the key features of the new institution more clearly, but it is equally necessary during the transition phase to ensure that the exchange-rate agreements are backed from the start by adequate credit facilities. These must be put into use, moreover, in the light of the key features it is intended the EMF should have. It is therefore best to recall the main points in the Bremen Annex bearing on this issue and then to describe the present state of the technical analysis and the negotiations.

According to the Bremen document, besides being the *numéraire* of the exchange-rate system, the ECU is also to become the instrument for settlements between central banks. For this to be possible, two ECU accounts will be created within the EMF.

The first will record central banks' freely available assets, to be issued against the deposit of gold and dollars. The size of the initial deposit will be 20 per cent of central banks' holdings of these reserve assets. The initial deposit will be inserted in a mechanism whereby new acquisitions (disposals) of dollars by central banks will generate new deposits (withdrawals) in an ECU creation (extinction) account with the EMF, again in a proportion of 20 per cent.

The second account will record ECUs issued against the deposit of national currencies. The total amount of ECUs in this account will be of roughly the same order of magnitude as that in the first. Use of the ECUs in the second account will be conditional on the amounts and maturities involved, though it is still intended that short-term credits (up to one year) shall be 'substantial'.

At the latest two years after the inception of the system, the agreements concluded and the institutions created are to be brought together in a European Monetary Fund, which, in particular, will replace the FECOM.

This formulation of the EMF issue leaves several important aspects inadequately defined. Some countries, for example, tend to have a minimalist view of the Fund, even in its final form. Italy's position on this issue is different. In particular, we have argued that the mechanisms for the activation of ECUs in the final phase cannot be a mere accounting fiction. Similarly, as regards the first ECU account, we believe that legal solutions need to be foreseen that will allow a real pooling of part of the reserves in the final configuration. As regards the second, Community countries would obtain ECU deposits against actual payments of national currency.

These deposits would not be freely available as are those of the first account. It would be possible to consider them as time deposits involving constraints, in the sense that a country wishing to use its deposits would have to submit to adjustment rules. However, once the ECUs of the second account were unfrozen, they would acquire all the attributes of those of the first account. Specifically, they would be fully utilisable for settlements between the central banks of the Community, with the proviso that the account would have to be reconstituted at the end of the period agreed when it was unfrozen.

These summary remarks on the various possible views regarding the form and functions of the European Monetary Fund clearly show that it would be impossible to build advanced and innovatory solutions into this institution in a short lapse of time. We must therefore foresee a longer period, first to permit a thorough discussion and hence a convergence of opinions, and second to cast outline agreements into their legal and institutional moulds. It has therefore been agreed to study technical formulas that in the immediate future will provide financial support for the exchange-rate agreements in accordance with the proposed principles for the working of the Fund.

Turning now to the creation of ECUs as the counterpart of reserve assets, there is a large measure of agreement that the initial creation should not involve transfers of ownership nor any redistribution of assets between central banks. Consequently, the proposal is for reserves not to be given up definitively and in practice for the central banks owning them to bear the exchange risk.

Technical discussions on the best way to achieve this short-term objective are still under way. If the solution put forward for the so-called 'transition phase' does not differ greatly from the guidelines we have suggested, Italy will enjoy the substantial advantage of mobilising its gold reserves more easily.

The financial support of the European exchange system during the transition phase would rely heavily on reciprocal credit agreements. In this phase there would therefore be neither a partial pooling of reserves, except in a purely fictitious form, nor the surrender of national currencies against the issue of ECUs.

The adaptation of existing facilities, at the same time as the exchange-rate agreements come into effect, involves the very-short- and short-term support mechanisms as well as that for medium-term financial assistance.

An over-all assessment of the issue requires a rapid review of the present form and scope of the mechanisms before examining the various hypotheses for change and enlargement that are being studied.

At present the very-short-term intra-Community facilities allow the central bank that has had to intervene in Community currencies within the framework of the Snake (so that Italy currently does not benefit from this form of support) to receive an unlimited amount of credit but for a limited period (thirty days from the end of the month). The right of automatic renewal, which allows the debtor country to extend the maturity to a maximum of three months, is restricted to the debtor quota of its central bank in the short-term monetary support mechanism. Subject to reciprocal agreement, there can be a second renewal limited to the amount of the debtor quota.

The *short-term* support mechanism was set up among the EEC central banks with the agreement signed on 9 February 1970, which was last revised on 13 December 1977. The debtor quotas, which determine the amount each bank can draw under the agreement, currently total 2725 million EMUAs; the creditor quotas total 5450 million EMUAs, while the creditor and debtor *rallonges* (the technical name for extensions and increases of credit and debt positions in the short-term support system) amount to 3000 million EMUAs (at present one EMUA is equal to about 1.2 EUAs (ECUs) and $1.6). As a general rule no bank can obtain more than half the total of the debtor *rallonges*, but the Governors may go beyond this limit if the special situation and needs of the borrowing country justify such action. Borrowing from this facility has a maturity of three months, but central banks may apply to have their loans renewed *once* for a further three months. The *medium-term financial assistance* mechanism was established by the EC Council of Ministers on 22 March 1971 and was last modified by the Council on 19 September 1977. The credit granted under this mechanism can have a maturity of between two and five years and is conditional on undertakings by the borrowing country in connection with domestic and external adjustment. The total amount of commitments is currently 5450 million ECUs. In practice this medium-term financial assistance can link up with the support provided by the short-term monetary facility.[1]

As regards the proposals for the strengthening of the credit facilities that are being examined, it is best to distinguish the very-short-term mechanism from the other two.

A number of countries, including Italy, have suggested that it would be useful if the unlimited very-short-term financing in connection with settlements within the Community were extended to ninety days from the end of the month. This would increase the likelihood of the debtor-country's position being reversed. As can easily be imagined, other countries – in particular Germany and the Netherlands – are against this proposal.

Turning now to short-term support and medium-term financial assistance, it is fairly generally agreed that these mechanisms should be strengthened to a total of 25 milliard ECUs, which would be equivalent to the amount involved in the deposit of 20 per cent of countries' foreign currency reserves in the Fund's first ECU account. None the less, there are widely differing opinions about the operational application of this principle. Specifically, these concern:

- how to divide the total increase between short-term support and medium-term assistance;
- whether the agreement is to cover the sum of creditor quotas and *rallonges* (or debtor quotas and *rallonges*) plus the maximum commitment to provide medium-term support, or, instead, the total amount of potentially available credit (meaning the maximum amount of credit that can be obtained from the system with the optimal configuration of debtors and creditors).

Several different formulas for the practical modification of the mechanisms in question are currently being discussed. The most restrictive is that put forward by the German monetary authorities, backed by those of the Netherlands. With this proposal the total credit of the system amounts to 25 milliard ECUs if reference is made only to the sum of the *credit* quotas of the short-term monetary support and the medium-term financial assistance (increased from 5.5 to 8.5 milliard ECUs). It is worth noting, moreover, that, apart from Germany and the Netherlands, all the other countries consider that the calculation of the total amount of credit should be based on the potentially available sum as defined above.

In practice the German proposal is to multiply the credit currently available for short-term support by 1.6 while leaving its maturity unchanged at three months (renewable once). The same factor is applied to the amount of medium-term financial assistance. This would mean that the Bank of Italy would be able to obtain, as the sum of the automatic part (the debtor quota) and the discretionary part (half the *rallonges*), 3.7 milliard ECUs, as against the 2.3 milliard available today.

Italy's proposals, which are also upheld by the UK, give preference to the increase in short-term support over that in medium-term assistance – in view of the delays the latter might encounter in the process of national parliamentary approval – and to the increase in (automatic) quotas over that in (discretionary) *rallonges*. The proposals also envisage the doubling of the initial maturity of short-term monetary support (from three to six months), with the possibility of renewing the credit for a further period of six months. With the Italian proposals it would therefore be possible in practice to link up the short-term support mechanisms within the date set for the establishment of the European Monetary Fund, where the short- and medium-term mechanisms would be brought together.

This scheme would effectively double the credits available to Italy (4.5 milliard ECUs as against 2.3 milliard). The automatic component would rise from the present 0.5 milliard ECUs to 2.2 milliard.

The Belgians, French and Irish have put forward alternative proposals for raising the amount of credit available, all of which involve a substantial increase in the existing facilities.

In considering these matters, it should be remembered that they are part of negotiations. It has none the less been stated – most recently by the Italian Treasury Minister, Mr Pandolfi, at the October ECOFIN meeting – that the availability of credit facilities totaling 25 milliard ECUs is a cornerstone that cannot be renounced in the negotiations. A substantial buffer appears indispensable if destabilising speculative attacks are to be countered and possibly discouraged.

I also believe Italian participation in the European Monetary System will prove valuable, provided it is possible to realise the three conditions announced in parliament by Mr Pandolfi and repeated here: that the System shall be immediately operational in the three aspects originally foreseen with regard to the exchange-rate agreements, the credit facilities and the measures in support of the less-prosperous economies; that each of these aspects shall be acceptable (so that, for example, an unsatisfactory exchange-rate agreement cannot be offset by more extensive credit facilities); and, finally, that the system shall be sufficiently flexible to allow Italy to come back into line with the stronger countries, without upheavals, as regards economic conditions and especially inflation.

The basic reason why each of these conditions must be realised separately, with no scope for offsets, lies in the enormous difference between the situation of a country which maintains an unrealistic exchange rate or undermines its development potential with a series of exchange-rate crises, and which receives aid from its partners, or some of them, to 'compensate' for this loss of competitiveness and potential, and that of a country which, partly because of a suitable exchange-rate policy, stays afloat and advances under its own steam.

NOTE

1. To date Italy is the only country to have used this financial assistance, having been granted a credit of 1159.2 million *units of account* in 1974. The money was made available in December the same year to coincide with the repayment of the short-term monetary support. The total amount, however, was less than the maximum obtainable since, in view of its own balance-of-payments difficulties, the UK did not participate in the loan, though for a certain period it maintained a credit line (403.3 million EUAs) equal to that granted to the Banca d'Italia under the short-term monetary support arrangement. The repayment of the medium-term financial assistance was made in four quarterly instalments and completed on 22 September, in advance of the scheduled maturity of 18 December 1978.

15 Foreign Capital and Domestic Planning*

Indraprasad G. Patel

INTRODUCTION

Actors in a joint production who have been assigned a part but are invited to write their own script are under strong temptation to steal each other's lines. In the hope of being able to avoid this temptation, I have defined the scope of this chapter rather narrowly and have attempted to deal in the main with two questions. Assuming that a country has embarked on a course of planned economic development, what is the difference that will – and should – be made to its plans by the availability of foreign capital? And, if the absorption of foreign capital into a process of planned economic progress is to be as smooth and beneficial as possible, are there any conditions that the availability of foreign capital must satisfy? The focus clearly is on a poor country receiving capital from abroad both from private as well as public sources.

It would of course be a mistake to assume that the current emphasis on planning as a precondition for aid has already led to a situation where most developing countries have well-articulated plans which look sufficiently far into the future. Nor have we reached a stage where the commitment to assist the poorer nations has assumed a degree of firmness and continuity which makes it meaningful to relate it to well-considered long-term aims. The giving and receiving of aid at present, with a few exceptions, is essentially an *ad hoc* affair based on the presumption that when the needs of the poorer countries are so many and so urgent every little help will somehow go to add up to something worthwhile. It would nevertheless be useful to assume that an examination of how foreign capital might best be related to domestic planning will provide a few pointers to a more rational policy towards foreign aid and private foreign investment.

*This chapter was originally published in J. H. Adler and P. W. Kuznets (eds), *Capital Movements and Economic Development* (London: Macmillan, 1967).

PLANNING WITHOUT FOREIGN CAPITAL

The necessity for planning has been impressed of late on the rich and the poor alike. There is, however, an essential difference between the kinds of plans that the two sets of countries need and this difference relates to the appropriate time span or horizon for planning. We plan for a certain period ahead; and despite the blandishments of saints, philosophers and model-builders, we hesitate to take in our stride the entire period from here to eternity. But how far into the future is far enough? For a rich country whose task in ordering the use of its resources over time is of a marginal nature, a limited time-horizon of four to five years at a time may well be sufficient. But for those left behind in the race for economic progress, there are a number of 'structural' problems which can be tackled only within a somewhat long-term perspective – of say, twenty to twenty-five years. Problems remain in life at all levels of well-being; and there is no guarantee that those who have already established themselves at a base camp at the foot of Mount Everest will succeed in all the subsequent series of assaults. But there are major deficiencies in poor countries from the point of view of their ability to cope with the ceaseless struggle for 'higher' economic aims; and the removal of these basic weaknesses constitutes the first stage in domestic planning – a stage which unhappily must extend over a number of decades.

Without endeavouring to be exhaustive or to arrange things in the order of their importance, we might say that the end of stage I in domestic planning would be reached and the country would be reasonably free from 'structural' weaknesses when:

(a) the bulk of its people have reached the standards of nutrition, clothing, shelter and health consistent with the requirements of efficiency;

(b) the bulk of its working force has acquired education and technical training of the kind that makes it possible for them to respond to changing techniques and circumstances;

(c) the rate of saving and investment is high enough – say 15 to 20 per cent – to permit a satisfactory rate of growth;

(d) the community at large includes a sufficient number of people imbued with the spirit of enterprise – that is the desire to lead, manage, push, cajole and experiment;

(e) the structure of production and the available stock of capital and trained personnel are sufficiently diversified to permit a considerable degree of transferability of resources from one use to another without much loss.

There is of course no natural order in which the different ingredients of the necessary minimum of economic strength are bound to appear. Japan in all probability had achieved high enough standards of saving, training and entrepreneurship before achieving the standard of well-being consistent with economic efficiency; and there are among less-developed nations today some which enjoy fairly satisfactory living conditions without achieving high enough rates of saving or enterprise. But if the first task of domestic planning in a poor country is to arrive at a perspective of where it ought to go in the first instance, it should not be difficult to define the broad contours of this perspective – so much food and clothing and shelter must be available per person, so many hospitals, doctors, teachers of various kinds and a certain minimum rate of saving. Even entrepreneurs can be trained and encouraged, if not manufactured with absolute certainty. The 'goals' then are easy to define; and the questions that remain in perspective planning are essentially two: how soon ought one to try to achieve these goals and what is the course along which the economy ought to be steered from year to year if it is to arrive at the goal at the appointed hour. The two questions, needless to say, are related and can only be answered simultaneously.

Artificial as it is, it might be instructive to inquire how these questions might be answered in a closed economy where both foreign trade and foreign capital are absent. At first sight, it might appear that the only relevant question for such a society is that of the pace at which the desired goals are to be achieved and that this in turn is a matter of the marginal rate of saving and investment to aim at. Since the goals are known and must be met from internal production, the marginal rate of saving will also uniquely determine the distribution of available investiable resources between investment for the investment-goods sector and investment for the consumer-goods sector. One can further disaggregate this model to take account of the pattern of consumption at different levels of income and saving and derive a complete time-profile of the distribution of resources till the predetermined goals are reached in terms of the desirable rate of saving and desired levels of *per capita* consumption in essential directions. The period over which the objectives of the perspective plan would be reached would depend on the marginal rate of saving and the productivity of capital in different fields. While this way of setting out the planning problem has relevance and merit it disregards at least four important aspects of the issue at hand.

The productivity of capital even within a given sector is not a fixed factor to be taken for granted. There is always a choice open for the method by which even a given basket of goods can be produced. Where savings are scarce and can be assumed to be determined independently by policy, it would make sense within each sector to choose the least capital-intensive method. But even this is not always a safe rule. Minor irrigation, for example (that is, wells, tanks, etc.), may be capital-saving in relation to major irrigation schemes involving the training of rivers which is a time-consuming affair. But if the scope for minor irrigation is limited, it would become necessary to make a start with major irrigation sooner or later – and this will have to be done before the scope for minor irrigation is fully exhausted. Much the same is true of expansion of existing industrial complexes as distinct from the initiation of new ones. Investment – and its productivity – are almost always associated not only with labour but also with certain geographical or geophysical factors; and the particular complex of investment which is most productive over time (even within a limited sector) cannot be determined with reference to simple criteria such as capital-intensity. But whatever the criteria for choice, the method of production to be chosen is an important area of planning as distinct from that of deciding on the rate of saving and investment.

Equally, if productivity is determined not only by investment but also by consumption and standards of training and enterprise, one has also to decide on the distribution of resources among all these productive uses. The normal national-income accounting conventions which represent consumption as a withdrawal from the potential stock of productive assets and treat much of the expenditure on education, training, health, extension activities, marketing advice, etc., as expenditure on consumption are grossly misleading in the context of a developing society. A step-up in investment (for example, irrigation facilities) unaccompanied by the necessary increase in training and entrepreneurship (for example, spread of knowledge of better techniques and their demonstration) would be hardly productive, whereas a smaller increase in investment accompanied by efforts to stimulate or create the supply of complementary factors may be far more productive. There has been a good deal of discussion of late of what has been called the 'absorptive capacity' for capital. In reality, what needs to be emphasised is not some absolute measure of the capacity to absorb capital in general but the need for associating the growth of capital in different sectors with the growth of other productive forces so that the over-all increase in productivity (per unit of capital) is sufficiently great. In this sense of the necessity for ensuring fuller realisation of the productive potential of capital, the need for attention to 'absorptive capacity' is a continuing one and not something which has a relevance only to countries at the lowest stage of development. Any country can absorb any kind of capital within wide limits; but the efficiency with which it can do so can also vary widely in accordance with the availability of complementary factors of skills, training and management. Domestic planning thus must pay as much attention to these factors as to the growth of capital.

Planning is not simply an exercise in dividing the cake at each stage between consumption and investment leaving the distribution of consumption between different items to individual choice. The speed with which the goals of the perspective plan are achieved will also depend on conscious attempts to alter the pattern of consumption either by the use of the market mechanism or by direct restraint on (or stimulus for) the production of certain goods. Without undue elaboration, we might assert that consumption of the kind that leads to greater efficiency should be encouraged, whereas consumption (and production) of items which act as a spur to the demonstration effect without adding correspondingly to efficiency or effort should be discouraged. Similarly, consumption of items which require capacities (or other scarce resources) of the kind that are particularly required for enlarging the capacity to invest and train might be discouraged. Unfortunately, excessive emphasis on analytical aggregates such as consumption, investment, capital–output ratios and the like have tended to obscure the vital importance of a rational policy towards the pattern of consumption. But the difference between successful and not-so-successful efforts to develop are often the result of the degree of attention paid to this particular area of policy.

Lastly, a perspective plan without a conscious policy for distribution of income fails to come to grips with some of the most relevant aspects of the alternatives that are open to a society bent upon growth. Here again, the habit of thinking in terms of marginal rates of saving and the like distracts attention from vital issues. It is possible, for example, that the initial distribution of income – and property – in a society is capable of a radical adjustment leading to an immediate increase in the rate of saving and investment and/or to an advance towards more satisfactory levels of consumption for the poorest sections of the community. For subsequent periods also, the pattern of distribution at which one aims will have a bearing on the supply of savings or entrepreneurship. Again, if a basic minimum standard for all consistent with requirements of efficiency is an essential objective of a perspective plan, one must at least inquire whether this is to be done with or without a change in the distribution of income. The quantitative significance of this consideration is so overwhelming that it is really surprising that so many plans in developing countries today can get by without being explicit on this point. Suppose, for example, that a country has an average *per capita* income of $60 per annum and that the minimum income consistent with efficiency is $180 per annum *per capita*. If, at one extreme, all incomes were equally divided all the time, one would need to increase total *per capita* income to only three times the present level. If, however, as is likely, the lowest 30 per cent of the population have only a 10 per cent share in total income to begin with, their *per capita* income would be only $20 per annum; and if they are to enjoy the basic minimum of $180 per person per year without any change in the distribution of income, *per capita* income for the community as a whole must rise to nine times the present level. In actual practice, the distribution of income cannot be changed at will without unfavourable repercussions. But one cannot plan for a certain perspective without any regard to this consideration.

Planning then, even in a closed economy, has to involve decisions on:

(a) the rate at which saving and investment are to be raised;
(b) the choice of the method of production in different fields bearing in mind the relative availability of factors over time, including natural factors, and the time it takes to develop most resources;
(c) growth of skills of various kinds and creation of an environment conducive to entrepreneurship by extension services, development of financial institutions, market facilities and the like;
(d) the manner in which the pattern of consumption might be suitably modified by direct as well as indirect measures;
(e) the distribution of income between different classes at different times.

Whether all these questions are capable of simultaneous solution at one fell swoop on the basis of some theoretical model or whether they can be answered at best in a tentative or rough and ready way need not deter us here. But it cannot be too strongly emphasised that domestic planning is a matter of establishing the right interplay between technical factors and issues of policy involving institutional, social and psychological considerations.

The assumption so far of a closed economy was only intended to focus attention on some of the issues which would be equally relevant even if possibilities of trade (but not of capital inflow) existed. International division of labour generally relieves particular scarcities so that the possibility of trade enhances the productivity of capital and shortens the time span for reaching desired goals. The potential for taking advantage of international division of labour would vary from country to country and will have to be built up over time in much the same way as the potential for investing larger and larger amounts and for absorbing more and more productive techniques. Foreign trade would make no difference to the pattern of availability at which a community ought to aim in terms of the growth potential it seeks to establish at the end of the first stage of its domestic planning. But its structure of production need not coincide fully with the desired pattern of availability. In the nature of things, there has to be substantial overlap between the two. Many things like power, water and transport are rooted in the soil and under present conditions at any rate it is not possible to buy or hire skilled personnel from abroad to any significant extent. But in an open economy, the perspective plan will have to include some idea of the nature and extent of exports and imports at different stages of growth, bearing in mind the need for a balance between the two in the absence of capital movements. Apart from lending a measure of extra efficiency to the whole operation, the possibility of trade will not do away with the importance of the different aspects of planning that we have discussed earlier – in fact, it might well underscore them. Thus, a conscious policy towards the pattern of consumption becomes all the more necessary if export earnings are to be maximised and used in particular for obtaining those imports which have the most beneficial effect on growth potential.

PLANNING WITH FOREIGN CAPITAL

Assuming that a country is operating on the basis of some perspective plan of development, what is the difference that could be made by the availability of foreign capital? The freedom to import foreign capital adds to the stream of resources; it imposes also an obligation to respond to some extent to the interests and judgements or prejudices of those who provide the capital. Beyond this, many other problems flow from the terms on which such capital might be forthcoming. It might be useful first to take the simplest case of capital inflow where a country has at its command a given lump sum of foreign capital which can be used in any manner it likes without any obligation to repay. Ideally, one might wish that even the amount of foreign capital was left to be determined by the developing country. But this would be clearly unrealistic. For the present, we may assume that there is no uncertainty regarding the amount of capital available, no limitations on its use and no considerations to take care of about the conditions to be satisfied after the absorption of the capital at hand.

Under these conditions, foreign capital can either shorten the time-span for achieving the desired results and/or can permit a different course for the economy in the interim period. But the situation that must emerge ultimately, that is, the pattern of production and foreign trade, must remain the same as before in so far as the stock of available foreign capital is limited and growth beyond the stage under consideration would require the same initial conditions. If foreign capital is absorbed in a manner which involves no gain of time, the entire difference it would make would be to the stream of consumption and the gain here may well be larger than what might be indicated by the purchasing power of the foreign capital. In ex-post national accounting terms, the inflow of foreign capital will represent a net addition to domestic savings; but this does not mean that it is investment rather than consumption that would be necessarily larger than in the alternative case. And the gain to consumption – when all the gain is so taken – may well be larger than the value of foreign capital because, as a versatile resource, foreign capital could be used in substitution of particularly scarce resources. Thus if a machine has to be imported and paid for by the export of food grains, it may well be that larger exports of food grains entail a deterioration in terms of trade. If the machine is imported by the use of foreign capital instead, the additional food grains released for domestic consumption may well be larger than the amount of food grains that can be purchased at home by the local currency value of the machine at the current exchange rate. Generally speaking, the absorption of foreign capital has a sort of 'multiplier' effect because it makes it possible to avoid deterioration in terms of trade and to postpone difficult acts of investment till such time as the economy is better able to realise their full productive potential by the development of complementary factors.

It is perhaps as well to recognise that the gain from foreign capital might go primarily to consumption and that this might be desirable or inevitable in certain circumstances. The very fact that the gain to consumption may be a multiple of foreign capital offers a justification to this course from the welfare point of view. For a country with very low incomes and savings, some immediate gain in consumption may have a productive significance. If the only way out of the vicious circle of low income, low savings and stagnation in the absence of foreign capital is a revolutionary redistribution of incomes, such a revolution may be thoroughly impracticable or destructive in the short run so that the injection of foreign capital initially may be required both for increasing consumption and investment. It may also be that in the absence of foreign capital, domestic planning may have to rely to a great extent on direct restraints on consumption of certain items (by import controls, licensing of production and the like) and some relaxation of these restraints on the basis of foreign capital may generate a better climate for expansion. But the dividing line between legitimate and other uses of foreign capital for assisting consumption is not easy to draw. Instances where the availability of foreign capital engenders undue complacency about redistributing incomes, or altering the pattern of consumption, or mobilising domestic savings or exploiting avenues for fruitful international division of labour are not unknown; and in many cases, such complacency is encouraged by the prejudices of the suppliers of capital. The case for assisting poor countries rests as much on the desire to put them on their feet as soon as possible as on the desire to help them avoid difficult social choices which might disrupt their political fabric. The very fact that there is this dual objective means that the claims of investment cannot have overriding significance over those of consumption. But the availability of foreign capital – even when it is on the generous terms we are postulating for the time being – cannot be allowed to supplant domestic discipline altogether.

Given the extent to which it is legitimate to utilise foreign capital for reducing the rigours of domestic planning, the rest of the gain must be taken in shortening the time-horizon for achieving the goals of the perspective plan. If foreign capital were to represent a fully versatile resource which could be employed for any purpose whatsoever, there would be much to be said for absorbing it as rapidly as possible for enlarging investment. This would give the whole process of development a head start. But unfortunately, there are things which cannot be purchased with foreign capital (for example, skills, managerial talent, etc.) and there are activities such as agriculture, small industry and the like where domestic productive agents cannot be replaced by foreigners. What is thus called lack of absorptive capacity can also be described as lack of capacity for absorption on the part of foreign capital. Whichever way one looks at it, there is clear need for migration of talent as well as for migration of capital. As it is, leaving private capital aside, foreign capital brings with it at best perfunctory advisory talent rather than a steady stream of talent for doing things; and unless this can be remedied, we shall always be left with a bit of a dilemma in deciding on the absorption of a given amount of foreign capital. If it is absorbed early, its contribution will multiply over a longer period; on the other hand, its initial contribution to higher productivity would be limited so that there would be greater temptation to embody it in higher consumption. The recent history of the liquidation of foreign exchange reserves accumulated during the war should provide an instructive illustration in this regard.

UNCERTAINTY

The assumption so far that we were concerned with the utilisation of a given lump sum of foreign capital was intended to do away with uncertainty regarding the availability of such capital. In real life, however, uncertainty presents one of the most baffling problems in relating foreign capital to domestic planning. A rational plan for development in a poor country must extend over a fairly long period of at least twenty to twenty-five years. Given the magnitudes of the tasks involved and the time it takes to remove some of the crucial shortages, a more limited time-horizon will not give any assurance that future growth will not be held back by lack of timely action in a number of directions. Foreign aid, on the other hand, is voted and distributed from year to year; and even the World Bank perhaps would react with consternation if not derision if it were asked for its plans and intentions over the next five years. In the nature of things, the flow of private investment must remain uncertain. What sense does it make then to speak of planning in the context of something which is so highly uncertain?

It is perhaps useful to distinguish between two kinds of uncertainty relating to foreign aid: one, where a country could be reasonably sure of aid over a sufficiently long period while having to reckon with fluctuations in aid from year to year, and the other, where there is a real danger of aid disappearing altogether (or getting drastically reduced) at any time. The first kind of uncertainty is clearly more easy to live with and is in itself diminished by the increase in the number of countries and institutions from whom a poor country draws its aid. A fair share in the burden of aid by all also makes for greater certainty and efficiency in the use of aid. One might even argue that this kind of uncertainty is no different from that which every country dependent on foreign trade has to reckon with and must be dealt with, therefore, by the use of reserves and resort to short-term credit facilities from the International Monetary Fund. Unfortunately, poor countries are seldom able to have reserves adequate enough to meet normal fluctuations in trade and payments, and instances are not lacking where aid-giving countries and even international institutions show scant recognition of the importance of reserves to the poor countries.

The International Monetary Fund has recognised in practice that its accommodation is available for meeting payments difficulties arising from fluctuations in aid-flows. The IMF clearly cannot provide long-term development finance. But when there are sudden or unexpected variations in the flow of such finance from other sources, it is a legitimate use of the Fund's resources to provide short-term relief to the country concerned so that worthwhile long-term plans are not upset suddenly and are adjusted, where necessary, in an orderly manner. Useful as the IMF is as an insurance against uncertain (that is, uneven) aid-flows, this usefulness is limited by the fact that accommodation from the IMF has to be repaid in a relatively short period. An alternative source of long-term but occasional finance for the developing countries is badly needed and the Horowitz plan for reactivating the international capital markets for the use of the developing countries can fill an important gap in this respect. Loans floated by the developing countries before the First World War in international capital markets had the great advantage that they could be used for any purpose – for buying more goods, for repaying old debts, for meeting sudden difficulties or even for adding to foreign exchange reserves. It would be too much to hope that even with interest subsidies this kind of foreign capital movement could now be revived on a large enough scale to meet a significant part of the need for long-term finance on the part of the poorer countries. But the

Horowitz plan can be adopted for the more modest purpose of providing from time to time fully liquid resources repayable over a fairly long period, to developing countries who find themselves in difficulties which cannot be overcome in the short run and for which other forms of long-term finance are not available at least for the time being. In short, the Horowitz plan could well be an adjunct to the Monetary Fund rather than to the World Bank and it could provide an answer to – or a reserve against – a part of the uncertainty that surrounds official capital movements to the developing world.

Where the uncertainty in question relates to the very existence of foreign aid, there is little that can be done to overcome it. Perhaps the only useful thing one can say is that when faced with such uncertainty, the poorer countries would be best advised to utilise such aid as is currently available for speeding up the pace of their development rather than for reducing the rigours of domestic planning. In the ultimate analysis, the only safeguard against the sudden cessation of all aid is international public opinion or conventions and agreements. From this point of view, the efforts of the United Nations and others to define the long-term tasks of development and the responsibility of all nations in meeting these tasks deserve all encouragement as also the efforts to channel as much aid as possible through international agencies. The consortium techniques developed by the World Bank whereby the needs of a few countries over a five-year plan period are assessed in general terms and some tentative assurance of assistance for meeting these needs obtained is also a step in the right direction. More or less firm commitments under the auspices of the UN and other international agencies to devote as a minimum a certain proportion of national income to foreign aid would also serve to reduce the area of uncertainty. For the rest, uncertainty concerning aid will continue to encourage its utilisation on an *ad hoc* and essentially unplanned basis.

LIMITATIONS ON USE

A country importing foreign capital is seldom free to utilise it as it likes in support of its plans. Private foreign investment is clearly available for specific purposes. Even official capital carries limitations on its use – much of it is tied to purchases within specific countries or to specific projects and purposes and often to specific methods of production. The conditions governing the use of aid sometimes extend even to the use of a country's own resources or to its general economic and social policies. Some of the issues involved here such as tied aid, aid tied to projects, etc., form the subject matter of other papers and we shall refer to them here only in so far as they have a bearing on domestic planning.

Much of developmental aid today is tied to purchases from the aid-giving countries. If aid did not have to be repaid, country-tying would present no real problem from the point of view of domestic planning. If costs in a particular country were high or if one had to buy in a certain market goods which could be bought cheaper elsewhere in order to utilise aid from that country fully, one would be simply making a mental note of the fact and reckoning that the flow was less than what appeared at first sight. Since there would be a number of countries giving aid, each insisting on the aid being used for buying goods produced in the country concerned, there would be a problem of deciding on how the purchases ought to be distributed between different countries. But this should not present insuperable difficulties. The real difficulty arises from the fact that although country-tying reduces the real value of aid, no allowance for this is made in the terms of aid including repayment. Thus a poor country might get only half or two-thirds of the value out of tied aid, but the debt is reckoned without taking this into account so that the real cost of aid is obscured. When foreign capital has to be repaid, an important planning problem that arises is that of determining how much capital at each of the terms available ought to be accepted from time to time; and country-tying makes it difficult to adopt a rational approach to this problem. Equally, there is asymmetry in insisting that the use of aid should not put pressure on the balance of payments of the aid-giving country whereas no such safeguard must be provided in repayment terms for the country receiving aid. Sooner or later, tied aid will lead to a demand for tied repayments.

The desire to tie aid sometimes assumes more sophisticated and far-reaching proportions. It has been argued that even when aid is country-tied, an aid-receiving country could divert its use to third countries by reducing its normal commercial purchases from the first country and shifting them to another. Aid is thus sought to be tied to conditions regarding the total value of imports from the aid-giving country. Indeed, it is not entirely unknown for countries to take the position that they should assist poorer countries only to the extent that is necessary to balance their accounts with each of them as otherwise aid would put pressure on the balance of payments of the aid-giving countries. Thus, if a poor country increases its exports to a particular rich country, the latter would be entitled to reduce its aid unless the former chooses to increase its imports correspondingly! If all rich countries were committed to giving such amount of aid as was required to balance their accounts with each developing country, there would perhaps be no great disadvantage in complete bilateralisation of aid. But as it is, bilateralisation is generally insisted upon only selectively to justify particular commercial interests or unwillingness to extend aid to particular countries to whom this argument fits. Domestic planning, in the context of such ferocious bilateralisation of aid, is bound to become a hand to mouth and uncertain affair bedevilled by constant bargaining with a number of countries. The jig-saw puzzle of trying to maximise aid by constant diversion of purchases from one source to the other would take up energies which could be better devoted to domestic planning.

Apart from country-tying, aid is often tied to particular uses such as import of complete equipment or even a particular kind of equipment. This problem also is perhaps dealt with at some length elsewhere in this volume. But it may be noted that except in cases where available aid is small in relation to the needed imports of the categories eligible for aid, purpose-tying is likely to be wasteful. For one thing, when combined with country-tying, it adds to the wasteful use of aid in the sense that even within the country the eligible categories may not be the most competitive – or least disadvantageous – things to buy. Where an aid-receiving country has reached a stage where import of complete equipment is no longer all that necessary, purpose-tying may lead to inefficient or insufficient use of capacity already created. In general, limitation on the use of foreign capital would lead to wasteful use of such capital. Even without any conscious limitation, the tendency to import inappropriate techniques along with the import of foreign capital is a real one not only when the import concerned represents private foreign capital but also when it is sponsored by official or international agencies who often insist on the designing and the engineering of the projects being done by firms accustomed to deal with problems in more advanced countries. The tendency to over-import or to import inappropriate forms of capital does not always need encouragement from foreigners either. Domestic entrepreneurs or local governments also attach a certain snob value to doing things as they are done in the best countries. And repercussions of foreign capital of this kind are difficult to regulate in any scheme of domestic planning unless it provides for a detailed scrutiny of each investment proposition – a remedy which can be worse than the disease.

Reference may be made here to one particular danger that arises from the fact that private foreign capital is necessarily available for only particular uses. In theory, it is easy to say that a country is free to decide which particular cases of private foreign capital to admit and which not; and it might be argued that those particular lines of consumption which need to be discouraged should not be allowed to be developed even with the help of foreign capital. But in practice, the general desire to prove that one welcomes foreign capital or the pressure of domestic vested interests in league with foreign investors or the fact that investment propositions from abroad often come in a package (oil-refining–cum–fertilizers–cum–synthetic fibres) leads to situations where foreign capital is allowed to set up industries where its contribution is essentially to the growth of inessential consumption based on a growing volume of imported raw materials and components. This danger is particularly great in the case of items whose imports are regulated on the ground of inessentiality but whose domestic (and often high-cost) production is not similarly discouraged. The general point that needs to be made is that in so far as foreign capital may be available only for specific uses, it might be advisable in some cases to reject it altogether.

It has been mentioned earlier that any society which relies on foreign capital must accept the fact that its domestic planning will have to respond to some extent to the wishes of those who supply the capital. This is true not only in respect of the particular use to which the foreign capital might be put but also of the general policies and plans of the aid-receiving country. Whether this particular aspect of the interaction between domestic planning and foreign capital represents a fruitful or healthy exercise in international economic co-operation is more than one can say on the basis of experience so far particularly when the use can turn so unpredictably on those irrational springs of action which still govern the conduct of nations as of individuals. We can only remind ourselves usefully that prejudice, irrationality and unwillingness to face facts and act upon them are not the special attributes of any particular group or nation, be it rich or poor; nor is any country or even an international agency likely to be altogether free from their hold.

PROBLEMS OF REPAYMENT

We turn now to consider the fact that only a small part of foreign capital that is available today to the poorer countries is in the form of gifts. By far the larger part consists of loans and investments bearing a liability to pay interest or remit profits as well as to repay and repatriate. One could argue that this fact should make no difference to the purposes for which aid is utilised except perhaps that it heightens the importance of enhancing the pace of progress as distinct from reducing the rigours of development. But essentially, since the servicing of loans and the ability to live without aid require the acquisition of the same kind of balance-of-payments strength, there should not be any special use of foreign capital which would be dictated by the fact that it carries the burden of interest charges and repayment.

The question, however, that arises is that of the amount of foreign capital that it is prudent to borrow and on what terms. The two aspects are clearly related as more capital can be prudently and profitably employed at more favourable terms and the other way around. Sir Roy Harrod in R. Harrod and D. Hague (eds), *International Trade Theory in a Developing World* (London: Macmillan, 1963), has worked out a number of instructive examples to show how much foreign capital can be absorbed with assurance of being able to repay and on what terms and under what conditions. Suffice to say here that given the terms on which foreign capital is available and the productivity of capital in general as well as the limitations on external markets and the minimum essential growth in consumption, it may not be possible for a country to service its debts without more and more external borrowing. Even where conditions are intrinsically favourable, repayment may pose a problem if aid or capital in necessary amounts is not forthcoming over a sufficiently long period. In this sense, there is generally a minimum amount of foreign capital that is necessary even for a successful case of 'assisted take-off' just as much as there might be cases where no reasonable amount of foreign capital might suffice for the purpose. In practice, it is rather unrealistic for a country to worry about whether it can afford to have foreign capital beyond a point because it can never be sure of how much capital it will ultimately receive over a number of years. Some projections over time of inflow of foreign capital and the feasibility of ultimately servicing it, however, would be useful both for creditors and debtors as long as the tendency to wishful thinking on either side is resisted. Such exercises could at least engender a realistic attitude towards what could be regarded as reasonable terms for assistance.

A great deal of attention has of late been devoted to this question of terms on which foreign capital ought to be made available if a crippling burden on the balance of payments of aid-receiving countries is to be avoided. Some improvement in this regard has also taken place. But much remains to be done. In a saner world, one might well advocate that whatever aid a country feels like giving should be by way of gifts and that this would make for a more rational aid policy as well as for more harmonious relations between aid-givers and aid-receivers even if it reduces the total flow of aid. But this is too much to aim at in the present circumstances. As it is, the desire to maximise aid flows in the short-run comes in the way of reducing or minimising reliance on 'hard' loans from some quarters and this sets up a tendency for others to harden their terms as well. Indeed, there is also a certain asymmetry in the attitude of aid-giving countries and international agencies in this regard. The World Bank and several governments, for example, rightly insist on aid-receiving countries avoiding suppliers' credits and other medium-term credits for development. At the same time, they encourage the maximum possible use of private foreign investment when it is abundantly clear that such investment imposes a very heavy burden of servicing charges on the balance of payments of the recipient countries. The truth, divorced from all ideological considerations, is that private foreign investment today makes sense in developing countries only when it comes for certain high-priority uses and when it forms in the aggregate only a small part of total foreign capital that is available by virtue of being accompanied by a much larger inflow of official capital on relatively 'soft' terms.

One important aspect of the burden of repayment is that it represents a first charge on the earnings of a country in good times as well as bad. Quite apart from anything else, the vital necessity of preserving the reputation as a good debtor makes it so. The inflow of foreign capital adds resources of the kind that would be in particularly short supply otherwise. But the reverse side of the medal is that repayment obligations take away the most valuable resource. Some mechanism of flexibility in respect of debt obligations is a vital need if the plans and programmes of developing countries are not to be thrown out of gear from time to time when they are faced with an additional temporary strain on their balance of payments. We have an excellent precedent here in the post-war Anglo-American and other loans where instalments of interest and repayments due in any year could be automatically deferred in the event of the debtor country being faced with a serious prospect of losing reserves. There is every justification for loans to developing countries, including those from international agencies, carrying a similar provision from the outset and laying down some definite procedure for the activation of the provision. This is a far better and more orderly course – generating more sense of confidence all round – than the practice of rescheduling debts and of arranging emergency balance-of-payments assistance which is already becoming quite frequent.

Sooner or later, problems of repayment of foreign capital will bring to the fore the question of planned access to the markets of the aid-giving countries. The UN Conference on Trade and Development has already highlighted the connection between trade, aid and development. But if domestic planning in developing countries has to take account of foreign capital and its repayment, some sort of long-term planning on the part of the aid-giving countries to ensure an orderly and adequate absorption of the repayments is also urgently called for. Otherwise, the best that one can say about relating foreign capital to a plan of development in the poorer countries would be that such aid should be used for meeting situations that arise from year to year leaving the long run to look after itself. From this point of view of planning the use as well as the return of foreign capital, the practice of allowing repayments at least in part in local currencies has much to recommend itself.

SUMMING UP

The arguments in this chapter, I am afraid, are generally suggestive and not conclusive so that it would be more appropriate to sum up the issues they raise for further discussion rather than to indicate the conclusions to which they point. Among the questions that might be profitably discussed are the following:

(a) Can foreign capital be related to domestic planning in the absence of a long-term perspective plan?
(b) What are the ingredients of a perspective plan that deserve emphasis?
(c) In what circumstances would it be legitimate to employ foreign

capital for reducing the rigours of domestic planning and when would it be more advisable to use it for shortening the time-horizon for achieving desired results?

(d) How useful is the concept of 'absorptive capacity' and what bearing does it have on the timing and extent of the use of foreign capital?

(e) Are there any ways in which the risks inherent in the uncertainty regarding the flow of foreign capital could be minimised?

(f) What are the special considerations that deserve emphasis in determining the nature and extent of private capital inflows?

(g) Among the possible conditions governing the use of aid, which are most harmful to rational planning at home and how can the legitimate interests of aid-giving countries in stipulating such conditions be safeguarded without the same harmful effects on aid-receiving countries?

(h) Is it possible to make an objective estimate of the amount of aid that a country can prudently and profitably absorb and on what terms?

(i) How can we improve upon the prospects of repayment of foreign capital without an undue strain on the poorer countries?

POSTSCRIPT (APRIL 1983)

Much water has flowed down the Ganges since this piece was written in the spring of 1964. Briefly, while the issues raised in relation to domestic planning have receded somewhat in the background, those concerning foreign capital are once again coming to the fore.

In most developing countries today, comprehensive long-term planning as outlined in this chapter is more an exception than the rule; and this is perhaps as it should be in a world where the pace of change has become so rapid and its sweep so wide. Horizons have become necessarily more short-term and planning, at best indicative, has yielded pride of place to economic policy. To some extent, this shift in emphasis signifies growing acceptance of some of the points made in the paper such as (i) the many dimensions of the structural weaknesses that planning – or better still, conscious developmental efforts – should seek to overcome and (ii) the need for planning to focus on decisions pertaining not just to the rate of saving and investment but also to choice of technology, growth of skills and entrepreneurship, a framework of efficient markets and institutions, influencing the pattern of consumption (and investment) and the distribution of income. There would now, I believe, be more general acceptance of the proposition that: 'domestic planning is a matter of establishing the right interplay between technical factors and issues of policy involving institutional, social, and psychological considerations'.

There is one area, however, where long-term or perspective planning is vital and yet generally neglected, namely, in planning for the use – and even more important, preservation and augmentation – of basic resources such as water, clean air, soil fertility, forests, sources of energy and the like. Here, nothing but a long-term view and remedial–cum–developmental measures well in time will do.

As far as foreign capital is concerned, regrettably, the considerable progress that had been made along lines recommended in the paper is now being rolled back under the impact of analytical myopia and ideological blindness. The progress that was made towards rational policies in regard to foreign capital – concessional and non-concessional, short-term and long-term – can perhaps best be illustrated by reference to two points made in the chapter. How wrong, for example, was the statement that 'even the World Bank perhaps would react with consternation if not derision if it were asked for its plans and intentions over the next five years'? In fact, that is exactly what it did – and with a very good track-record of matching its intentions with actual achievements – under the leadership of Mr McNamara.

Or consider the suggestion that 'the Horowitz plan could well be an adjunct to the Monetary Fund rather than to the World Bank and it could provide an answer to – or a reserve against – part of the uncertainty that surrounds official capital movements to the developing world'. In a sense, that is exactly what happened under the leadership of Mr Witteveen after the first oil crisis when initiatives such as the Trust Fund and Interest Subsidy and mobilisation of special resources for medium-term assistance through gold sales and otherwise did so much to avoid extreme hardship for many countries, particularly the poorest among the non-oil developing countries. One cannot help feeling that the tragic waste and suffering during the second oil crisis are due in no small measure to the fact that the armoury assembled in 1974 was wilfully disbanded around 1980. Today, the sentiment in favour of 'aid' is on the retreat almost everywhere; and the current trend towards protectionism is reviving many of the restrictive practices described in the section on 'Limitations on Use'. While paying lip-service to freer access to markets and multilateralisation of trade and aid, there is feverish behind-the-scenes activity towards bilateralisation of trade and aid and one can only hope that wiser counsels will prevail soon.

This is not to deny that some problems mentioned in the chapter will always remain and that their solution in any given context cannot be altogether free from controversy. For example, the point made that induction of foreign capital generally has a dual objective (namely, to augment investment as well as help to avoid difficult social choices) and that a balance has to be kept between the two, has now become familiar as the balance between adjustment and finance around which the current controversies about conditionality revolve. A similar conflict – or hard choice – arises even when there is a fortuitous induction of resources due to other reasons, for example, better terms of trade as for the OPEC countries in recent years; and this was foreshadowed in the chapter (p. 286) when it was remarked that:

> we shall always be left with a bit of a dilemma in deciding on the absorption of a given amount of foreign capital. If it is absorbed early, its contribution will multiply over a period; on the other hand its initial contribution to higher productivity would be limited so that there would be greater temptation to embody it in higher consumption.

Such is the beauty of economic theory that despite its comparative simplicity and the vast complexity of economic phenomena, it does have continuing relevance. Only, the pace of change and the natural propensity to believe in what is convenient in the short run obscure our vision.

16 Monetary Policy, Capital Movements and Underdevelopment*

David Horowitz

MONETARY POLICY IN UNDERDEVELOPED COUNTRIES

The analysis made in this chapter does not necessarily have universal application. It refers to a certain type of underdeveloped country which, however, recurs frequently.

1. The central phenomenon in the economic and social development of underdeveloped nations is the growth of their populations. Preventive medicine and the application of hygiene and infant care have caused a steep decline in mortality rates, particularly as regards infant mortality. The birth rates have not declined at the same pace, and the resulting increase in the excess of births over deaths has inevitably generated economic problems as the rapidly expanding populations have exerted pressure on limited resources. The accumulation of local capital and the rate of saving are rather slow when nations live on a subsistence level, while their capital imports cannot match their rapid demographic expansion. Thus, the utilisation of existing natural resources is inadequate.

2. The above trend, with all its economic implications, is aggravated by sociological and psychological factors resulting from the dynamics and the pattern of modern civilisation. The larger national income in the highly developed and mature economies of Europe and the Western hemisphere, the high level of consumption and the tendency to consume conspicuously, are conveyed to the underdeveloped countries through modern media of mass communication and have widespread social and economic repercussions, establishing new

* Originally published as 'Monetary Policy in Underdeveloped Countries', in *The Challenge of Development* (Jerusalem: The Hebrew University, 1958); and as 'The Affluent Society and the Third World', in B. Schefold (ed.), *Floating, Realignment, Integration* (Tübingen: Mohr, 1972).

standards and arousing economic and social desiderata hitherto virtually unknown in backward countries.

This 'demonstration effect' of high-standard modern civilisation on the psychology and the demands of underdeveloped nations exerts a far-reaching influence on economic policy and determines the nature of development projects encompassed by economic planning. The attempts to utilise existing – and mobilise new – resources, with a view to accelerating the process of economic development, become – under these circumstances – imperative.

3. The process of primary accumulation of capital is extremely slow and is made even more difficult by the increasing pressure of populations growing at a rate of 2–3 per cent per annum. The propensity to save is of course reduced if the population expands more rapidly than national income, so that real income per capita decreases. The rate of saving being low, due to a relatively small excess of real income over and above the subsistence level, the process of accumulation is further restricted by the fact that institutional saving is in its embryonic stage, while the use of money as a medium of exchange is rather limited.

4. The supplementing of the limited and slowly accumulated resources of local capital and saving by capital investments from abroad is utterly inadequate. The theoretical assumption that the surplus of capital in the mature and developed economies of the West is attracted by higher returns in countries possessing underdeveloped resources, cheap labour and unexploited sources of raw materials, does not materialise. Considerations concerning the security of the capital invested are only one of the factors militating against extensive imports of capital to underdeveloped countries. The low productivity of labour, as well as the lack of skilled labour both in general and in particular sectors, likewise discourage foreign investment. The difference in returns per unit of capital invested tends on the whole to favour mature economies and encourages their economic expansion. Apart from the exploitation of oil resources, which constitute an exception, the flow of private capital between developed and underdeveloped countries does not reflect any spectacular surplus of capital inflow into the latter. Even the existing scope of investment is to some extent affected by artificial stimuli, such as the activity of the International Bank and grants-in-aid. In fact, little capital flows to underdeveloped countries via the natural processes of economic gravitation, except to finance oil.

5. Capital shortages due to influences retarding the formation and

influx of capital are not the only factors bearing on the utilisation of existing resources. Lack of 'know-how', managerial ability and entrepreneurial initiative are likewise conducive to stagnation, especially under conditions of increasing demographic pressure on limited resources and social desiderata determined by the 'demonstration effect' of Western civilisation.

6. Under these circumstances, economic policies and activities are largely determined by two main tendencies: (i) to substitute state enterprise for private initiative, and (ii) to substitute so-called 'inflationary saving' for the formation or influx of capital. The former is intended to overcome the difficulties caused by lack of 'know-how', managerial ability and entrepreneurial intiative, the latter to overcome the handicaps of a low rate of saving and capital accumulation, and inadequate capital imports from mature economies.

7. Inflationary financing as a substitute for capital and capital imports is a trend influenced by a certain interpretation of Keynesian theory. Attempts are made to reinforce the tendency towards monetary expansion on a theoretical basis. The application of Keynesian theory under the particular conditions of the inter-war period, against an economic background of unutilised capacity and disequilibrium between effective demand and investment as well as between the propensity to consume and the propensity to save, is being experimented within circumstances peculiar to underdeveloped countries. However, this application takes insufficient account of the Keynesian analysis of disequilibrium, which under different conditions may reach diametrically opposite conclusions from the same premises. The comparison between a policy applied on the basis of Keynes's *General Theory of Employment, Interest and Money* and a policy based on the principles of the treatise *How to Pay for the War* would demonstrate that, while the basic assumptions in both cases are identical, the different conditions under which they are applied result in diametrically opposite courses of action. It must be stressed that the policy formulated on the basis of Keynesian theory during the inter-war period was not identical with the theory itself, but reflected only an application of this theory under specific economic conditions. This policy is unapplicable, (i) in countries with a very adverse trade balance, which further deteriorates under conditions of monetary expansion, and (ii) in underdeveloped countries with a scarcity of unutilised resources and dormant factors of production which could be activated by fiscal and monetary policies. In these two types of countries the unexploited production capacity which can be brought

into action by monetary expansion is either limited or non-existent. Under these circumstances, it is not advisable to expand the money supply before developing resources, since this has an adverse effect on the balance of payments, as well as on the gold and foreign currency reserves. In consequence, the limited foreign currency reserves decline and thus the country's ability to obtain capital equipment necessary for the development of its unutilised resources is reduced.

A one-sided interpretation of Keynesian theory when formulating economic policy in underdeveloped countries, may lead to inflationary development distorting the price structure and to a deterioration in the balance of trade.

The demands to accelerate economic development to an extent requiring more resources than are created by the formation or influx of capital, create a situation in which monetary policy has to be applied as a restraining force.

8. Physical controls are frequently imposed to restrict inflationary pressures. Sometimes, attempts are made to substitute such controls for sound monetary policies. These attempts lead in most cases to a disparity between the official rate of exchange and the real value of local currency as reflected by internal price fluctuations. This involves a discrepancy between the internal and external price and usually creates an unofficial market where currency is sold at rates different from those officially fixed and implemented by the foreign-exchange control authorities.

The first and inevitable result of the said discrepancy is to stimulate imports and penalise exports. The relative price levels of locally produced and imported goods are changed, creating actual price differentials in favour of imported goods. Exports are adversely affected by the disparity between a level of costs dominated by inflationary pressures and prices in the international market, which is reflected in distortions caused by the unrealistic official exchange rate, and actually diminishes the returns of the exporter. Moreover, the expanding effective demand absorbs any increment of output produced by the export industries and diverts it into local consumption.

The deterioration of the trade balance is further aggravated by subsidies and price controls, which increase the disequilibrium between effective demand and the quantities of goods available at prevailing prices. The floating purchasing power is thus augmented by an artificially low price level imposed on the economy by means of price controls and subsidies.

Apart from causing a general distortion of prices, the above development also tends to distort the structure of investment. The order of priorities for the allocation of scarce resources is influenced by the fact that the artificial expansion of effective demand may foster uneconomic production and discourage investments on an economical basis. The treatment of symptoms reflected by rising price levels, instead of the basic roots of monetary expansion, further distorts the price structure and the composition of investments in underdeveloped countries, thus causing an additional worsening of the trade balance. At the same time, the rate of saving is further reduced by uncertainty as to the future of the currency and by inflationary expectations.

The attempt to overcome the shortage of capital by monetary expansion also results in some countries with occupational mobility in an alteration of the occupational structure, shifting a part of the labour force from the primary and secondary to the tertiary stages of production, that is, to services. Purchasing power released by the slower rate of saving and the scarcity of goods tends to be directed to the purchase of services. High money incomes, representing not real income derived from the production of goods and services, but mainly the results of dissaving and the disinvestment of foreign currency reserves, have repercussions similar to those in mature economies where the shift to services is based on a larger volume of income. This tendency is reinforced by the fact that prices of services are not easily subjected to controls, and their sale, therefore, becomes increasingly profitable.

In underdeveloped countries, such a shift in the occupational structure defeats the very purpose for which monetary expansion was initiated.

9. The success of monetary policy applied by central banks is to a great extent dependent on co-ordination with fiscal policy. However, budgetary deficits cannot be neutralised by the monetary policy of the central bank alone. Usually, the central bank has to execute its monetary policy under the pressure of monetary expansion caused by budgetary deficits; for central banks in underdeveloped countries are almost invariably subject to governmental interference although endowed with a certain autonomy. If budgetary deficits cause the money supply to expand, a central bank can hardly refuse to implement such an expansion. The only alternative is to compensate for the resultant increase in incomes by a tight money policy and credit restrictions. The orthodox means of influencing money markets, such as an open market policy or the manipulation of interest rates, are

not very effective in underdeveloped countries. An open market policy presupposes the existence of a money market, which in underdeveloped countries is either limited or non-existent.

Rates of interest exercise relatively little influence for the following reasons: (i) in underdeveloped countries, the availability of credit is more important than its cost, because in protected internal markets the higher cost can largely be shifted to the consumers; (ii) the fluctuations in the level of income and employment are so extensive that they can only be influenced by changes in interest rates, so wide as to be socially and politically unacceptable; and (iii) high income tax rates enable business enterprises, to shift part of their expenditure on interest to the income tax account, thus further reducing the effectiveness of the demand for money and changes in interest rates as regulators of the quantity of money and the volume of credit.

Thus, the sensitivity of monetary expansion and contraction to the impact of changes in the cost of credit is comparatively low. Central banks, therefore, have to resort to quantitative and qualitative credit controls and to liquidity ratios and similar devices to keep the quantity of money in check. High liquidity ratios imposed on commercial banks may prevent further inflationary increases of bank credit. However, the degree of effectiveness of such a policy will depend on the measure of quantitative expansion of central bank credit to government. If the government resorts to the central bank on a large scale, this expansion will invariably exceed the reserves accumulated in the central bank through the imposition of high liquidity ratios on commercial banks, and the attempts to sterilise excess money reserves will be unsuccessful or only partly successful. Moreover, the central bank can only apply its policy of monetary contraction and credit restrictions within certain limits. If these limits are exceeded, large-scale unemployment may be caused, defeating the purpose of this policy and compelling the central bank to reverse it. The extent to which such a reversion may become imperative will depend on the use of the resources to which the government has access through the central bank. If these resources stimulate productive economic activity, this may to some extent compensate for the inadequate normal activity of the economy.

Given scarce resources, which are the rule in underdeveloped countries, the central bank will hardly be able to confine itself to quantitative controls. The exigencies of the situation will inevitably require the simultaneous application of qualitative controls, with a view to facilitating credit for purposes of essential production.

Qualitative controls, however, have considerable shortcomings and limitations: (i) as only a partial control of credit is possible, the controlling of essential credit and its substitution for inessential credits do not necessarily reduce the volume of the latter; indeed, the usual result is that inessential credits simply appropriate a larger share of the uncontrolled section of credit extended by the banks; (ii) of course, control extends only over the first stage in the utilisation of credits, and as these percolate into the economy, the monetary expansion retains its detrimental character and forms a fundamental factor of monetary conditions which is not affected by the control in the first stage; (iii) even if very strict measures are taken to channel the available credit to 'productive' activities, there is a time lag between the monetary expansion which takes place immediately and the increase in real output promoted by such credit; (iv) owing to the lack of unexploited resources, there is no guarantee that the hypothetical increment of production will correspond to the increment of effective demand caused by the monetary expansion. The limitations of quantitative controls due to political and other external pressures, and the inherent limitations of qualitative controls, do not warrant the conclusion that monetary policy is ineffective in curbing inflationary pressures and neutralising the detrimental effects of monetary expansion. It is probably the most effective means available for the partial neutralisation of the harmful influences of excessive quantities of money generated by attempts to overcome the difficulties created by the shortage of real resources derived from internal saving and the influx of capital. The full effectiveness of monetary policy will depend on its co-ordination with budgetary and fiscal policies and the elimination of the fundamental factors generating inflationary pressures.

THE AFFLUENT SOCIETY AND THE THIRD WORLD

The problem of development with which the World Bank – as the foremost global institution in this field – is confronted is conventionally regarded as that of the gap between the developed and underdeveloped nations. This gap will inevitably widen, for, according to a projection for 1980, GNP *per capita* will by then average $ 245 in the developing world and $ 3280 in the developed world, as compared with $ 175 and $ 1964 respectively in 1968; in other words, the disparity will increase from elevenfold to thirteenfold. This will be due mainly to the rapid population growth in the developing countries, which will swallow up part of their 5.2 per cent annual gain in GNP.

However, the malady lies much deeper than that. For the affluent society itself is suffering from a malaise, which could be alleviated by responding to the great challenge of helping to build up the under-developed nations.

One-third of humanity – the developed world – has fallen prey to hedonistic tendencies, worshipping the idol of consumption and status symbols, and enslaved to a multiplicity of modern gadgets, turning its back on human and spiritual values. Considerable segments of the affluent society manifest all the symptoms of internal disintegration and spiritual degeneration: violence, delinquency, drug addiction; guided to a great extent by the ancient Roman principle *homo homini lupus est*. This society is torn by internal strife and contradictions, mired in a socio-psychological crisis and intellectual confusion. In addition, over-consumption, with its attendant discharge of noxious waste and its endless accumulation of disused materials, has become a primary source of pollution of water and air, soil and sea, ruining the beauty of the natural environment, and perniciously affecting human life in the noisy, grimy megalopolis with all its environmental and ecological problems.

The $ 2 thousand milliard economy of this affluent society can spare only $ 13.6 milliard a year, that is, about three-quarters of one per cent, for the development of the two-thirds of humanity which has to subsist on only half a thousand milliard dollar gross national product – a distribution of wealth of about 80 per cent for one-third of mankind and 20 per cent for the other two-thirds.

There is the frightening spectre of a clash between the over-affluent society, which has largely abandoned its humanistic and rationalistic achievements, and the two-thirds of humanity steeped in misery, hunger and disease, engaged in a struggle for their very physical existence, made resentful by the demonstration effect of the affluent Western civilisation.

After the Second World War, the victorious powers proved equal to the challenge posed by the ruin and destruction of the European continent. The Marshall Plan and the establishment of the World Bank and the International Monetary Fund at Bretton Woods amply bear out the truth of this contention. But today, a swelling volume of factors of production and a technology enabling man to reach the moon and explore outer space, to devise instruments of both life and destruction, are inadequate to meet the challenge of hunger, ignorance and disease plaguing two-thirds of mankind.

This is a dangerous situation. The technological achievements and the deteriorating quality of life contrast too glaringly to be tolerable for any length of time. Destitution breeds despair and despondency.

But in the third world it is not only the low standard of life, which has improved only slightly in the past decade, but also unemployment that is the curse of the underdeveloped nations. It is mounting twice as fast as the growth of the population.

Moreover, the urbanisation of masses of starving, underemployed people alienated from the rural economy leads to a proliferation of slums and a situation in which hundreds of thousands of persons without shelter, living literally in the street, is of frequent occurrence. This tremendous potential source of production is not being tapped because of insufficient capital.

Whatever the rationalisation of the reluctance to allocate more than a tiny fraction of the annual incremental gross national product of the developed world to promoting the economic growth of the third world, capital availability is the foremost and an indispensable precondition for any attempt to break the vicious circle of underemployment and subhuman standards of life.

There are only two possible ways to activate the potential factors of production of the developing world – domestic capital formation and capital import. Domestic capital formation is obviously constrained by the low margin of subsistence in the developing nations and has reached its limits. But the two thousand milliard dollar economy of the developed world, with its $ 100 milliard annual increase of gross national product, with all its affluence and over-consumption, does not find it possible to export sufficient capital, skill and know-how to foster and stimulate economic growth in the underdeveloped world. It should be stressed in this context that, by providing work for hundreds of millions of underemployed and unemployed, this would increase the wealth of the world as a whole and facilitate a tremendously expanded production of capital goods in the advanced industrial nations for export to the underdeveloped nations. Such a development would, in the final analysis, redound to the benefit of the developed, no less than of the developing, nations.

Today, some four-fifths of total capital investment in the developing world is derived from domestic capital formation. This is obviously the limit. More cannot be squeezed out of the underdeveloped economies of these countries, with their precariously narrow margin of subsistence – certainly not under a democratic regime, nor under the influence of the demonstration effect of high standards of life in the West.

The challenge is to telescope a process which should normally take half a century into two decades. This can be done, with an adequate import of capital, skill and know-how and with a motivation transcending material incentives. For capital will not flow to the developing world as a result of the operating of economic forces alone. Political instability, illiteracy, low standards of education and the risk of war and internal conflict preclude this.

I would like to cite the example with which I am familiar – that of Israel – as proof that it can be done. In a country of 8000 square miles, three-quarters of them desert and barren hills, with a pronounced scarcity of natural resources, devoid of coal, oil, timber and ores and almost all other natural resources, with a limited quantity of water and a small cultivable area, contending with a difficult geopolitical situation and the quadrupling of the population within two decades, Israel has achieved an annual GNP growth of 10 per cent per annum since its establishment, and within two decades real GNP has multiplied sevenfold. The standards of life and private consumption have increased two and a half times per head in the same period. Agricultural production has been stepped up to a level where it now supplies 85 per cent of the requirements of the vastly larger population. What is more, Israeli agriculture has achieved the highest rate of growth in the world and in some branches yields have attained a world record. Exports of goods and services have increased from $ 46m in 1950 to $ 1500m in 1971. The labour force has expanded by three times, and while agricultural production has increased more than eightfold during this period, the number of persons engaged in farming has declined from 17 per cent of the total labour force to 10 per cent. Productivity per worker in the economy as a whole has improved at the rate of 4.5 per cent per annum. The process of industrialisation has brought up the number of persons employed in manufacturing to 26 per cent of the total labour force. Exports constitute 29 per cent of the country's GNP and of these about 90 per cent consist of manufactured goods and services and only 10 per cent of agricultural produce and raw materials. This is an impressive record of growth and progress, and proof that the challenge of development can be met.

The indispensable ingredients of such progress are sufficient, even plentiful, capital, adequate levels of skilled labour, science, technology and expertise, and the imponderable of motivation. This is the key to the enigma of economic growth, and all these ingredients can, and should, be reproduced on a world scale.

First consider capital supply. It is not the sole ingredient of a policy of development; capital alone cannot do the job. On the other hand, the argument frequently voiced that capital is the least relevant of the elements is patently fallacious, as is borne out by the experience of all those countries that have undergone vigorous economic growth – all of which have been distinguished by a large capital import. The claim that capital is of little significance too frequently serves as a convenient rationalisation of the fact that only a trickle is being diverted to the underdeveloped nations.

Since the World Bank is responsible for this particular aspect of development, this is the proper forum to dwell on this problem.

There are presently under discussion two methods of augmenting the flow of development capital, which are not contradictory but complementary: the so-called Horowitz Plan, and a link between the creation of SDRs and development.

As to the Horowitz Plan, it could be implemented by the World Bank alone. There would be little, if any, difficulty in very substantially increasing the Bank's borrowings if its bonds yielded a higher return. Raising the interest rates on such bonds would enable them to supplant some of the issues of lower priority, which serve to increase investments in the already overheated economy of the developed world, contributing to inflationary pressures and tendencies. The time is particularly propitious, as some $ 60 milliard of speculative Eurodollars crowd the money markets of the world and to some extent this constitutes one of the major causes of financial fluctuations and disturbances. This source of capital could be tapped by an appropriate management of the interest rate of World Bank bonds. The additional amounts so procured could be lent by the World Bank to IDA, and the interest differential covered from the interest equalisation fund, which would consist of three component elements: the profits of the World Bank, the income surplus of the IMF and relatively small allocations from the budgets of the developed nations, even if these are at the expense of the IDA replenishment. Considering the heavy indebtedness of the underdeveloped nations, IDA must become a much more important instrument of development than it is today, and should therefore have an ample supply of capital at its disposal. Such funds cannot be obtained on an adequate scale by going, year after year, hat in hand to the governments and parliaments of the world with a request for replenishment. They can be obtained by direct access to the capital markets, provided that exaggerated interest rate considerations do not militate against this course of action and that replenishment funds are partly utilised for this purpose.

Only large-scale borrowing, particularly on the Eurodollar market, could put at the disposal of the World Bank sufficient funds, which could then be lent to IDA, using the interest equalisation fund to free the Bank from the constraints of a too low interest rate accruing to holders of its bonds. Even the relatively smaller amounts now being allocated by the various governments to IDA could serve a much more useful role as an ignition spark releasing massive amounts of capital to IDA through access to the capital markets.

The diversion for this purpose of Eurodollars and other funds procured on the capital markets is a cheap and simple way of stepping up the flow of capital to developing nations without detrimentally affecting the advanced nations.

The committees that examined this proposal in an objective manner – the Pearson Committee, appointed by the World Bank, the Perkins and Peterson Committees, appointed by the President of the USA, and more recently a comprehensive and well-reasoned report that had been commissioned by UNCTAD from Harry Bell, Economic Consultants – all recommended one variant or another of this plan.

The latter study makes the point that implementation of the Horowitz Proposal is easier, as larger amounts could be raised on the capital markets of the world.

Paragraph 14 of the summary (document TD/B/361) states:

An examination of the major capital markets shows that their size is a very large multiple of the total requirements envisaged under proposals for a multilateral interest equalization scheme.

In previous discussions one of the difficulties mentioned was the necessity of making multi-year budgetary commitments. On this point the study came to the following conclusions:

None of the countries studied appears to have experienced difficulty in making multi-year budgetary commitments of interest subsidies for domestic programmes (paragraph 11).

Another way of mobilising capital for the developing nations is the establishment of a link between the creation of SDRs and development.

Here I would like to stress that it is not suggested that SDRs should be created for purposes of development. As far as I know, nobody has suggested this unorthodox method of financing development. However, if SDRs are created to increase world liquidity, there is no reason why allocation according to IMF quotas – that is, substantially more to the rich and less to the poor nations – should be sacrosanct. The same ends could be served by using part of the SDRs to buy World Bank bonds, which would enormously enlarge the World Bank's capacity to finance IDA.

Apart from the ultraorthodox argument that there should be no connection between development and the creation of liquidity, for which it is difficult to find a rational explanation, much is made of the threat of inflationary pressures liable to be generated by such a policy. Inflation is, of course, one of the greatest dangers facing the world economy at the present juncture and should be combated by all possible means, and certainly I would not advocate an indulgent attitude toward inflation. However, it is hard to comprehend why the creation of SDRs for allocation on a quota basis to various countries is less inflationary than their utilisation for development purposes. A good case can be made out that the opposite is true, as in the developing nations there are still dormant or idle factors of production which could be galvanised by additional capital and thereby expand world production. Further, it hardly seems plausible that in the 2.5 thousend milliard dollar world economy, one milliard dollars per year – which is a fraction of one pro mille – could have any inflationary impact. Similar arguments were raised when the Board of Directors allocated part of the profits of the World Bank to IDA for the first time, and much was made of the argument that the creditworthiness of the Bank in the money markets would be affected by such an unorthodox method. The resolution was adopted by the Board of Directors, but later it was rescinded under the influence of this specious argument and after some time readopted. As we are now fully aware, that step has not had the slightest effect on the credit-worthiness or credibility of the World Bank.

For the priests of ultraorthodoxy, Keynes might just have not been born at all. Motivation by fears and anxieties, superstition and myth, carried over from the era of animism into the economics of modern life is irrational and remote from reality. We shall make no headway in facilitating the economic growth of the developing nations if we are guided by obsolete doctrines which hold that any redistribution of the world's GNP is anathema. In view of the mounting frustration felt by the leaders of the developing nations, the complacency and short-sightedness of these attitudes is a source of great peril, which is not confined solely to the economic aspect.

We must liberate ourselves from the fetters of bureaucratic advice and conventional wisdom. We cannot afford to be guided by the same doctrine and theory which, under different conditions and in a different way, brought on the great economic crisis of the 1930s. By contrast, the post-war era, by breaking the vicious circle of conventional wisdom, assured humanity a long period of progress and prosperity, which is now being imperilled by the same attitudes which determined policies in the first four decades of this century. Experience, the philosophy of humanism and sound horse sense indicate the correctness of the new policy.

Poverty, the scourge of man from time immemorial, is, in our age of modern technology and new economics, a superfluous and preventable affliction. It has ceased to be the remorseless and inescapable subject of mysterious and ungovernable forces. By conscious human effort and control it can be abolished as a function of global economic policy.

The accumulation of capital and productivisation of the millions of underemployed people in the developing nations may transform a Utopian dream of rapid, prosperous development into reality. The projection of a world economy with a $ 6 thousand milliard GNP by the end of the century suggests what can be attained by wise and bold policies, by vision combined with realism.

We are aware, of course, that, apart from capital supply, there are other problems that must be solved. If the proliferation of the human race proceeds at the present rate, the damage to the ecology and the ruining of the environment may destroy us, quite apart from economic disasters which are well-nigh inevitable.

The brilliant statements made by the President of the World Bank, Mr McNamara, his intuition and leadership, inspire some confidence that the immobilism and inflexibility of the present situation may be overcome.

Let us hope that human wisdom and vision, the spirit of innovation which brought man to the moon and endowed humanity with incredible technological achievements, will also be applied to the crucial problem of development with which the world is confronted.

Notes on the Contributors

Alessandro Roselli

Paolo Baffi was born at Broni (Pavia) on 5 August 1911; he graduated in Economics from the Bocconi University in Milan in 1932. He was a student of Professor Giorgio Mortara from 1928 and began to work with him in 1930. Baffi was an assistant lecturer from 1933 to 1936, first at the Bocconi University with Professor Mortara and then at the State University in Milan. He contributed to the *Bibliografia economica italiana*, of which he was also the editor.

Baffi entered the Bank of Italy in March 1936 and was assigned to the Research Department, of which he was the head from 1944 to 1956. During the three years from 1945 to 1947 he carried out several studies and missions on behalf of the Italian government and the Bank of Italy: at the Ministry of Foreign Affairs to analyse the economic problems connected with the Peace Treaty; at the Ministry of the Constituent Assembly as a member of the Economic Commission; in the Soleri Commission to study the problems inherent in a monetary reform; in Paris as a member of the Italian delegation in the negotiations that led to the establishment of the OEEC; and at Basle with the Bank for International Settlements.

In 1956 he was appointed Economic Adviser at the Bank of Italy and in November of the same year he was appointed as an external economic adviser of the Bank for International Settlements.

Baffi contributed to both the planning and the drafting of the Bank of Italy's Annual Report from 1936 to 1955 and to that of the Bank of International Settlements from 1956 to 1959, especially as regards the study of the factors underlying changes in the money supply, flows of funds and the financial and liquidity situation of the various economic sectors, European economic integration and Italy's economic development.

During the academic year 1959–60 he was Visiting Professor of International Economics at Cornell University (Ithaca).

In 1960 Baffi was appointed Director General of the Bank of Italy and Governor in June 1975, a post he was to hold – together with several international appointments (World Bank, Asian Development Bank, EEC Governors' Committee) – until October 1979. Of special note in the international sphere is Paolo Baffi's membership of the Board of Directors of the Bank for International Settlements. First appointed in 1960, he was a member of the Board – albeit with different roles – until October 1979 and then resumed office in February 1980. At present he is also honorary Governor of the Bank of Italy.

Baffi, who was external lecturer in Monetary History and Policy at the Political Sciences Faculty of Rome University from 1970 to 1980, is a national member of the Accademia dei Lincei, Chairman of the Ente per gli Studi Monetari, Bancari e Finanziari 'Luigi Einaudi', member of the Management

Committee of the Fondazione Raffaele Mattioli per la Storia del Pensiero Economico, and member of the Editorial Board of the *Giornale degli economisti*. From 1980 to 1983 he was Chairman of the Società Italiana degli Economisti, of which he is at present Deputy Chairman.

Arthur F. Burns was born at Stanislau in Austria on 27 April 1904. When still very young he went to the USA, where he received his Master of Arts degree in 1925 from Columbia University (where he also obtained his Ph.D. in 1934). In 1927 he moved to Rutgers University of New Brunswick (New Jersey) to take up a post as economics instructor. In 1930 he was appointed Assistant Professor; in 1933, Associate Professor; and in 1943, Professor. A year later he left Rutgers to return to Columbia, where he had already been Visiting Professor since 1941 and where he was appointed Professor in 1944. From 1959 to 1969 he was John Bates Clark Professor at Columbia, where he is now Professor Emeritus. From 1978 to 1981 he was Distinguished Professorial Lecturer at Georgetown University. In parallel with his academic career Burns worked as an economist at the National Bureau of Economic Research. He entered the Bureau in 1930, was appointed Director in 1945, President in 1957 and Chairman in 1967, a post he held for two years. In the meantime, in the early 1950s, he firmly established an academic reputation as an expert on the economic cycle.

Burns's life is marked, however, by the constant intertwining of two strands: his academic work on the one hand and his public activity on the other. In 1953 Eisenhower appointed him Chairman of the Council of Economic Advisers, a position he held until 1956. During the 1950s and 1960s he was a member and sometimes also chairman of various economic advisory commissions appointed by the US Administration. In 1969 President Nixon invited him to act as his Counselor and in February 1970 he succeeded McChesney Martin to begin the first of his four-year mandates as Chairman of the Board of Governors of the Federal Reserve System, a post which he gave up in March 1978. Though he could have continued as a member of the Board until 1984 (Federal Governors are appointed for fourteen years), he resigned because he felt his presence on the Board would be 'a complicating distraction'.

Burns's leading position in American academic and public life is amply evidenced by his participation in numerous societies and associations: the American Statistical Association, the Econometric Society, the Philosophical Society, the American Academy of Arts and Sciences, the American Economic Association (President in 1959), and the Academy of Political Sciences (President from 1962 to 1968). In addition, he was awarded numerous honorary degrees.

After leaving the Federal Reserve, Burns was a consultant with Lazard Frères and in Washington was associated with the American Enterprise Institute for Public Policy Research as Distinguished Scholar in Residence. From 1981 until May 1985 he was US Ambassador to the German Federal Republic.

Guido Carli was born in Brescia on 28 March 1914 and graduated in Law from the University of Padua in 1936. He joined Istituto per la Ricostruzione

Industriale (IRI) in 1937 and was appointed secretary of the Commission for the Standardisation of Company Accounts established at the Confederazione Generale dell'Industria Italiana (Confindustria) in 1939. In 1945 he was made a member of the National Council and appointed to the Board of Directors of the Italian Foreign Exchange Office (of which he was made Consultant General three years later). In this period he also started to gain international experience as Italy's Executive Director at the IMF in 1947 and as a member of the Management Committee of the European Payments Union from 1950 to 1958 (for the first two years he was also Chairman). In 1956 he became adviser to the Ministry of Foreign Affairs on the extension of non-military co-operation within NATO. In 1957–8 he was Minister for Foreign Trade in the Zoli Cabinet.

Carli's career in public sector banking started in 1952, when he was appointed Chairman of the Istituto Centrale per il Credito a Medio Termine. In 1959 he became Chairman of Consorzio di Credito per le Opere Pubbliche (Crediop) and Istituto di Credito per le Imprese di Pubblica Utilità (Icipu). He joined the Bank of Italy in 1959 as Director General and concurrently became a member of the Board of Directors of the Bank for International Settlements and the EEC Monetary Committee. A year later Carli was appointed Governor of the Bank of Italy and consequently acquired several other positions in Italy and abroad. He left the Bank in 1975, in which year he was a member of the group of experts set up within the OECD to study non-inflationary development.

From 1976 to 1980 Carli was Chairman of the Confindustria, the Italian industrialists association. In 1979 he was Deputy Chairman, and from 1980 to 1984 he has been President of the European Industrialists Federation. Since 1978 he has been President of the LUISS University in Rome. In addition, Carli is the Chairman of several companies, including Impresit International, Impresit SpA. In June 1983 he was elected to the Italian Senate.

Carlo A. Ciampi was born in Livorno on 9 December 1920. He graduated from the University of Pisa with a degree in Classics in 1941 and a second degree in Law in 1946. He also obtained a diploma in Classics from the Scuola Normale Superiore of Pisa in 1941.

Ciampi joined the Bank of Italy in 1946 and spent the early years of his career performing administrative duties and bank inspections in various branches of the Bank. In 1960 he moved to the Bank's Research Department, where he worked on cyclical and structural analysis as well as being specifically concerned with the national accounts. He was made head of the Research Department in 1970, promoting, among other initiatives, a comprehensive study of the changes in the Italian productive system since the creation of the EEC, research on a regional basis and a restructuring of the Bank's Annual Report. Ciampi subsequently continued his career in the Bank, as Secretary General in 1973; Deputy Director General in 1976; and Director General in 1978. Since October 1979 he has been Governor of the Bank of Italy.

Ciampi has held numerous important positions in various domestic and international organisations, including the EEC, where he was Deputy Chairman of the Economic Policy Committee. Among the positions he holds at present are: member of the Board of Governors for Italy of the IBRD, the IDA, the IFC and the Asian Development Bank; he is also a member of the Group of Ten, the Board of Directors of the BIS, the Governors' Committee of the EEC and the Board of Directors of FECOM. In addition, he is a member of the Advisory and Executive Committees of the Italian National Research Council.

Lord Cobbold was born Cameron Fromanteel Cobbold in London on 14 September 1904. He was educated at Eton and King's College Cambridge, and was awarded an honorary degree in Law by McGill University and in Economics by London University.

Most of his career was at the Bank of England, where he was Adviser from 1933 to 1938, Executive Director from 1938 to 1945, Deputy Governor from 1945 to 1949. He was appointed Governor in 1949, the youngest for over a hundred years and the third youngest in the Bank's history.

When Cobbold was appointed for a third five-year term as Governor in 1958, he accepted on the understanding that he would step down as soon as the Radcliffe Commission had completed its analysis of the UK financial system, and in fact, he resigned from the Bank of England in 1961. He was subsequently Lord Chamberlain (from 1963 to 1971) and since 1971 he has held an honorary position as Lord-in-Waiting to the Queen.

He has been a director of British Petroleum, Hudsons Bay Company and Guardian Royal Exchange Assurance, and has served as Chairman of the International Committee of the Chemical Bank of New York and also for a short time as Chairman of the Italian International Bank in London.

Luigi Einaudi was born at Carrù (Cuneo) on 24 March 1874. While studying Law at Turin University, he began to contribute to the review *Critica sociale*. He took his degree in 1895 and became a journalist, joining the Turin newspaper *La Stampa*, and interspersing this activity with teaching several hours a day at the School of Commerce.

At the age of 24 Einaudi qualified to teach Economics at Turin University. The acquisition of this qualification was followed in 1902 by his appointment as Assistant Professor in Public Finance at the University of Pisa, from where he transferred almost simultaneously to Turin. He later held other academic posts, teaching Economics at the Turin Politecnico and public finance at the Bocconi University in Milan. He was made a full Professor of Public Finance and Financial Law at the University of Turin in 1907. The academic fame he had achieved in so short a time led to his being made a correspondent-member of the Accademia dei Lincei in 1906 (full membership was to follow twenty years later). Shortly afterwards he was made a member (and Treasurer) of the Turin Accademia delle Scienze.

Einaudi continued his copious journalistic activity in parallel with his academic career. Starting in 1900 he began to contribute (sporadically in the early years) to *Corriere della Sera* in addition to *La Stampa*. He later left the latter to devote all the time left by his other commitments to *Corriere*. This collaboration – strengthened by his friendship with Luigi Albertini – was to last until 1925 when Albertini was forced to resign as editor and Einaudi simultaneously departed from the paper. In 1915 Einaudi started to write for *The Economist* and was to do so more regularly after the 1920s.

In the dissemination of scientific knowledge, Einaudi played a major role as the editor of *Riforma sociale* from 1908 on. This review published important contributions by the leading economists and social scientists of the period and was closed down in the end by the fascist regime. In 1936 Einaudi created *Rivista di storia economica*, which came out until 1943.

Einaudi's entry into public life in the broader sense came in 1919, when he was elected to the Senate. He was unswervingly critical of the fascist regime. When fascism collapsed in 1943, he was appointed Rector of Turin University but, with the establishment of the Italian Social Republic, he was forced to take refuge in Switzerland for over a year. In Switzerland he renewed his journalistic activity and taught Italian refugee students at Geneva University and the Lausanne School of Engineering.

The government invited him to return to Italy at the end of 1944 and then appointed him Governor of the Bank of Italy in January 1945. On 2 June 1946 he became a member of the Constituent Assembly, where he was active in ensuring that the Constitution recognised the need both for a consistent management of the country's finances and for the defence of the stability of the currency. In May 1947 he was appointed Deputy Prime Minister in De Gasperi's Cabinet. For a short time he was Minister of Finance and the Treasury (the two ministries had been unified under fascism). When the Ministry of the Budget was created, Einaudi was put at its head but, under a special law, remained Governor of the Bank of Italy, though his functions were delegated to the Director General.

In April 1948 he was re-elected to the Senate. In May of the same year he was elected President of the Italian Republic. In 1948 he was honorary Chairman of the Lincei and received honorary degrees from the Universities of Paris and Algiers. Immediately after his seven-year term as President of the Republic he also received honorary degrees from the Universities of Oxford, Basle and Geneva. When Einaudi's Presidency came to an end in 1955 he not only became a life senator by law but was also specially authorised to exercise his university professorship for the rest of his life. In 1960 he gave the copyright of all his writings to endow a fund to provide grants to post-graduate students in subjects of an economic and historical nature. He died in Rome on 30 October 1961.

Otmar Emminger, born in Augsburg, Bavaria, on 2 March 1911, studied Law and Economics at the Universities of Berlin, Munich, Edinburgh and London. In 1950 Emminger started his association with the Bank Deutscher Länder, the institution that acted as the central bank in the Federal Republic until the monetary reform of 1957, when it acquired the name and structure of today's Deutsche Bundesbank. In 1953 he was appointed member of the Directorate, in 1970 Vice President and, with effect from 1 June 1977, President. He retired from the position of President of the Bundesbank at the end of 1979.

Emminger represented his country on the Executive Board of the International Monetary Fund, on the Monetary Committee of the European Economic Community, and on various committees of the Organisation for Economic Co-operation and Development. He took part in the negotiations on the European Payment Union (1949–50), the European Monetary Agreement (1955), the General Arrangements to Borrow with the IMF (1961–2), the Special Drawing Rights in the IMF (1966–8) and the various negotiations on the Reform of the International Monetary System (1972–6). As President of the Bundesbank he was a member of the Board of the Bank for International Settlements in Basle, as well as Governor of the International Monetary Fund for the Federal Republic of Germany.

Emminger is now Chairman of the Board of Directors of Deutsche Pfandbriefanstalt (the biggest German mortgage bank), member of several boards of directors and international advisory groups. He is a founding member of the Group of Thirty (International Consultative Group) and an Honorary Fellow of the London School of Economics.

Erik Hoffmeyer was born at Raarup in Denmark on 25 December 1924. Educated at Copenhagen University, he joined Danmarks Nationalbank in 1951. He spent the academic year 1954–5 studying in the USA on a Rockefeller Fellowship. On his return to Denmark he became a lecturer in Economics at the University of Copenhagen, completing his D.Sc. in Economics in 1958 with a thesis on the dollar shortage and the structure of US foreign trade. Subsequently he became a professor at the same university from 1959 to 1964.

Hoffmeyer was Economic Counsellor to Danmarks Nationalbank from 1959 to 1962 and General Manager of Bikuben Savings Bank from 1962 to 1964. He has been Chairman of the Board of Governors of Danmarks Nationalbank since 1965. From 1973 to 1977 he was a Director of the European Investment Bank. At present Hoffmeyer is a member of the EEC Governors' Committee and Governor for Denmark of the IMF. He is also Deputy Chairman of the Danish Export Finance Corporation.

In addition, as an economist and man of learning he has been a member of numerous other organisations: President of the Association of Political Economy (1951–3); member of the Board of Directors of the Danish Economic Association (1960–6); member of the Presidency of the Economic Council (1962–5); member of the Board of the Academy of Technical Sciences (1963–); member of the Economic Council (1965–), member of the Board of the Danish Science Advisory Council (1965–72) and member of the Group of Thirty (1984–). He is also Chairman of the C. L. David Collection, the Nationalbank Anniversary Foundation and the Foundation for Trees and Environment Protection.

David Horowitz was born at Drohobycz in Poland on 15 February 1899. He went to live in Palestine in 1920 after studying in Vienna and Lwow. In Palestine he worked as a journalist from 1927 to 1932 and then became the Economic Counsellor of the American Economic Commission for Palestine. From 1935 to 1948 he was head of the economic service of the Jewish

Agency. In the period after the war he was a member of the Israeli delegation to the 1947 General Assembly of the United Nations. When the state of
Israel was established in 1948 Horowitz played an active part in the economic
and financial negotiations with the UK in connection with the ending of the
British mandate. In the same year Horowitz was appointed Director General
of the Ministry of Finance, a post he held until 1952. However, Horowitz did
his most important work in the new state's central bank. He can well be
called the founding father of the Bank of Israel and remained at its head
without interruption for seventeen years, until 1971. He made a fundamental
contribution to the development of the Bank and to the conduct of monetary
policy, starting almost from scratch. The role which Horowitz played in
Israeli public life thus makes him one of the heroes of the new state.

Horowitz's fervent activity as a central banker was backed, moreover, by
solid learning. His studies and his close links with the academic community
are reflected in the important positions that he held in various cultural
organisations: he was a member of the Board of Directors of the Hebrew
University, Tel Aviv University and many other institutions; in 1968 he was
also awarded the Israel Prize for Social Sciences. In recognition of his ability
in economics and of the results he achieved in public life, the Hebrew
University awarded him an honorary degree in 1967. Tel Aviv University
conferred a similar honour on him three years later. He was also honorary
Chairman of the Istituto per le Relazioni Internazionali in Rome.

In economics his position was basically Keynesian and he paid special
attention to the problem of economic growth, with regard not only to the
young state of Israel but also more generally to the vast area of underdeveloped countries. The results of his thinking in this field are contained in
the well-known Horowitz Plan for the financing of developing countries,
which was given careful consideration at the conference on trade and development organised by the United Nations in 1964. He died on 10 August
1979.

Reinhard Kamitz was born in Halbstadt in Austria on 18 June 1907. He
studied at the Hochschule für Welthandel in Vienna. He obtained his
diploma in 1929 and a Ph.D. in Economics in 1934. In the same year, after
going on missions to Czechoslovakia and France, he joined the Institute for
Research on the Economic Cycle in Vienna, where he completed his training
as an economist under the guidance of its head, Oscar Morgenstern.

When the First Republic collapsed in 1939 after the annexation of Austria
by Germany, Kamitz left the Institute and joined the staff of the Vienna
Chamber of Commerce. In 1939 he also started working as an assistant
lecturer at the Hochschule für Welthandel, and was Lecturer in Political
Economy there from 1944 to 1946. At the end of the war Kamitz was
appointed head of the economic policy department of the newly-created
Federal Chamber of Industry and Commerce, where he later became Deputy
Secretary General. However, he accepted greater political responsibilities in
1952, when he was appointed Minister of Finance, a post he held until 1960.

After accomplishing the priority tasks of freeing Austria from the inflationary mentality that had gripped it until then, by ending price- and wage-

indexation mechanisms, and of stabilising the external value of the schilling at a level judged able to resist the play of market forces, Kamitz moved on to remove the web of administrative controls hampering the economy, reduced taxation and kept public expenditure within limits compatible with adequate private investment. Kamitz did not change his approach when, in 1960, he left the Ministry of Finance to become Chairman of the Austrian National Bank, a post he filled with great distinction and international acclaim until 1968.

The appreciation of Kamitz as policy-maker went hand in hand with academic recognition. In 1960 he was elected Professor and taught Political Economy, Economic Policy and Public Finance at Vienna University. Further evidence of his commitment to learning is to be found in the suggestion he put forward at a meeting of the Akademikerbund in 1963 to create a *cité universitaire* and his decisive support for the establishment of a fund for scientific research on the occasion of the National Bank's 150th anniversary in 1966. He was awarded an honorary degree by the University of Los Angeles and was Chairman of the Institute for Advanced Studies and of the Committee of the Friends of the Alpbach European Forum, a valuable cultural organisation operating in the social sciences and with an especially open policy in its seminars to participants from abroad. Kamitz is also a member of the Boards of the Austrian Economic Research Institute and the Institut d'études politiques in Vaduz.

Donato Menichella was born at Biccari (Foggia) on 23 January 1896. He graduated in Political and Social Sciences from the Istituto Cesare Alfieri in Florence in 1920.

An official of the Bank of Italy and the National Foreign Exchange Institute in the early 1920s, he moved to Banca Italiana di Sconto when it was in the process of being liquidated and thus began to acquire the vast range of experience that was to enable him to make a fundamental contribution between the two world wars to the delicate separation made in Italian banking between special (medium- and long-term) credit intermediation and ordinary (short-term) credit business. Banca Italiana di Sconto, a typical investment bank, which owed part of its growth to meeting the needs of Ansaldo during the First Word War, had been overwhelmed by the reconversion of the economy when the war ended and placed in liquidation in the last part of 1921. Menichella joined the bank in 1923, when the liquidation was in the hands of the Consorzio per le Sovvenzioni sui Valori Industriali before being entrusted in 1926 to the Istituto di Liquidazioni.

Subsequently, Menichella was involved in the complicated disposal of the equity interests of Credito Italiano after joining Banca Nazionale di Credito as a manager in 1929. In 1930 the latter was merged with Credito Italiano. Credito Italiano took over the short-term assets and liabilities of Banca Nazionale di Credito, while the equity interests of the two banks were taken over initially by the re-established Banca Nazionale di Credito and then passed, in 1931, to Società Finanziaria Italiana, of which Menichella was made General Manager.

Menichella, however, also played a key role in the subsequent reform of Italy's financial and credit structure. In 1933 he was asked to join the newly-founded Istituto per la Ricostruzione Industriale (IRI) as head of the Disposals Department, and from 1 May as General Manager. This was the moment when IRI took over Società Finanziaria Italiana (and Sofindit, the finance company of Banca Commerciale Italiana) and developed a comprehensive industrial strategy. Under the guidance of Beneduce and Menichella, IRI succeeded in replacing the Italian investment banks without harmful effects on industrial output. Indeed, it brought new organisational vigour and obvious advantages for the country's financial structure. The same persons who had created IRI then undertook the institutional reform of the Italian banking system with the Banking Law of 1936. This completed the implementation of the plan to separate short-term from long-term lending and created the foundations upon which the Italian credit system still rests today.

The second important phase of Menichella's career was more directly concerned with the conduct of monetary policy and started in 1946, when he returned to the Bank of Italy as Director General under Einaudi. He became Governor in 1948 and held this post until 1960. From then until his death on 11 August 1984 he was honorary Governor of the Bank of Italy.

Lord O'Brien of Lothbury was born Leslie Kenneth O'Brien on 8 February 1908 in London. He spent the whole of his career at the Bank of England, to which he went directly from Wandsworth School when still very young in 1927. He rose through the Bank (for a time he was also private secretary to Montagu Norman) and was appointed Chief Cashier in 1955. Seven years later in 1962 he became a member of the Bank's Court of Directors. In 1964 he was appointed Deputy Governor and in 1966 he succeeded Lord Cromer as Governor. He was the first person with an all-bank career to have been appointed to this post, in breach of the long-standing tradition whereby the Governor was a leading figure from the City or had held only senior positions in the central bank.

Lord O'Brien left the Bank of England before the end of his second five-year term in 1973, in conformity with his intention of retiring from the Governorship at 65. He has none the less continued to play a leading role in banking: from 1973 to 1980 he was President of the British Bankers' Association; from 1974 to June 1983 he was a Director of the Bank for International Settlements, of which he was also Vice President from 1979 to 1983. He was awarded an honorary doctorate in Science by the City University in 1969 and one in Law by the University of Wales in 1973. He is honorary Treasurer of several artistic and cultural bodies and is a Fellow of the Royal College of Music. He has been awarded the Italian Grand Cross of the Order of Merit and is a Grand Officer of the Order of the Crown of Belgium.

Indraprasad G. Patel was born in Baroda in India on 11 November 1924 and studied at King's College, Cambridge and Harvard University.

Professor of Economics at the University of Baroda in 1949–50, he subsequently joined the staff of the International Monetary Fund in Washington for four years. Upon his return to India he became Deputy Economic Adviser in the Ministry of Finance and held this post until 1958. He then returned to the IMF as Alternate Executive Director for India. In 1961 he was back in India as Chief Economic Adviser in the Ministry of Finance, a post he held until 1968 except for a short interruption when he was Visiting Professor of Economics at the University of Delhi in 1964.

His civil-service career continued with his appointment to the post of Special Secretary in the Ministry of Finance in 1968, followed by his appointment as Secretary in 1969. He held this office until 1972, when he was asked to tackle the problems of underdevelopment as Deputy Administrator of the UN Development Programme, a position he held until 1977. From 1977 to 1982 Patel was Governor of the Reserve Bank of India.

Patel has published widely on economics, writing principally on the problems of developing countries, inflation and world trade. In October 1984 he became Director of the London School of Economics and Political Science.

Louis Rasminsky was born in Montreal on 1 February 1908 and studied at Toronto University and the London School of Economics.

In 1930 he entered the economic and financial section of the League of Nations as an expert in monetary and banking problems. In 1938 he was appointed Secretary of the League's Financial Committee and then worked with the Committee on food problems and headed a mission to Bolivia in 1939. In 1940 he continued to co-operate with the League of Nations on fiscal problems and with the League's delegation on economic depressions.

Also in 1940 Rasminsky joined the staff of the Bank of Canada, which had been established as Canada's central bank six years earlier. In this period of reorganisation of Canada's new monetary structure, Rasminsky set up the Research and Statistical Section of the Foreign Exchange Control Board. Two years later in 1942 he became Alternate Chairman and Chief Executive Officer of the Board. From 1943 to 1954 he also held the post of Executive Assistant to the Governor of the Bank of Canada.

As the Chairman of the Drafting Committee Rasminsky played a leading role in the Bretton Woods negotiations leading to the setting up of the International Monetary Fund, and he was an Executive Director of the Fund from its inception until 1962. He was also an Executive Director of the World Bank from 1950 to 1962, of the International Finance Corporation from 1956 to 1962, and of the International Development Association from 1960 to 1962. His active contribution to international economic and financial relations is also demonstrated by his membership of numerous Canadian delegations to important international conferences, including that of the United Nations in San Francisco in 1945 and those of the UN General Assembly and the Economic and Social Council in 1946. He has also taken part in numerous financial conferences of the Commonwealth countries as well as being on mixed Canadian–US and Canadian–UK commissions.

Rasminsky was appointed Deputy Governor of the Bank of Canada in 1955 and then Governor in 1961. He remained in this post until February 1973.

He received numerous tokens of recognition for his work in the international field and as a central banker: in 1953 he was awarded an honorary degree by the University of Toronto and in 1960 he was elected Honorary Fellow of the London School of Economics. He subsequently received honorary degrees from several Canadian universities as well as from the Hebrew Union College of New York.

Henry C. Wallich was born in Berlin on 10 June 1914 and studied in England (Oxford, 1932–3) and the USA (Harvard, Ph.D. in Economics in 1944). In 1944, ten years after leaving Germany, he became a US citizen.

From 1933 to 1935 he worked in the private sector in Argentina and Chile, specialising in export business and banking. From 1935 to 1940 he was a securities analyst with various Wall Street firms, including Chemical Bank. In 1941 he entered central banking with a post in the Foreign Research Division of the Federal Reserve Bank of New York, of which he was appointed Chief in 1946. He held this post until 1951, when he left the Federal Reserve Bank of New York to take up an academic career as Professor of Economics at Yale University. He continued to teach at Yale until 1974 and during the last four years (1970–4) was Seymour H. Knox Professor of Economics.

While at Yale, Wallich none the less took leaves of absence to fill posts in the public sector: in 1958–9 he was Assistant to the Secretary of the Treasury, from 1959 to 1961 he was a member of the President's Council of Economic Advisers, and from 1969 to 1974 he was Senior Consultant to the Secretary of the Treasury. His appointment to the Board of Governors of the Federal Reserve System came in 1974 and at the time of writing he still holds the post.

Wallich has also performed numerous other public duties as a member of the Advisory Committee of the Arms Control and Disarmament Agency, as the US representative in the United Nations study group on the consequences of the arms race, and as a member of the Advisory Committee of the Economic Development Commission.

One of Wallich's outstanding contributions to central banking has been his unrelenting effort to inform public opinion, as clearly and widely as possible, about the aims and operational methods of the various aspects of monetary policy. This view of the central banker and his role is perhaps coloured by Wallich's experience as a journalist. As an editorial writer for the *Washington Post* (1961–4) and a columnist for *Newsweek* (1965–74) he had made a name with the American public even before he joined the Federal Reserve System.

Jelle Zijlstra was born on 27 August 1918 in Barradeel in the Netherlands and studied at the Netherlands School of Economics in Rotterdam. Zijlstra's career was multi-faceted since he achieved prominence not only as a banker but also as an economist and statesman.

He obtained his Ph.D in 1948 with a thesis on the velocity of circulation of money. Zijlstra had already been appointed Assistant at the School in 1945 and in 1947 was promoted to Lecturer. In 1948 he moved to the Free University of Amsterdam as Professor of Economic Sciences, a post he held until 1952. He returned to the Free University in 1963 and taught Public Finance until 1967.

Zijlstra began his political career in the 1950s as a member of the Calvinist Party and became Minister of Economic Affairs in 1952. He held this post until 1958. In 1959 he was made Minister of Finance. In 1963 he was elected to the Senate in the list of the Calvinist Party and for a short period (October 1966–March 1967) he was both Prime Minister and Minister of Finance.

In May 1967 Zijlstra succeeded Holtrop as President of the Netherlands Bank and in the same year he was elected President of the Bank for International Settlements, the second Dutchman to hold this post since the end of the Second World War. Zijlstra retired from both positions in 1981.

Index